最新国防科技信息源大全

电子技术、通信技术

秦利　高丽　王新　闫庆红　童欣　主编

国防工业出版社

·北京·

内 容 简 介

《最新国防科技信息源大全——电子技术、通信技术》一书是在长期跟踪研究国防科技信息源的实践积累基础上，针对电子技术、通信技术领域的国外研究机构进行研究、编译、整理而成，共收录 17 个国家和地区的 120 个学协会、企业、研究机构、出版机构等，主要呈现所述机构的中英文名称、网址、简介、会议信息、出版物等信息，为关注电子技术、通信技术领域发展的科研人员提供重要的信息源参考。同时，也有助于信息服务机构系统地把握信息资源情况，使其在信息资源建设中能够事半功倍，提高信息资源服务水平。

图书在版编目（CIP）数据

最新国防科技信息源大全：电子技术、通信技术/高丽，
闫庆红，童欣主编．—北京：国防工业出版社，2016.6
ISBN 978-7-118-10847-7

Ⅰ.①最… Ⅱ.①高… ②闫… ③童… Ⅲ.①国防科技工业—信息源—世界 Ⅳ.①F416.48

中国版本图书馆 CIP 数据核字（2016）第 118530 号

※

图防工業出版社出版发行

（北京市海淀区紫竹院南路 23 号　邮政编码　100048）

新华书店经售

*

开本 710×1000　1/16　印张 15¾　字数 292 千字
2016 年 6 月第 1 版第 1 次印刷　印数 1—2000 册　定价 59.00 元

编写人员

主　　编　秦　利　高　丽　王　新　闫庆红
　　　　　童　欣

参编人员（按姓氏笔划排序）
　　　　　王俊英　王晓云　齐　洋　李法勇
　　　　　张　晓　周　倩　易利华

前　言

信息源研究是信息资源建设工作的一项重要的基础性工作。对信息源的研究与挖掘，有助于信息服务机构更系统、更准确地把握信息资源情况，在信息资源建设中能够事半功倍，从而更好地开展信息资源服务工作。同时，信息源研究的成果能够协助相关领域的科研人员，快速定位所关注领域的相关信息，为其开展科研工作提供重要参考。

本书是在长期跟踪研究装备与国防科技信息源研究的实践积累基础上，将电子技术、通信技术领域的国外研究机构相关情况进行研究、编译、整理，为相关读者提供参考。这些机构包括相关的学（协）会、企业、研究院（所）和出版社（集团）等。

本书共汇集了17个国家/地区的110个电子技术、通信技术领域的机构信息。在结构编排上，各国机构均以中文译名或中文名称编入，按国家/地区顺序排列。机构的中文名称和机构的简称以通行/常用为准。一些非英语国家机构简称系本语言简称，与英文名称相比可能存在不对应现象。

机构信息部分，包括机构名称、网址、简介、会议信息和出版物等。

会议信息部分，列出了机构网站公布的近期该机构主办或赞助的学术会议信息，供读者参考。

出版物部分，列出了机构相对正式的出版物，如期刊与杂志、图书、会议录、报告、标准及简讯等，同时还包括博客和数据库等其他类型有价值的资源。

由于专业水平有限，且在编译过程中涉及英、法、德、日、俄等多种语言和众多专业词汇，书中难免有疏漏或欠妥之处，敬请批评指正。

编著者
2016 年 2 月

目　录

第一部分　国际机构

第二部分　美洲机构

第三部分　欧洲机构

第四部分　亚洲机构

第五部分　大洋洲机构

附录：机构中英文名称对照表

第一部分

国际机构

国　际

国　际

IPC 国际电子工业连接协会

英文名称：Association Connecting Electronics Industries，ACEI

网　　址：http：//www.ipc.org/

机构简介

IPC 国际电子工业连接协会成立于 1957 年，是一家全球非营利性电子行业协会，总部位于美国伊利诺伊州班诺克本。作为会员驱动型组织，IPC 国际电子工业连接协会提供的服务主要有行业标准、培训认证、市场研究和公共政策支持，并且通过开展各种类型的工业项目来满足全球产值达 2 万亿美元的行业需求。

IPC 国际电子工业连接协会包括了 64 个国家和地区的近 3 700 家会员公司，在深圳、北京、苏州、成都、新墨西哥州陶斯、弗吉尼亚州阿灵顿、斯德哥尔摩、莫斯科、班加罗尔、曼谷等地都设有办事机构，代表着包括设计、印制电路板生产以及电子封装的电子内联工业的方方面面。

出版物

1）期刊与杂志

❏ SMT 设备与技术，双月刊。

2）标准

❏ World PCB Production Report for the Year 2011；ISBN：978 - 1 - 61193 - 517 - 2.

❏ Generic Standard on Printed Board Design；ISBN：978 - 1 - 61193 - 069 - 6.

❏ Design - Richtlinie für flexible Leiterplatten（German language）；ISBN：978 - 1 - 61193 - 084 - 9.

❏ Cover and Bonding Material for Flexible Printed Circuitry；ISBN：978 - 1 - 61193 - 079 - 5.

❏ Specification for Electroless Nickel/Electroless Palladium/Immersion Gold（ENEPIG）Plating for Printed Circuit Boards；ISBN：978 - 1 - 61193 - 081 - 8.

❏ Requirements for Printed Electronics Functional Conductive Materials；ISBN：978 - 1 - 61193 - 070 - 2.

❏ Design and Assembly Process Implementation for BGAs；ISBN：978 - 1 -

61193 – 080 – 1.

❑ Requirements for Power Conversion Devices for the Computer and Telecommunications Industries; ISBN: 978 – 1 – 61193 – 072 – 6.

❑ IPC/WHMA – A – 620B Requirements and Acceptance for Cable and Wire Harness Assemblies; ISBN: 978 – 1 – 61193 – 066 – 5.

❑ Proceedings of Conflict Minerals Seminar.

❑ IPC International Technology Roadmap for Electronic Interconnections – CD – ROM 2013.

❑ Latin America: Regional Outlook for the Electronics Industry.

❑ A nedvességre/újraömlesztésre érzékeny felületszerelt alkatrészek kezelése, csomagolása, szállítása és használata (Hungarian); ISBN: 978 – 1 – 61193 – 082 – 5.

❑ Handhabung, Verpackung, Transport und Einsatz feuchtigkeits –/reflow – und/oder prozessempfindlicher Bauteile (German); ISBN: 978 – 1 – 61193 – 086 – 3.

❑ Требования к паяльным пастам (Russian); ISBN: 978 – 1 – 61193 – 032 – 0.

❑ IPC Sample Master Ordering Agreement for EMS Companies and OEMs.

❑ IPC Executive Compensation Study for the North American Electronics Industry 2011—2012; ISBN: 978 – 1 – 61193 – 519 – 6.

❑ 焊膏要求; ISBN: 978 – 1 – 61193 – 088 – 7.

会议信息

❑ 2015 International Printed Circuit & APEX South China Fair; 2015. 12. 02—04; 中国深圳.

❑ IPC APEX EXPO 2016; 2016. 03. 13—17; Las Vegas, NV, USA.

NATO 军事科学与技术组织

英文名称：NATO Science and Technology Organization，NATO – STO
网　　址：http：//www. sto. nato. int/

机构简介

NATO 军事科学与技术组织由成立于 1998 年的 NATO 研究与发展组织（NATO Research and Technology Organization，NATO – RTO）发展而来，NATO – RTO 是由航空航天研究与发展咨询集团（Advisory Group for Aerospace Research and Development，AGARD）和国防研究集团（Defence Research Group，DRG）合并而成。

NATO 军事科学与技术组织是北约主要的国防科学技术组织，总部位于布鲁塞尔，是北约领导层的高级科学顾问，致力于共同研究和信息交流，发展并维护北约的长期研究和技术战略，为北约的所有研究和技术问题提供建议，由科学技术委员会、首席科学家和 3 个执行委员会组成。

- ❏ 首席科学家办公室（Office of the Chief Scientist）位于布鲁塞尔，为首席科学家提供行政和执行支持。
- ❏ 联合支持办公室（Collaboration Support Office，CSO）位于巴黎，为其 2 线委员会和 3 线小组的活动提供行政和执行支持。
- ❏ 海军研究与实验中心（Centre for Maritime Research and Experimentation，CMRE）位于意大利拉斯佩齐亚，组织实施科学研究和技术的发展，进行创新性的科学研究，满足北约国家对防务和安全的需求。

NATO 军事科学与技术组织下设 8 个技术小组：

- ❏ 运载器应用技术委员会（Applied Vehicle Technology Panel，AVT）。
- ❏ 人为因素和医学委员会（Human Factors and Medicine Panel，HFM）。
- ❏ 信息系统技术小组（Information Systems Technology Panel，IST）。
- ❏ 系统分析和研究小组（System Analysis and Studies Panel，SAS）。
- ❏ 系统概念与集成小组（Systems Concepts and Integration Panel，SCI）。
- ❏ 传感器和电子科技委员会（Sensors and Electronics Technology Panel，SET）。
- ❏ 建模与仿真小组（NATO Modelling and Simulation Group，NMSG）。
- ❏ 信息管理委员会（Information Management Committee，IMC）。

出版物

NATO 军事科学与技术组织的每个小组每年都会召开会议、出版会议文集和报告，其中与国防科技相关性高的领域有运载器应用技术、人为因素与军事医学、信息系统技术、系统分析与研究、系统概念与集成等。

1）会议录

2）报告

❑ Technical Reports.

❑ CMRE Reports.

❑ Annual Report.

3）简讯

❑ STO Newsletter.

❑ The Centre Quarterly.

4）技术备忘录

5）其他出版物

❑ CMRE Fact Sheets.

会议信息

❑ Lecture Series on "C2 to Simulation Interoperability（C2SIMI）"（MSG – 141）；2015. 10. 05—06；Hants，UK.

❑ Specialists Meeting on "Intelligence & Autonomy（Robotics）"（IST – 127）；2015. 10. 06—08；Bonn，Germany.

❑ C2 to Simulation Interoperability（C2SIMI）；2015. 10. 08—09，Arcueil，France.

❑ Lecture Series on "Advanced Algorithms for Effectively Fusing Hard and Soft Information"（IST – 134）；2015. 10. 12—13；Wachtberg，Germany.

❑ Symposium on "Health Surveillance and Informatics in Missions：Multidisciplinary Approaches and Perspectives"（HFM – 254）；2015. 10. 12—14；Paris，France.

❑ Specialists Meeting on "Augmented Reality for Improved Situational Awareness and Survivability of Combat Vehicles"（AVT – 256）；2015. 10. 12—14；Prague，Czech Republic.

❑ Specialists Meeting on "Munitions Related Contamination"（AVT – 244）；2015. 10. 12—14；Prague，Czech Republic.

❑ Specialists Meeting on "Future Rotorcraft Requirements"（AVT – 245）；2015. 10. 12—15；Prague，Czech Republic.

❑ Fall 2015 AVT Panel Meeting Week Enrolment Link for AVT Panel Members，Technical Team Members and Invited Guests to Technical Teams and Exploratory Teams（AVT – 36TH）；2015. 10. 12—16；Prague，Czech Republic.

- ❏ Lecture Series on "Advanced Algorithms for Effectively Fusing Hard and Soft Information" (IST – 134); 2015. 10. 15—16; Salamanca, Spain.
- ❏ Lecture Series on "Cognition and Radar Sensing" (SET – 216); 2015. 10. 19—20; Prague, Czech Republic.
- ❏ Lecture Series on "Cognition and Radar Sensing" (SET – 216); 2015. 10. 22—23; Wachtberg, Germany.
- ❏ Lecture Series on "Advanced Algorithms for Effectively Fusing Hard and Soft Information" (IST – 134); 2015. 11. 16—17; Adelphi, MD, USA.
- ❏ Lecture Series on "Advanced Algorithms for Effectively Fusing Hard and Soft Information" (IST – 134); 2015. 11. 19—20; Ottawa, Canada.
- ❏ Lecture Series on "Space Debris Reentry and Mitigation" (AVT – 262); 2015. 11. 30—12. 04; VKI, Belgium.

国际船舶电子公司协会

法语名称：Comité International Radio – Maritime，CIRM

英文名称：International Association for Marine Electronics Companies

网　　址：http：//www. cirm. org/

机构简介

国际船舶电子公司协会最初由 8 个从事海洋无线电应用的公司于 1928 年在西班牙建立，1948 年在比利时进行重组，随后迁往伦敦。

国际船舶电子公司协会已成为船舶电子的公司的主要国际协会，拥有来自全世界 29 个国家的 90 个成员公司，其职能是：①代表国际船舶电子工业的利益，在解决监管问题以及提升船舶电子产业方面协调成员的观点和行动，向国际监管组织提供技术和工业建议；②为成员提供专业信息服务，提供一个交流信息和商业机会的私人平台，使成员能够参与影响他们产品和服务的国际法规和标准的制定。

国际船舶电子公司协会是 1949 年认证的 9 大原始国际实体之一，是一个为国际海事组织（International Maritime Organization，IMO）提供咨询服务的非政府组织。国际船舶电子公司协会是国际电信联盟（International Telecommunication Union，ITU）的部门成员，是国际标准化组织（Organization for Standardization，ISO）和国际电工技术委员会（International Electrotechnical Commission，IEC）的联络会员。国际船舶电子公司协会与以下组织是相互观察员：国际水文组织（International Hydrographic Organization，IHO）、国际航标协会（International Association of Lighthouse Authorities，IALA）、国际集装箱协会（International Chamber of Shipping，ICS）以及美国海上无线电技术委员会（US Radiotechnical Commission for Maritime，RTCM）。

出版物

技术论文

国际船舶电子公司协会每年都会召开一些技术会议，并出版会议报告和技术论文。

会议信息

❑ IMO/ITU Joint Experts WG；2015. 10. 05—10. 9；IMO London.

❑ WG6 – Interfaces；2015. 10. 14—16；Busan，Korea.

❑ TC80 – Plenary；2015. 10. 19—20；Busan，Korea.

❑ IALA ENAV 17；2015. 10. 26—30；Paris，France.

❑ PT – BAM；2015. 12. 08—10；BSI London.

国际电信联盟

英文名称：International Telecommunication Union，ITU

网　　址：http：//www. itu. int/en/pages/default. aspx

机构简介

国际电信联盟是联合国的一个专门机构，也是历史最悠久的一个国际组织，简称"国际电联"、"电联"或"ITU"。

国际电信联盟的前身是 1865 年 5 月 17 日在巴黎创立的国际电报联盟，是世界上历史最悠久的国际组织，总部设在瑞士日内瓦，其主要任务是制定标准，分配无线电资源，制定各个国家之间的国际长途互连方案，并负责确立国际无线电和电信的管理制度和标准。

作为主管信息通信技术事务的联合国机构，国际电信联盟是世界范围内联系各国政府和私营部门的纽带，通过其麾下的无线电通信、标准化和发展的电信展览活动，是全球高峰会议的主办机构。

国际电信联盟的成员包括 193 个成员国和近 800 个部门成员及部门准成员。2011 年，该联盟第 18 届全权代表大会通过重要决议：邀请大学和科研单位作为其学术会员参加国际电联的活动，第一批获准成为国际电信联盟学术成员的 5 所高校及科研单位包括中国南京邮电大学、清华大学，日本早稻田大学以及突尼斯的两所大学。

出版物

1）会议录

❑ Proceedings of ITU Kaleidoscope.

❑ Resolutions and Decisions of the Council of the International Telecommunication Union.

❑ Collection of the Basic Texts of the International Telecommunication Union adopted by the Plenipotentiary Conference.

❑ World Radiocommunication Conferences.

❑ World Telecommunication Standardization Assembly Proceedings.

2）期刊与杂志

❑《国际电联新闻月刊》。

3）报告

❑ The CPM Report to the 2015 World Radiocommunication Conference（WRC – 15）.

❑ Measuring the Information Society.

4）法规

☐ Radio Regulations.

5）标准

☐ ITU – R Recommendations and Reports – DVD – ROM.

6）数据库

☐ ITU Terms & Definitions Database.

☐ World Telecommunication/ICT Indicators Database CD – ROM.

7）图书

☐ ITU – R propagation prediction methods for interference and sharing studies.

☐ Radiometeorology.

☐ Amateur and amateur – satellite services.

☐ Radio Astronomy.

☐ Handbook on Global Trends in International Mobile Telecommunications.

☐ Guidance for bilateral/multilateral discussions on the use of frequency range 1350 MHz ~ 43. 5 GHz by fixed service systems.

☐ Handbook on Global Trends in International Mobile Telecommunications.

☐ Ground Wave Propagation.

☐ Space Network Systems (SNS).

☐ Security in Telecommunications and Information Technology.

8）年鉴

☐ Yearbook of Statistics – Telecommunication/ICT Indicators.

9）其他出版物

☐ List V – List of Ship Stations and Maritime Mobile Service Identity Assignments.

☐ BR International Frequency Information Circular (BR IFIC) – Space Service.

☐ BR International Frequency Information Circular (BR IFIC) – Terrestrial Services.

会议信息

☐ ITU Telecom World 2015；2015. 10. 12—15；Budapest, Hungary.

☐ Radiocommunication Assembly 2015 (RA – 15)；2015. 10. 26—30；Geneva, Switzerland.

☐ World Radiocommunication Conference 2015；2015. 11. 02—27；Geneva, Switzerland.

☐ World Telecommunication/ICT Indicators Symposium (WTIS)；2015. 11. 30—12. 02；Hiroshima, Japan.

国际电子技师协会

英文名称：Electronics Technicians Association，International，ETA

网　　址：http：//www. eta－i. org/

机构简介

国际电子技师协会成立于1978年，位于美国印第安纳州格林卡斯尔，是一个非营利性机构，是一个世界范围内的联盟，为技术职业人员提供支持。

国际电子技师协会代表从技师和教育者到企业机构的整个电子行业，其电子认证项目被广为人知，并被国际认证认可委员会（International Certification Accreditation Council，ICAC）所认可，帮助电子技师提升他们的知识水平，并使他们能在其领域内脱颖而出，并将雇主和电子专业人员紧紧联系在一起。

国际电子技师协会在各种电子领域已经颁发了150 000多个技术证书，涵盖80多个认证项目，拥有600多位服务于各种行业咨询委员会的主题专家（Subject Matter Experts，SME）以及1 000多个认证管理员（Certification Administrators，CA）。

出版物

1）期刊与杂志

❏ The High－Tech News，bi－monthly.

2）学习指南

❏ EM3 Analog Basics.

❏ EM4 Digital Basics.

❏ EM Bulk Rates.

❏ EM1－DC Basics.

❏ EM2 AC Basics.

会议信息

❏ 2015 Wireless Leadership Summit；2015. 10. 07—09；Atlanta，Georgia，USA.

❏ ACTE CareerTech Vision 2015；2015. 11. 19—22；New Orleans，Louisiana，United States.

国际对地观测卫星委员会

英文名称：Committee on Earth Observation Satellites，CEOS
网　　址：http：//www. ceos. org

机构简介

国际对地观测卫星委员会创建于 1984 年，是空间地球观测活动国际合作的中心，主要目标是改进空间观测系统的功能，通过充当地球观测活动国际合作的中心，给予其成员及用户以帮助，交流相关政策和技术，关注地球观测领域普遍关心的问题。

国际对地观测卫星委员会的成员主要是对正在进行或即将进行的卫星地球观测系统相关活动给予资助或承担项目责任的国家或国际政府机构，包括国家海洋和大气管理局（National Oceanic and Atmospheric Administration，NOAA）、美国国家航空航天局（National Aeronautics and Space Administration，NASA）、欧洲航空航天局（European Space Agency，ESA）、欧洲气象卫星开发组织（European Organization for the Exploitation of Meteorological Satellites，EUMET-SAT）、日本航空航天局（Japan Aerospace Exploration Agency，JAXA），以及澳大利亚、巴西、加拿大、中国、法国、德国、印度、意大利、日本、瑞士、俄罗斯、乌克兰、英国等国家对应的空间地球观测系统。支持国际对地观测卫星委员会的成员机构可被邀请为观察员，如来自比利时、加拿大、新西兰和挪威的机构。其他国际卫星合作组织和国际政府间机构的成员地位已得到世界粮农组织（Food and Agriculture Organization）、全球气候观测系统、全球海洋观测系统、国际科学联合会（International Council of Scientific Unions）、国际地圈生物圈计划、政府间海洋地质委员会、联合国环境规划署、联合国外层空间事务办公室、世界气候研究计划和世界气象组织的认可。

国际对地观测卫星委员会的标准化和合法化工作组（Working Group on Calibration and Validation，WGCV）致力于标准化/合法化运动的合作，技术信息的交流，设备、资源和人才的优化与共享，设有 4 个小组，研究内容分别为 SAR 标准化、微波传感器、地形图、红外线光学传感器。

国际对地观测卫星委员会的信息系统和服务工作组（WGISS）提供有关数据加工、数据管理、数据获取、数据存储及数据传播方面的信息，其目的在于扩大信息服务范围，设有数据检索、数据管理和网络维护等 3 个小组。

出版物

1）简讯
❑ 每年的 2 月和 8 月出版。

2）其他出版物

- ❏ CEOS Constellations for GEO Process Paper.
- ❏ CEOS Flyer for GEO－5.
- ❏ CEOS Brochure.
- ❏ CEOS Flyer for GEO－4.
- ❏ CEOS Implementation Plan（IP）.
- ❏ CEOS Response to the GCOS Implementation Plan（IP）.
- ❏ CEOS Earth Observation（EO）Handbook，每三年出版一次。
- ❏ CEOS Terms of Reference.
- ❏ SIT Terms of Reference.
- ❏ LSI Declaration of Intent & Annexes.
- ❏ OCR Implementation Plan.
- ❏ OSVW Implementation Plan.
- ❏ PC Implementation Plan.
- ❏ ACC Concept Document & Draft Workplan.
- ❏ WGClimate Terms of Reference.
- ❏ WGISS Terms of Reference.
- ❏ WGEdu Terms of Reference.
- ❏ WGCV Terms of Reference.
- ❏ WGCV Atmospheric Composition Subgroup Terms of Reference.
- ❏ WGCV Infrared and Visible Optical Sensors Subgroup Terms of Reference.
- ❏ WGCV Land Product Validation Subgroup Terms of Reference.
- ❏ WGCV Microwave Sensors Subgroup Terms of Reference.
- ❏ WGCV Synthetic Aperture Radar Subgroup Terms of Reference.
- ❏ WGCV Terrain Mapping Subgroup Terms of Reference.

会议信息

- ❏ WGCapD：Civil Security & EO Workshop；2015.10.29；Quebec City, Canada.

国际公共安全通信官协会

英文名称： Association of Public Safety Communications Officials International, APCO

网　　址： https：//www. apcointl. org/index. php

机构简介

国际公共安全通信官协会成立于1935 年，是世界上历史最悠久、规模最大的公共安全通信专业人士组织，为世界范围内的公共安全通信领域的领导者和通信专家及公众提供完整公共安全通信经验、专业开发、技术帮助等。

出版物

1）期刊与杂志

❑ Public Safety Communications.

2）年度报告

❑ APCO Annual Report.

3）标准

❑ Public Safety Communications Common Status Codes for Data Exchange.

❑ Best Practices for the Use of Social Media in Public Safety Communications.

❑ Multi – Functional Multi – Discipline Computer Aided Dispatch（CAD）Minimum Functional Requirements.

❑ Standard Channel Nomenclature for the Public Safety Interoperability Channels.

❑ Standard for Telecommunicator Emergency Response Taskforce（TERT）Deployment.

❑ Public Safety Answering Point（PSAP）Service Capability Criteria Rating Scale.

❑ Wireless 9 – 1 – 1 Deployment and Management Effective Practices Guide.

❑ Common Incident Disposition Codes for Data Exchange.

❑ Establishment of a Quality Assurance and Quality Improvement Program for Public Safety Answering Points.

会议信息

❑ Emerging Technology Forum；2015. 11. 17—18；Atlanta, GA, USA.

❑ 2016 APCO Western Regionals Conference；2016. 03. 08—10；Portland,

Oregon, USA.

- ❑ DAS & Small Cells Congress Europe; 2016. 05. 16—18; Las Vegas, NV, USA.
- ❑ APCO Annual Conference & Expo; 2016. 08. 14—17; Orlando, FL, USA.
- ❑ APCO Annual Conference & Expo; 2017. 08. 13—16; Denver, CO, USA.
- ❑ APCO Annual Conference & Expo; 2018. 08. 05—08; Las Vegas, NV, USA.
- ❑ APCO Annual Conference & Expo; 2019. 08. 11—14; Baltimore, MD, USA.
- ❑ APCO Annual Conference & Expo; 2020. 08. 02—05; Orlando, FL, USA.
- ❑ APCO Annual Conference & Expo; 2021. 08. 15—18; San Antonio, TX, USA.
- ❑ APCO Annual Conference & Expo; 2022. 08. 07—10; Anaheim, CA, USA.

国际海事卫星组织

英文名称：Inmarsat plc

网　　址：http：//www.inmarsat.com/

机构简介

国际海事卫星组织是海运国家为提高船舶通信效率而共同投资筹建的一个技术运营机构，实质上是一个总投资额为 3 亿美元的国际合营股份公司，其宗旨是为改进海上通信而提供所必需的空间段，从而有助于改进海上紧急通信和海上公众通信，并提高船舶效率和无线电定位能力。

1973 年 11 月 23 日，政府间海事协商组织（简称海协，现改称国际海事组织）第 8 届全体大会通过决议：召开国际海事卫星系统筹建会议。经过准备，海协于 1975 年和 1976 年先后召开了 3 次会议，并在第 3 次会议上通过了《国际海事卫星组织公约》和《国际海事卫星组织业务协定》。此后，海协又相继召开了 5 次筹备会议，前后共有 57 个国家派代表或观察员、19 个国际组织派观察员出席了会议。《国际海事卫星组织公约》于 1979 年 7 月 16 日正式生效，同年 10 月在伦敦召开的国际海事卫星组织第 1 届全体大会，宣告国际海事卫星组织正式成立，总部设在伦敦。

国际海事卫星组织的主要活动有：讨论海事卫星通信的要求，制定地面站和船站接入国际海事卫星组织空间段的标准和批准程序，确定空间段方案和卫星轨道，制定财务政策。

国际海事卫星组织的最高负责人为总干事，总干事领导下的执行局负责处理日常事务，并设有大会、理事会、财务委员会、技术委员会和执行局。大会是最高权力机构，每两年召开一次。理事会由 26 个理事国组成，其中 22 个理事国为拥有股份最多的国家，其余 4 个是由地区选出的代表。理事会每年召开 4 次会议。

国际海事卫星组织自 1999 年起由一个政府间组织变更为一个私人公司——国际海事卫星公司（Inmarsat plc），并于 2005 年在伦敦证券交易所上市。

中国于 1979 年加入国际海事卫星组织，并在第一届第三次全体大会上当选为理事，指定北京船舶通信导航公司作为经济实体参加这一组织的经营管理。

出版物

手册

❑ EXPLORER Push to Talk.

❑ Haiti Earthquake Aftermath.

❑ TCP Payload Compression.

❑ Seven Questions to ask before Building your Satellite SCADA Network.

❑ Satellite Services.

❑ Type Approved Systems SwiftBroadband.

❑ Inmarsat Satellite Services for Utilities.

会议信息

❑ 7 th AIDF Global Disaster Relief Summit 2015；2015. 09. 11—12；ashington D. C. , USA.

❑ Geo Hack Day；2015. 09. 05；City Road HQ, London.

国际静电放电协会

英文名称： Electrostatic Discharge Association，EDA

网　　址： http：//www. esda. org/

机构简介

国际静电放电协会建立于 1982 年，是一个专业志愿协会，致力于避免静电放电理论和实践的进步研究。它由最初的不到 100 个会员发展到如今在全世界范围内超过 2 000 个会员。最初，国际静电放电协会的工作重点在电子元件的静电放电效应上；如今，它将工作范围扩展到诸如纺织品、塑料、网络处理、洁净室以及图形艺术等领域。

国际静电放电协会的成员任职于协会标准委员会，在每年的 EOS/ESD 座谈会上发表技术论文，并为其他国家的相似组织提供通信联系。该协会已与各个国家的相似组织建立了非正式和正式的关系，正式的关系包括日本可信赖度中心、新加坡生产力标准局、日本电子工业联合会、德国静电放电论坛、欧洲电子器件可信度和时效物理与分析研讨会，以及巴西电磁兼容协会等。国际静电放电协会在国际电工委员会的静电领域代表美国的利益。

出版物

1）通讯

❑ Threshold.

2）会议录

❑ EOS/ESD Symposia Proceedings.

3）教程说明

❑ 12 TUT（Basic）.

❑ 12 TUT（On – Chip）.

❑ 12 TUT（ESD Design & IO）.

❑ 12 TUT（System Level：Principles & Testing）.

❑ 12 TUT（Sunday，Monday，Thursday）.

4）其他出版物

❑ ESD DS1. 1 – 2013 Wrist Straps；ISBN：1 – 58537 – 235 – 8.

❑ ANSI/ESD STM4. 2 – 2012 ESD Protective Worksurfaces – Charge Dissipation Characteristics；ISBN：1 – 58537 – 208 – 0.

❑ ESD DSP14. 1 – 2012 System Level Electrostatic Discharge（ESD）Simulator Verification；ISBN：1 – 58537 – 215 – 3.

❑ ANSI/ESD S8. 1 – 2012 Symbols – ESD Awareness；ISBN：1 – 58537 – 233 – 1.

❑ ESD DSTM12. 1 – 2013 Seating – Resistive Measurement；ISBN：1 – 58537 –

230 - 7.

- [ ] ANSI/ESD STM11. 31 – 2012 Bags；ISBN：1 – 58537 – 209 – 9.
- [ ] ANSI/ESD S11. 4 – 2012 Performance Limits for Bags；ISBN：1 – 58537 – 238 – 2.
- [ ] ESD DSTM5. 2 – 2012 Electrostatic Discharge Sensitivity Testing – Machine Model（MM） – Component Level；ISBN：1 – 58537 – 212 – 9.
- [ ] ESD DSP5. 2. 1 – 2012 Human Body Model（HBM）and Machine Model（MM）Alternative Test Method：Supply Pin Ganging – Component Level；ISBN：1 – 58537 – 213 – 7.
- [ ] ESD DSP5. 2. 2 – 2012 Human Body Model（HBM）and Machine Model（MM）Alternative Test Method：Split Signal Pin – Component Level；ISBN：1 – 58537 – 214 – 5.
- [ ] ANSI/ESD SP3. 3 – 2012 Periodic Verification of Air Ionizers；ISBN：1 – 58537 – 236 – 6.
- [ ] ANSI/ESD SP3. 4 – 2012 Periodic Verification of Air Ionizer Performance Using a Small Test Fixture；ISBN：1 – 58537 – 233 – 1.
- [ ] ANSI/ESDA/JEDEC JS – 001 – 2012 ESDA/JEDEC Joint Standard for Electrostatic Discharge Sensitivity Testing – Human Body Model（HBM） – Component Level；ISBN：1 – 58537 – 211 – 0.
- [ ] ESD DSTM2. 1 – 2013 Garments – Resistive Characterization；ISBN：1 – 58537 – 234 – X.
- [ ] ESD DLB7. 1 – 2013 Resistive Characterization of Materials – Floor Materials；ISBN：1 – 58537 – 228 – 5.

会议信息

- [ ] Electro Optical System/Electro – Static Discharge（EOS/ESD）Symposium and Tutorials；2015. 09. 27—10. 02；Reno，NV，USA.
- [ ] Integrated Reliability Workshop（IIRW）2015；2015. 10. 11—15；Fallen Leaf Lake，CA，USA.
- [ ] Electrostatic Discharge Association（ESDA）Certified TR53 Technician's Certification Training；2015. 11. 03—05；NY，USA.
- [ ] Electro – Static Discharge（ESD）Device Design Essentials；2015. 11. 11—12；Munich，Germany.
- [ ] Advanced Electro – Static Discharge（ESD）Characterization and Test Methods；2015. 11. 13；Munich，Germany.
- [ ] Electro – Static Discharge（ESD）Association Meeting Series；2016. 04. 12—

19；Garden Grove, California, USA.

❑ 2016 International ESD Workshop；2016. 05. 16—19；Tutzing, Germany.

❑ Advanced Electro – Static Discharge（ESD）Association Meeting Series/ EOS/ESD Symposium and Tutorials；2016. 09. 08—16；Garden Grove, California, USA.

❑ EOS/ESD Symposium；2016. 09. 11—16；Garden Grove, California, USA.

❑ Electro Optical System/Electro – Static Discharge（EOS/ESD）Symposium and Tutorials；2017. 05. 09—14；Tucson, AZ, USA.

❑ Electro Optical System/Electro – Static Discharge（EOS/ESD）Symposium and Tutorials；2017. 09. 07—15；Tucson, AZ, USA.

❑ EOS/ESD Symposium；2017. 09. 10—15；Tucson, AZ, USA.

❑ Electro – Static Discharge（ESD）Association Meeting Series；2018. 04. 10— 15；Reno, NV, USA.

❑ Electro Optical System/Electro – Static Discharge（EOS/ESD）Symposium and Tutorials；2018. 09. 20—28；Reno, NV, USA.

❑ EOS/ESD Symposium；2018. 09. 23—28；Reno, NV, USA.

国际全球导航卫星系统协会

英文名称：International Global Navigation Satellite Systems Society Inc. , IGNSS

网　　址：http：//www. ignss. org/Default. aspx

机构简介

国际全球导航卫星系统协会成立于 2004 年，位于澳大利亚昆士兰，是一个非营利性组织，关注的领域涉及导航技术在空、天、陆地和海洋的应用，还通过组织研讨会、座谈会、会议或贸易展及其他成员要求的活动来为其成员提供服务。其宗旨是：

（1）鼓励全球导航卫星系统的研发；

（2）鼓励终端用户全球导航卫星系统应用的开发；

（3）提高公众对全球导航卫星系统的总体认识；

（4）鼓励协助成员间、成员与研究机构、政府和企业建立联系；

（5）收集成员感兴趣并有益于成员的信息；

（6）为会员提供倾听来自研究机构、企业和政府的高质量演讲的机会；

（7）成为会员继续教育与培训的联系枢纽。

出版物

会议录

❏ IGNSS conference & exhibition 会议录。

国际通信卫星组织

英文名称：International Telecommunications Satellite Organization，Intelsat S. A.

网　　址：http：//www. intelsat. com/

机构简介

国际通信卫星组织于 1964 年由 11 个国家共同成立，是一个政府间的全球性商业通信卫星机构，其宗旨是建立和发展全球商业卫星通信系统，供世界各国平等使用。2001 年，国际通信卫星组织完成私有化，成为一个私有公司。2006 年，国际卫星通信组织兼并了 PanAmSat，并荣获"全球最佳传送服务提供商"称号。2007 年，BC Partners 公司宣布持有国际卫星通信组织 76% 的股份。2013 年，国际卫星通信组织更名为 Intelsat S. A.，并在纽约证券交易所上市。

2014 年，国际卫星通信组织收入达到 24. 72 亿美元，约有员工 1 100 人，为全球 50 多个卫星和 1 500 多客户如电信公司、网络服务提供商等提供服务。

出版物

简讯

❏ Intelsat Insider Newsletter，季刊，内容分为 5 个地区，即 Africa，Asia Pacific，Europe and Middle East，Latin America and Caribbean，North America。

会议信息

❏ Digital Ship Singapore 2015；2015. 10. 13—14；Singapore.

❏ Congresso Latino – Americano Satelites 2015；2015. 10. 15—16；Rio de Janeiro，Brazil.

❏ Digital Ship Korea 2015；2015. 10. 22；Busan，Korea.

❏ CASBAA 2015；2015. 10. 26—28；Hong Kong，China.

❏ Futurecom 2015；2015. 10. 26—29；Sao Paulo，Brazil.

❏ Digital TV CEE 2015；2015. 10. 27—28；Warsaw，Poland.

国际微电子组装与封装协会

英文名称：International Microelectronics Assembly and Packaging Society，iMAPS

网 址：http：//www. imaps. org/

机构简介

国际微电子组装与封装协会的前身是成立于 1967 年的国际混合微电子协会（International Society for Hybrid Microelectronics，ISHM）。1996 年，国际混合微电子协会与国际电子与封装协会（International Electronic and Packaging Society，IEPS）合并，成立了国际微电子组装与封装协会。

国际微电子组装与封装协会是全球最大的致力于通过专业教育来推动微电子和电子封装技术发展进步的协会，每年举办多达 30 次会议，为微电子和封装专业领域的人员提供教育和市场机会；此外，还成立了微电子基金会，每年为电子封装领域的学生提供资助。该协会在北美有 23 个分会，在北美之外的世界其他地方有 21 个分会，在美国拥有 3 000 多名会员，在世界其他地方有 3 000 多名会员。

出版物

1）期刊与杂志

❏ Advancing Microelectronics Online，双月刊。

❏ Journal of Microelectronics and Electronic Packaging Online，季刊；ISSN：1551－4897。

2）在线图书馆

❏ IMAPS On－line Library——iKNOW Microelectronics，有 3200 多种出版物，包括期刊与杂志文章、会议录、小组 PPT、网络视频、CD－ROM 等。

会议信息

❏ IMPACT 2015；2015. 10. 21—23；Taipei，CH.

❏ IMAPS 2015－48th International Symposium on Microelectronics；2015. 10. 26—29；Orlando，California，USA.

国际无线电科学联盟

法语名称：Union Radio – Scientifique Internationale，URSI
英文名称：International Union of Radio Science
网　　址：http：//www. ursi. org/en/home. asp

机构简介

国际无线电科学联盟成立于 1919 年，常设机构设在比利时布鲁塞尔。该联盟是国际无线电科学领域的非政府非营利性学术组织，是国际科学理事会（International Council for Science，ICSU）的下属机构。其宗旨是在无线电科学领域内促进国际合作，协调国际研究，讨论和传播研究成果，促进观测方法和仪器的统一与标准化。

国际无线电科学联盟下设 9 个学术委员会：电磁度量、场和波、信号和系统、物理电子学、干扰环境、非电离媒质中的波现象、电离层无线电波传播、等离子体中的波、射电天文学。联盟每 3 年召开一次全会，各委员会在此期间组织学术活动，并组织经常性的专题学术讨论会。此外，联盟负责国际无线电科学联盟数据广播和世界日服务工作，进行日地物理数据的快速交换，组织或参与全球性观测研究活动等。国际无线电科学联盟同国际无线电通信咨询委员会（International Radio Consultative Committee，CCIR）、电气和电子工程师协会（Institute of Electrical and Electronics Engineers，IEEE）、世界气象组织（World Meteorological Organization，WMO）、国际空间研究委员会（Committee on Space Research，COSPAR）、国际日地物理委员会（Scientific Committee on Solar – Terrestrial Physics，SCOSTEP）、世界数据组织（World Data Center，WDC）有咨询和学术联系。

出版物

国际无线电科学联盟的主要出版物有《URSI 简讯》、《无线电科学》以及每一届的会议录、有关的学术讨论会文集、科学专论等，其中会议论文可以免费下载。

1）期刊与杂志

❑ URSI Newsletter，URSI 简讯，双月刊，通过电子邮件发布。

❑ Radio Science Bulletin，季刊，每年 3、6、9、12 月出版。

❑ Radio Science Journal，由 URSI 主办，由美国地球物理联盟（American Geophysical Union，AGU）出版。

❑ Journal of Atmospheric and Terrestrial Physics.

2）白皮书

❑ URSI white paper on SPS – Book version.

❑ URSI white paper on SPS – Book version – Appendices.

❑ Report of the SPS Inter – Commission Working Group.

❑ Report of the SPS Inter – Commission Working Group – Appendices.

❑ White Paper on Solar Power Satellites.

3）会议录

❑ Proceedings of the URSI General Assembly.

❑ Proceedings of the URSI Anniversary Symposium.

❑ Proceedings of the Corsendonk Conference.

会议信息

❑ 2nd Symposium of the Committee on Space Research（COSPAR）: Water and Life in the Universe（COSPAR 2015）; 2015.11.09—13; Foz do Iguacu, Brazil.

❑ 2nd URSI Regional Conference on Radio Science（URSI – RCRS 2015）; 2015.11.16—19; New Delhi, India.

❑ 2016 National Radio Science Meeting（NRSM 2016）; 2016.01.06—09; Boulder, CO, USA.

❑ European Conference on Antennas and Propagation 2016（EuCAP 2016）; 2016.04.10—15; Davos, Switzerland.

❑ 11th European Conference on Synthetic Aperture Radar（EUSAR 2016）; 2016.06.06—09; Hamburg, Germany.

❑ 41st Scientific Assembly of the Committee on Space Research（COSPAR）and Associated Events（COSPAR 2016）; 2016.07.30—08.07; Istanbul, Turkey.

❑ 2016 URSI Commission B International Symposium on Electromagnetic Theory（EMTS 2016）; 2016.08.14—18; Espoo, Finland.

❑ Nordic HF Conference with Longwave Symposium LW 13（HF13）; 2016.08.15—17; Faro, Sweden.

❑ 2016 URSI Asia – Pacific Radio Science Conference（AP – RASC 2016）; 2016.08.21—25; Seoul, Korea.

❑ 2016 International Symposium on Antennas and Propagation（ISAP 2016）; 2016.10.24—28; Okinawa, Japan.

❑ XXXIInd URSI General Assembly and Scientific Symposium（URSI GASS 2017）; 2017.08.19—26; Montreal, Canada.

❑ 2019 URSI Commission B International Symposium on Electromagnetic Theory（EMTS 2019）; 2019.05.27—31; San Diego, CA, USA.

国际无线电与电信电磁工程师协会

英文名称：International Association for Radio, Telecommunications and Electromagnetics, iNARTE

网　址：http://www.inarte.org/

机构简介

国际无线电与电信电磁工程师协会由成立于1982 年的原美国无线电与电信工程师协会（National Association of Radio and Telecommunications Engineers, NARTE）发展而来。NARTE 是非营利的电磁  兼容、静电放电、电信、产品安全等领域优秀工程师和技术员级专家认证组织。1994 年国际静电放电协会选择 NARTE 实施和执行静电放电控制工程师和技术员的认证。2007 年 NARTE 在全球设立考试中心，并更名为 iNARTE，并且在中国北京和南京两地设立了静电放电和电磁兼容考试中心并批准了培训中心。2012 年 6 月 30 日，国际无线电与电信电磁工程师协会并入全球最大的非营利性国际化人力认证组织——2004 年成立的美澳联合人员培训和注册机构（RABQSA International），组成了 Exemplar Global，但是组成 Exemplar Global 的两个机构仍然独立运行。Exemplar Global 在全球审核员范围内享有非常高的声誉，是国际领先的认可人才与培训认证机构，致力于人才与培训认证项目的设计、开发、管理与运作，并提供配套的职业发展服务。美澳联合人员培训和注册机构于 2004 年由美国注册认可委员会（Registrar Accreditation Board, RAB）和澳大利亚质量协会（Quality Society of Australasia, QSA）合并而成，在悉尼、密尔沃基、东京、台北、河内、吉隆坡、奥克兰等地设有办事处。

国际信息处理联合会

英文名称：International Federation for Information Processing，IFIP

网　　址：http：//www.ifip.org/

机构简介

国际信息处理联合会于 1960 年在联合国教育、科学及文化组织（UNESCO）的支持下正式成立，位于奥地利拉克森堡，是一个非政府非营利性组织。

国际信息处理联合会的宗旨是推动信息科学和信息技术的发展，加强信息处理领域的国际合作，促进信息处理的研究、开发及其在科学和人类活动中的应用，普及和交流信息处理方面的情报，扩大信息处理方面的教育事业。

国际信息处理联合会代表着 5 大洲 56 个国家或地区的 IT 协会，将 3 500 多名在学术界和产业界的科学家联系起来，每年赞助或主办的会议约 100 个，以促进会员间的交流，促进信息处理技术的发展与提高。

国际信息处理联合会每两年召开一次其标志性的大会——世界计算机大会（World Computer Congress，WCC），1959 年召开的第一届世界计算机大会也促成了该联合会的成立。

国际信息处理联合会下设 13 个技术委员会：

- ❏ TC－1 计算机科学基础（Foundations of Computer Science）。
- ❏ TC－2 软件理论与实践（Software：Theory and Practice）。
- ❏ TC－3 教育（Education）。
- ❏ TC－5 信息技术应用（Information Technology Applications）。
- ❏ TC－6 通信系统（Communication Systems）。
- ❏ TC－7 系统模型与优化（System Modelling and Optimization）。
- ❏ TC－8 信息系统（Information Systems）。
- ❏ TC－9 信息通信技术与社会（ICT and Society）。
- ❏ TC－10 计算机系统技术（Computer Systems Technology）。
- ❏ TC－11 信息处理系统安全与保护（Security and Protection in Information Processing Systems）。
- ❏ TC－12 人工智能（Artificial Intelligence）。
- ❏ TC－13 人机交互（Human－Computer Interaction）。
- ❏ TC－14 娱乐计算（Entertainment Computing）。

出版物

IFIP 建设有数字图书馆（International Federation for Information Processing－Digital Library），网址为 http：//dl.ifip.org/index.php/index/index，IFIP 与

SPRINGER（AICT）、SPRINGER（IFIP LNCS）、ELSEVIER 建立有良好的合作关系，其出版物多由这三家机构出版。

1）期刊与杂志

❑ IFIP Journal：Education and Information Technologies，由 Springer 出版。

❑ IFIP Journal：Computers & Security，由 Elsevier 出版。

❑ IFIP Journal：International Journal of Critical Infrastructure Protection，由 Elsevier 出版。

❑ Entertainment Computing，由 Elsevier 出版。

2）简讯与通报（IFIP Newsletter and Bulletin）

❑ Newsletter，每年出版四期。

❑ Bulletin，每年出版一期。

3）声明（Declarations）

❑ Gabarone Declaration.

❑ Stellenbosch Declaration.

❑ Lyon declaration for digital solidarity.

4）图书

❑ IFIP 及其技术委员会出版图书有 400 多种。

会议信息

❑ Latin American Network Operations and Management Symposium；2015. 10. 01—03；João Pessoa，BR.

❑ The 23rd IFIP World Computer Congress；2015. 10. 04—07；Daejeon，KR.

❑ 9th International Workshop on Communication Technologies for Vehicles；2015. 10. 05—07；Munich，DE.

❑ 16th Working Conference on Virtual Enterprises；2015. 10. 05—07；Albi，FR.

❑ IFIP/IEEE International Conference on Very Large Scale Integration；2015. 10. 05—07；Daejeon，KR.

❑ 7th International Workshop on Reliable Networks Design and Modeling；2015. 10. 05—07；Munich，DE.

❑ Wireless and Mobile Networking Conference；2015. 10. 05—07；Munich，DE.

❑ 2015 International Conference on Cyberworlds；2015. 10. 07—09；Gotland，SE.

❑ History and Philosophy of Computing；2015. 10. 08—11；Pisa，IT.

❑ IFIP I3E2015，e－business，e－service，e－society；2015. 10. 13—14；Delft，NL.

❑ International Symposium on Computer Architecture and High Performance

Computing; 2015. 10. 18—21; Florianopolis, BR.

❏ International Conference on Parallel Architectures and Compilation Techniques; 2015. 10. 18—21; San Francisco, US.

❏ 11th International Conference on Network and Service Management; 2015. 10. 26—30; Barcelona, ES.

❏ IFIP WG 11. 4 Workshop – iNetSec 2015; 2015. 10. 29—30; Zurich, CH.

❏ SIGGRAPH Conference and Exhibition on Computer Graphics and Interactive Techniques in Asia; 2015. 11. 02—05; Kobe, JP.

❏ International Conference on Natural Disasters and Emergency Management; 2015. 11. 04—06; Sofia, BG.

❏ 8th IFIP WG 8. 1 working conference on the Practice of Enterprise Modelling; 2015. 11. 10—12; Valencia, ES.

❏ International Conference on Application of Information and Communication Technology and Statistics in Economy and Education; 2015. 11. 13—14; Sofia, BG.

❏ Wireless Days; 2015. 11. 16—18; Toulouse, FR.

❏ The 21st IEEE Pacific Rim International Symposium on Dependable Computing (PRDC 2015); 2015. 11. 18—20; Zhangjiajie, CN.

❏ International Conference on Testing Software and Systems; 2015. 11. 23—25; Sharjah/Dubai, UAE.

❏ Digital Enterprise and Smart Technologies; 2015. 12. 14—17; Canberra, Australia.

❏ Wireless On – demand Network systems and Services; 2016. 01. 20—22; Cortina d`Ampezzo, IT.

❏ The 8th International Precision Assembly Seminar 2016; 2016. 02. 14—17; Chamonix, France.

❏ IFIP Information Security & Privacy Conference; 2016. 05. 30—06. 01; GHENT, BE.

❏ Twelfth International Conference on Open Source Systems; 2016. 05. 31—06. 01; Gothenburg, Sweden.

❏ 8th IFAC Conference on Manufacturing Modelling, Management & Control; 2016. 06. 28—30; Troyes, France.

❏ ICNPAA 2016: Mathematical Problems in Engineering, Aerospace and Sciences; 2016. 07. 05—08; La Rochelle, France.

❏ IFIP WG 11. 11 International Conference on Trust Management；2016. 07. 18—22；Darmstadt，Germany.

❏ 12th IFIP TC9 Human Choice and Computers Conference；2016. 09. 07—09；Manchester，UK.

❏ INTERACT 2017；2017. 09. 27—29；Mumbai，India.

❏ INTERACT 2018；2018. 09. 03—07；Paphos，CY.

机电制造与绕线协会

英文名称：Electrical Manufacturing & Coil Winding Association，EMCWA

网　　址：http：//www. emcw. org/

机构简介

机电制造与绕线协会成立于 1974 年，位于美国加利福尼亚州帝王海滩，是一个非营利性志愿组织。

机电制造与绕线协会致力于电气产品概念、研究、设计、生产、营销和使用的进一步推进，其涉及的内容包括激光器、信号处理、模糊逻辑与神经网络、打印技术、计算机、控制系统、电路与设备、一般信息、数学、物理及无线技术等。协会还提供一系列教育机会来加强电气技术和产品的开发、知识和使用，并通过年度峰会来展示技术、产品、思想和创意等。

机电制造与绕线协会的会员由其核心产业、相关产业、科学团体、学院的成员以及其他感兴趣的个体构成，每一个成员都是专业人士，大多是工程师、公司总裁、经理、生产专家、设计师等。

出版物

期刊与杂志

❑ Circuit Cellar，monthly.

❑ Laser and Optronics；ISSN：0892 – 9947.

❑ Communications News.

❑ Lightwave.

❑ Computer Reseller News.

❑ Mobile Computing and Communications.

❑ Computer Shopper.

❑ Network Computing Online.

❑ Data Communications.

❑ Networking Solutions Online.

❑ Data Management Review.

❑ Nuts and Volts.

❑ Dr. Dobb's Portal.

❑ PC Magazine Online.

❑ Electronic Component News.

❑ PC Today Online.

❑ Electronic Products.

❑ PC AI.

❑ Embedded Systems Programming.

❑ Physics Today.

❑ HP Professional.

❑ Scientific American Website.

❑ Information Week Online.

❑ Unix Review.

❑ Industrial Computing.

❑ Web Review.

❑ Job Shop Technology.

会议信息

❑ Electrical Manufacturing & Coil Winding Expo;2016.05.11;Milwaukee, Wisconsin,USA.

教育通信与技术协会

英文名称：Association for Educational Communications and Technology，AECT
网　　址：http：//www. aect. org/newsite/

机构简介

　　教育通信与技术协会于1923年作为美国国家教育委员会可视化教学部成立，位于美国印第安纳州布卢明顿市，已发展成一个由成千上万的教育者和其他业务为直接通过技术改进教学的人员组成的专业协会，会员大多来自大学、军队、博物馆、图书馆、医院等许多正在进行教育变革的地方。

　　教育通信与技术协会活跃于教学设计以及学习系统方法设计领域，为成员和目标受众提供一个交流和传播思想的国际平台，是教学改善的国家和国际发言人。

　　教育通信与技术协会拥有美国24个州分支机构和6个国际分支机构，是该领域最早成立的机构，并一直保持着其在该领域内的核心位置，促进学术研究和实践的高标准，拥有9个部门和一个研究生大会，代表着该领域的广度和深度。

出版物

　　1）期刊与杂志

❑ Educational Technology Research and Development；bimonthly；ISSN：1042 – 1629（print version）；ISSN：1556 – 6501（electronic version）.

❑ TechTrends—Linking Research and Practice to Improve Learning；bimonthly；ISSN：8756 – 3894（print version）；ISSN：1559 – 7075（electronic version）.

❑ International Journal of Designs For Learning；ISSN：2159 – 449X；online.

❑ The Journal of Applied Instructional Design；ISSN：2160 – 5289；online.

❑ Instructional Science；ISSN：0020 – 4277（print version）；ISSN：1573 – 1952（electronic version）.

❑ The Quarterly Review of Distance Education；Quarterly.

❑ The Interpersonal Computing and Technology Journal（IPCT – J）；2/3 times a year.

　　2）通讯

❑ iTech Digest：International Electronic Newsletter；Quarterly.

　　3）会议录

❑ 2012 Annual Convention Proceedings – Louisville：Volume #1 and #2.

4）标准

❑ AECT Standards for Professional Education Programs （2012 version）；2012. 07. 16.

会议信息

❑ Accelerate Learning：Racing into the Future；2015. 11. 03—07；Indianapolis，Indiana.

❑ AECT International Conventions；2015. 11. 03—07；Indianapolis，IN.

❑ AECT International Conventions；2016. 10. 17—21；Las Vegas，NV，USA.

❑ AECT International Conventions；2017. 11. 06—11；Jacksonville，FL，USA.

❑ AECT International Conventions；2018. 10. 23—27；Jacksonville，FL，USA.

❑ AECT International Conventions；2020. 11. 03—07；Jacksonville，FL，USA.

欧洲卫星运营商协会

英文名称：European Satellite Operator's Association，ESOA

网　　址：https：//www.esoa.net/

机构简介

欧洲卫星运营商协会成立于 2002 年 3 月，是一个由 CEO 推动的机构，其宗旨是为全球范围内的卫星运营商提供一个共同的平台，确保运营商不断取得成功并拓展决策者的机遇，提高卫星服务水平，应对商业卫星通信带来的机遇与挑战。

欧洲卫星运营商协会由 21 个成员单位的 CEO 组成的董事会进行管理，代表了欧洲主要卫星机构的利益，如欧盟委员会以及欧洲航空航天局（European Space Agency）等。

出版物

其他出版物

❑ Crisis Management& Satellites – Links for Life.

❑ Satellites & Spectrum – The Right Wavelength.

❑ Broadband Connectivity via Satellite.

❑ Satellite Communications For Aid And Emergency.

❑ Satellite Communications For Sustainable Development.

❑ Satellites and the Digital Switchover.

欧洲电气标准化委员会

法语名称：Comité Européen de Normalisation Électrotechnique，CENELEC
英文名称：European Committee for Electrotechnical Standardization
网　　址：http：//www. cenelec. eu/

机构简介

欧洲电工标准化委员会创立于 1973 年，由原欧洲电工标准协调委员会共同市场小组（CENELCOM）和原欧洲电工标准协调委员会（CENEL）合并组成，是在比利时法律下建立起来的一家非营利性机构。

欧洲电工标准化委员会由欧洲国家的国家电工委员会组成，被指定为欧洲标准组织，负责电气工程领域的标准化，并制定推荐标准，便利不同国家间的贸易，创造新的市场，降低合规成本，支持欧洲单一市场的发展。

欧洲电工标准化委员会与欧洲标准化委员会（The European Committee for Standardization, French：Comité Européen de Normalisation，CEN）和欧洲电信标准研究院（European Telecommunications Standards Institute，ETSI）等联合组成了欧洲标准化组织（European Standards Organisations，ESOs）。

欧洲电工标准化委员会在德累斯顿协议下，通过与国际电工委员会的紧密合作，采用可行的国际标准，不仅在欧洲层面上也在国际水平上创建了市场准入。通过该委员会成员、专家、行业联合会以及消费者的努力，欧洲标准得以创造以鼓励技术开发，确保互操作性以及消费者的安全健康，并提供环境保护。

出版物

1）通信

❑ CONNECT.

2）目录

❑ CENELEC Catalogue, twice a year in February and July.

3）技术活动报告

❑ CENELEC Report on Technical Activities, twice a year in May and November.

欧洲气象卫星开发组织

英文名称：European Organisation for the Exploitation of Meteorological Satellites，EUMETSAT

网　　址：http：//www. eumetsat. int/

机构简介

欧洲气象卫星开发组织成立于 1986 年，总部设在德国达姆施塔特，是一个政府间组织。该组织的主要目标是建立、维护和利用欧洲业务气象卫星系统，同时尽可能考虑世界气象组织的建议。经修正的公约的另一项目标是为实际监测气候和探测全球气候变化做出贡献。除了气象和气候监测这些优先活动之外，该组织还计划将其业务服务范围扩大到有关的环境监测活动。

欧洲气象卫星开发组织目前有 30 个成员国和一个合作国家，成员国和合作国可以共享该组织的数据和服务，由成员国根据其国民生产总值缴纳的会费来运行。

出版物

1）简讯

❏ IMAGE Newsletter，每年出版 2 期。

2）会议录

❏ EUMETSAT Meteorological Satellite Conference.

❏ EUMETSAT 9th User Forum in Africa.

❏ Tenth International Winds Workshop.

3）报告

❏ Annual Report 2004 ~

4）小册子

❏ EUMETSAT – Monitoring weather and climate from space（COR. 01，Version 1，January 2011）.

❏ EUMETSAT Strategy：A global operational satellite agency at the heart of Europe（COR. 02，Version 1，October 2011）.

❏ Climate Monitoring – EUMETSAT's Contribution（CLM. 01，Version 1，December 2010）.

❏ EUMETSAT SAF Network – A Network for Europe（COP. 01，Version 1，September 2010）.

❏ GMES – EUMETSAT：Contributing to Global Monitoring for Environment and Security（COP. 02，Version 1，September 2010）.

❑ AMESD – Safeguarding the future of a continent, its environment and natural resources (AMESD. 01, Version 2, April 2009).

❑ GEONETCast – Delivering environmental data to users worldwide (GNC. 01, Version 1, February 2009).

❑ CEOS – Ocean Surface Topography Constellation Strategic Workshop (E. 02, Version 1, December 2008).

❑ Meteosat (1977—2040) – Europe's geostationary meteorological satellites (PRG. 01, Version 1, September 2010).

❑ EUMETSAT Polar System – Keeping a closer eye on weather and climate (PRG. 02, Version 1, May 2012).

❑ Jason – 2 – Global ocean data for global weather and climate monitoring (JSN. 01, Version 2, March 2008).

5）视频出版物

❑ EUMETSAT – Monitoring weather and climate from Space.

❑ Climate Monitoring – Meeting the global challenge.

❑ GMES – Global Monitoring for Environment and Security.

❑ The Ocean Odyssey – An introduction to the Ocean Surface Topography Mission (OSTM).

❑ EUMETSAT Polar System – Taking Meteorology to a new level.

❑ PUMA, AMESD, GMES and Africa – Environmental monitoring for sustainable development in Africa.

6）资料单

❑ WMO – CGMS Virtual Laboratory (VLab) – A contribution to education and training in satellite meteorology (COP. FS. 02, Version 1, June 2010).

❑ DAWBEE——Data Access for Western Balkan, Eastern European and Caucasian Countries (COP. FS. 01, Version 1, March 2011s).

❑ Meteosat Third Generation – Europe's future geostationary meteorological satellites (PRG. FS. 01, Version 1, September 2010).

❑ DevCoCast – GEONETCast applications for and by developing countries (FS. 01, Version 1, April 2009).

❑ AÏDA——Advancing ICT for Disaster Risk Management in Africa (FS. 02, Version 1, April 2009).

❑ AMESD in the ECOWAS region – Water management for cropland and rangeland management (FS. 03, Version 1, April 2009).

❑ AMESD in the CEMAC region – Water resource management (FS. 04, Version 1，April 2009）．

❏ AMESD in the IOC region – Coastal and marine management（FS. 05，Version 1，April 2009）．

❏ AMESD in the SADC region – Agricultural and environmental resource management（FS. 06，Version 1，November 2009）．

❏ AMESD in the IGAD region – Land degradation mitigation and natural habitat conservation（FS. 07，Version 1，November 2009）．

❏ EUMETSAT Data Centre – Long – term records for essential environmental and climate monitoring data（FS. 16，Version 1，November 2009）．

❏ Meteosat Data Collection Service – Accurate support for meteorology and weather prediction（FS. 17，Version 1，March 2010）．

会议信息

❏ PV 2015 Conference；2015. 11. 03—05；Darmstadt，Germany.

全球导航卫星系统国际委员会

英文名称：International Committee on Global Navigation Satellite Systems（GNSS），ICG

网　　址：http：//www. unoosa. org/oosa/en/SAP/gnss/icg. html

机构简介

全球导航卫星系统国际委员会成立于2005 年，从属于联合国外层空间事务委员会（United Nations Office for Outer Space Affairs，UNOOSA）。全球

导航卫星系统国际委员会旨在促进全球导航卫星系统、区域系统的提供者之间的合作，以提高兼容性、互通性和透明度，促进全球卫星导航系统及相关系统服务的使用及未来的发展，推动民用卫星监测、导航、测试以及其他相关服务的合作。

出版物

1）会议录

❑ International Committee on Global Navigation Satellite Systems（ICG）2006—2011.

2）其他出版物

❑ 10 Years of Achievement of the United Nations on Global Navigation Satellite Systems.

会议信息

❑ National Space – Based Positioning，Navigation，and Timing Advisory Board；2015. 10. 30—31；Boulder，Colorado，USA.

❑ 10th Meeting of the International Committee on Global Navigation Satellite Systems（ICG – 10）；2015. 11. 01—06；Boulder，Colorado，USA.

❑ 10 th Annual Rin Baska GNSS Conference；2016. 05. 08—10；Krk Island，Croatia.

❑ 2016 European Navigation Conference；2016. 05. 30—06. 02；Helsinki，Finland.

第二部分

美洲机构

美　国

加拿大

美　国

ASM 电子设备故障分析学会

英文名称：ASM Electronic Device Failure Analysis Society，EDFAS

网　　址：www. asminternational. Drg/web/edfas

机构简介

ASM 电子设备故障分析学会是美国材料信息学会（ASM International）的下属学会，成立于 1998 年，其宗旨是推动故障分析领域的教育交流和技术进步，提高电子产业设备和材料的可靠性。

出版物

1）会议录

❏ 历年会议的会议录。

2）期刊与杂志

❏ Electronic Device Failure Analysis，季刊。

3）简讯

❏ EDFA eNewsletter，月刊。

会议信息

❏ 41st International Symposium for Testing and Failure Analysis（ISTFA）；2015. 11. 01—05；Portland，OR，USA.

IEEE 超声学、铁电体与频率控制协会

英文名称：Ultrasonics, Ferroelectrics, and Frequency Control Society, IEEE UFFC

网　　址：http：//www. ieee – uffc. org/

机构简介

IEEE 超声学、铁电体与频率控制协会是 IEEE 的一个分会，历史可追溯至 1953 年成立的无线电工程师学会（Institute of Radio Engineers，IRE）的超声工程专业小组。1963 年，无线电工程师学会与美国电气工程师学会（American Institute of Electrical Engineers）合并，该小组更名为声能学与超声学专业小组（Professional Group on Sonics and Ultrasonics），1984 年更名为 IEEE 超声学、铁电体与频率控制协会。

IEEE 超声学、铁电体与频率控制协会拥有 2 200 多名技术工作者会员，每年举办 3 个会议，目的是通过多学科的技术会议、讲座等为该领域的技术发展和技术进步提供机会，以促进其所关注领域的交流与合作。该协会关注与以下内容相关的理论、技术、材料和应用：

- ❑ 超声波及相关现象的产生、传播和探测。
- ❑ 医疗超声即相关技术。
- ❑ 铁电体、压电、压磁材料。
- ❑ 频域的产生和控制，计时，时间协调和分布。

出版物

1）会议录

- ❑ IEEE Transactions on UFFC.
- ❑ Proceedings of IEEE International Ultrasonics Symposium.
- ❑ Proceedings of IEEE International Symposium on Applications of Ferroelectrics.
- ❑ Proceedings of IEEE International Frequency Control Symposium.
- ❑ UFFC – S AdCom Minutes，每年出版 2 次。

2）简讯

- ❑ UFFC – S Newsletter，每年一期。

会议信息

- ❑ 2015 IEEE International Ultrasonics Symposium；2015. 10. 21—24；Taipei, Taiwan.
- ❑ 2016 IEEE International Frequency Control Symposium；2016. 05. 09—12；

New Orleans, Louisiana, USA.

❑ 2016 Joint IEEE International Symposium on the Applications of Ferroelectrics, European Conference on Applications of Polar Dielectrics & Workshop on Piezoresponse Force Microscopy (ISAF/ECAPD/PFM); 2016. 08. 22—25; Darmstadt, Germany.

❑ 2016 IEEE International Symposium on Applications of Ferroelectrics; 2016. 08. 24—27; Darmstadt, Germany.

❑ 2016 IEEE International Ultrasonics Symposium; 2016. 09. 17—21; Tours, France.

IEEE 航天与电子系统协会

英文名称：Aerospace & Electronic Systems Society，AESS
网　　址：http：//ieee - aess. org/

机构简介

IEEE 航天与电子系统协会成立于 1973 年，源于 1965 年成立的航天与电子系统小组，是 IEEE 的分会之一。IEEE 航天与电子系统协会每年举办各种会议、研讨会，并出版期刊杂志和会议录等，
促进学术交流。该协会为航空航天、电子和防务领域的企业、机构和研究中心以及电子系统领域的工程师们提供了一个专业的交流平台，涉及航天、航空、海洋、地面环境，包括硬件、软件、一体化和其他方面的工程业务。

出版物

1）期刊与杂志

❑ Aerospace&Electronic Systems Magazine，月刊；ISSN：0885 - 8985。

❑ AESS Systems Magazine Tutorials，年刊。

❑ IEEE Transactions on Aerospace and Electronic Systems，季刊，ISSN：0018 - 9251。

2）报告

❑ Radar Conference Report.

❑ Quality of Life：ISACONAS information.

❑ Preliminary Program ISACONAS.

❑ ISaCoNaS Report.

❑ ISaCoNaS Final Brochure.

❑ AUTOTESTCON Conference Report.

❑ IEEE/ION PLANS.

❑ ESTEL.

❑ Galileo Special Panel Report.

❑ RAST.

会议信息

❑ 2015 Sensor Data Fusion：Trends，Solutions，Applications（SDF）；2015. 10. 06—08；Bonn，Germany.

❑ 2015 IEEE Electrical Power and Energy Conference（EPEC）；2015. 10. 26—28；London，Canada.

❑ 2015 IEEE Radar Conference；2015. 10. 27—30；Johannesburg，South Africa.

❏ 2015 IEEE International Conference on Microwaves, Communications Antennas and Electronic Systems (COMCAS); 2015. 11. 02—04; Tel Aviv, Israel.

❏ 2015 IEEE AUTOTESTCON; 2015. 11. 02—05; Washington D. C, MD, United States.

❏ 2015 IEEE Wireless for Space & Extreme Environments Conference (WISEE); 2015. 12. 14—16; Orlando, FL, United States.

❏ 2016 IEEE Aerospace Conference; 2016. 03. 05—12; Big Sky, MT, United States.

❏ 2016 IEEE/ION Position, Location and Navigation Symposium (PLANS); 2016. 04. 11—16; Savannah, GA, United States.

❏ 2016 IEEE Radar Conference (RADARCONF); 2016. 05. 01—06; Philadelphia, PA, United States.

❏ 2016 European Navigation Conference (ENC); 2016. 05. 30—06. 02; Helsinki, Finland.

❏ 2016 23rd Saint Petersburg International Conference on Integrated Navigation Systems (ICINS); 2016. 05. 30—06. 15; St. Petersburg, Russia.

L-3 通信公司

英文名称：L-3 Communications Holdings，Inc.，L-3

网 址：www. l-3com. com

机构简介

L-3 通信公司成立于 1997 年，总部位于纽约，是世界五百强之一。L-3 通信公司是一家通信设备生产商，提供综合安全通信系统及特殊通信产品，公司产品包括数据传输率通信系统、微波组件、航空计算机、航海产品和遥感勘测、仪器及太空产品，其产品用于连接各种航天、地面及海上通信系统，是 C^3ISR（Command，Control，Communications，Intelligence，Surveillance and Reconnaissance）、飞机现代化维护和政府服务的主要承包商，也是高技术产品、子系统和系统的领先提供者。

2014 年，L-3 通信公司的销售额达 121 亿美元，拥有员工约 45 000 人，在澳大利亚、加拿大、德国、意大利、挪威、阿联酋、英国和美国等地设有分公司或分支机构。

出版物

报告

❑ Annual Report.

Skybox Imaging 公司

英文名称：Skybox Imaging, Inc.

网　　址：http：//www. skyboximaging. com/

机构简介

Skybox Imaging 公司成立于 2009 年，位于加利福尼亚州山景城，现有员工约 125 人。2013 年 11 月，公司成功发射第一颗卫星 SkySat – 1，2014 年 7 月成功发射第二颗卫星 SkySat – 2，公司计划发射 24 颗卫星。2014 年 8 月，Skybox Imaging 公司被谷歌公司收购，成为谷歌公司的子公司。

Skybox Imaging 公司是一家革新性地利用卫星图像的公司，主要提供商业高清地球观测卫星图像、高清视频和分析服务。其产品可以分为两类：工业和应用。工业类产品包括在线地图，石油天然气探测、场址选择、油垫计数、设施和管道监测，野生森林管理、侵略性物种监测、碳信用计算，水资源管理、火灾预防、人类行为生态影响的检测等。应用类产品包括土地使用管理、监测、可视化仿真、应急反应、计数与分析、探测与选址等。

Skybox Imaging 公司与 L – 3 通信公司、海克斯康地理空间部门（Hexagon Geospatial）、日本空间影像公司（Japan Space Imaging）、欧洲空间成像公司（European Space Imaging）等有合作。

出版物

1）技术规范

❑ Satellite Imagery Product Specifications.

❑ RapidEye Mosaics™ Product Specifications.

❑ Spectral Response Curves of the RapidEye Sensor.

❑ Apparent Cloud Shift in RapidEye Image Data.

2）手册

❑ EyeFind™ User Guide.

3）报告

❑ White Paper：The RapidEye Red Edge Band.

❑ Spectral Response Curves of the RapidEye Sensor.

❑ Apparent Cloud Shift in RapidEye Image Data.

4）小册子

❑ General Brochures.

❑ High – Resolution Satellite Imagery.

❑ RapidEye Satellite Constellation.

- ❑ RapidEye Mosaics™.
- ❑ EyeFind™/ Online Archive Discovery Tool.
- ❑ RapidEye's ArcGIS Premium Services.
- ❑ RapidEye for REDD + .
- ❑ RapidEye for Agriculture.
- ❑ RapidEye for Visualization & Simulation.
- ❑ RapidEye Mosaics™ Country Brochures.
- ❑ Bangladesh; Brazil, State of Sao Paulo; Congo, Democratic Republic; Eritrea, Malawi; North Korea; Oman; Nigeria; Pakistan; Somalia; Uzbekistan; USA – Hawaii.

Technica 公司

英文名称：Technica Corporation, Technica

网　　址：http：//technicacorp. com/

机构简介

Technica 公司成立于 1991 年，由两个工程师 Miguel Collado 和 Bill Groah 创立，位于弗吉尼亚州杜勒斯。该公司主要向美国与全球商业电信运营商提供专业产品与服务，工程解决方案是该公司的核心业务之一，主要涉及系统工程、软件工程和信息保障。该公司的其他产品解决方案涉及数据解决方案、企业软件解决方案、安全解决方案和统一通信等。

Technica 公司近年为美国国防部、联邦法律情报机构提供了一系列大规模的网络服务。例如，2013 年 3 月，公司获得美国国防信息系统局（DISA）一份价值 900 万美元的合同，以"软件服务"的模式向国防部提供赛门铁克数据恢复平台。

会议信息

❑ 2015 Alamo ACE；2015. 11. 16—19；San Antonio, TX, US.

❑ FBI HQ Technology Expo；2015. 12. 09；Washington, DC.

❑ GEOINT 2016 Symposium；2016. 05. 15—18；Orlando, Florida.

鲍尔航空航天技术公司

英文名称：Ball Aerospace & Technologies Corporation，BATC
网　　址：http：//www.ballaerospace.com

机构简介

鲍尔航空航天技术公司成立于 1956 年，是鲍尔公司（Ball Corporation）在航空航天领域的子公司。

鲍尔航空航天技术公司是设计、开发、制造创新的航空航天系统的领导者，业务涉及航天器、仪器和传感器、红外和微波技术等。该公司生产的产品包括备用的发电机、天线、低温设备、飞轮、燃料电池、工业流体、激光、运动控制器、光学镜、卫星通信设备、科学成像、摄像机等。

鲍尔航空航天技术公司仪器因航空航天和地球科学探索、国家安全和情报项目上的贡献而闻名于世，在商业遥感市场、图像系统生产、用于制图的航天器等方面也同样走在前列，多次与 NASA 合作，曾获得 NASA 为期 5 年、金额超过 1 亿美元的卫星探测项目合同。2012 年，鲍尔航空航天技术公司向 NASA 提出任务概念研究，将在太空之中展示太阳能电力推进技术。

2014 年，鲍尔航空航天技术公司的销售收入达 9.348 亿美元，有员工约 2 800 人，包括工程师、科学家、技师和支持职员等。

鲍尔公司是全球金属及塑料包装的主要供应商之一，其包装产品主要面向饮料、食品企业。鲍尔公司战略是通过产品生产、市场营销、产品服务来满足饮料、食品行业对于金属及塑料包装的需求。鲍尔公司 90% 的销售额来自包装业务，包括各类饮料、食品的金属容器，以及 PET（塑料）容器等。

出版物

1）简讯

❑ Uplink Newsletter，季刊，在线版。

2）其他出版物

❑ Print materials，免费下载，是鲍尔航空航天技术公司在天线、无线电、防务、情报、航空航天技术等方面的材料。

得克萨斯仪器公司

英文名称：Texas Instruments Inc. ，TI

网　　址：http：//www. ti. com/

机构简介

得克萨斯仪器公司也称得州仪器，历史可追溯至成立于 1930 年的地球物理服务公司（Geophysical Service Incorporated），1951 年改名为得克萨斯仪器公司，并于 2011 年收购了国家半导体公司（National Semiconductor）。

得克萨斯仪器公司是美国的防务承包商之一，主要从事光学、电子学、红外线、激光、半导体等方面的研究工作，控制着激光制导炸弹和制导炮弹领域的研制，近年还开发了炮射导弹。该公司业务包括研制导弹制导、红外探测器、红外透镜、红外线窗、陆军空中用夜视监视系统、坦克用热成象瞄准具、导弹用热象瞄准器、空对地导弹雷达制导系统等，还生产空中交通控制器、工业控制设备、小型计算机、电子计算机等。

2014 年，得克萨斯仪器公司的收入约为 130 亿美元，有员工约 31 000 人，拥有 41 000 多项专利。

蒂尔集团咨询公司

英文名称：Teal Group Corporation

网　　址：http://www.tealgroup.com/

机构简介

蒂尔集团咨询公司成立于 1988 年，位于弗吉尼亚州费尔法克斯，是一家航空航天和防务领域的咨询公司，旨在分析飞机、发动机、军用电子、导弹、灵巧炸弹、无人系统、空间系统在内的各领域市场，同时邀请分析家发表独立的见解和预测，为有关国家、政府和公司提供市场情报和专业帮助。

蒂尔集团咨询公司的信息来源多样，通过收集、分类、分析信息，并加入深度分析和预测，形成专业的报告（纸本、CD 或在线形式），为客户提供重要的决策参考。其重要客户包括空中客车集团、通用电气、洛克希德·马丁公司、波音公司、诺斯洛普·格鲁曼公司、霍尼韦尔公司等。

出版物

1）简报

❑ Defense & Aerospace Agencies Briefing.

❑ Defense & Aerospace Companies Briefing.

❑ International Defense Briefing.

❑ Military Electronics Briefing.

❑ World Military & Civil Aircraft Briefing.

❑ World Missiles & UAV Briefing.

❑ World Power Systems Briefing – Aero Gas Turbines.

❑ World Power Systems Briefing – I & M Gas Turbines.

❑ World Power Systems Briefing – Two Binder Set.

❑ World Space Systems Briefing（WSSB）.

以上出版物每月出版纸质版，每季度出版 CD – ROM 版。

2）简讯

❑ Defense Business Briefing，每周通过 Email 传送，每月出版 CD – ROM 版。

3）报告

❑ Business Aircraft Overview.

❑ Commercial Jet Transport Overview.

❑ Fighter/Attack Aircraft Overview.

❑ Military Transport Aircraft Overview.

- ❏ Regional Aircraft Overview.
- ❏ Special Mission Aircraft Overview.
- ❏ Trainer/Light – Attack Aircraft Overview.
- ❏ World Aircraft Overview.
- ❏ World Rotorcraft Overview.

4）其他出版物

- ❏ Aircraft Markets Forecasts and History.
- ❏ Missile and UAV Market Forecasts.
- ❏ Defense Business Briefing Contract Awards.
- ❏ Worldwide Mission Model Online.

电子文档系统协会

英文名称：Xplor International, The Electronic Document Systems Association

网　　址：http：//www. xplor. org/

机构简介

施乐打印联络机构（国际）（Xplor 全称 Xerox Printing Liaison Organization），即电子文档系统协会，起源于 20 世纪 70 年代后期的施乐 9700 用户小组（Xerox 9700 User Group），1981 年成为一个正式的非营利性组织。

电子文档系统协会由会员管理其各地的分支机构，使命是成为信息共享的一致选择，满足会员对网络共享的需求，为文献系统的发展和顾客通信产业的发展提供领导。除了举办年度会议，该协会每年还举办多场在线会议和研讨会来促进成员之间的交流。

会议信息

❏ The emergence of Omni – Channel Communications；2015. 09. 15；Chicago，IL，USA.

❏ Xplor Webinars.

电子显微镜与分析小组

英文名称：Electron Microscopy and Analysis Group，EMAG

网 址：http：//www. iop. org/activity/groups/subject/emag/

机构简介

美国物理协会电子显微镜与分析小组原是成立于 1946 年的电子显微镜小组（Electron Microscopy Group），1962 年改为现名。

美国物理协会电子显微镜与分析小组的会员来自多个学科领域，如物理、材料科学、化学、工程等。该小组每两年举办一次大型会议，包括电子显微镜及相关技术的大型贸易展，有效促进了电子显微镜领域新技术的发展，鼓励了新技术的更广泛应用。

出版物

简讯

❑ Electron Microscopy and Analysis Group newsletter，每年 2 期。

碟形网络公司

英文名称：Dish Network Corporation，DISH

网　　址：http：//www. dishnetwork. com/

机构简介

碟形网络公司源于 1980 年成立的回声星通信公司（Echo Star）。1995 年，回声星通信公司成功发射"回声星1 号"卫星，并于 1996 年确立了 DISH Network 的品牌。2008 年 1 月，回声星与其子公司碟形网络公司拆分成两家独立的公司——碟形网络公司（DISH Network）与回声星公司（EchoStar Corporation）。回声星公司目前是碟形网络公司重要的技术合作伙伴，为后者提供机顶盒和其他电视技术。

碟形网络公司是美国著名的直播卫星服务提供商，总部位于科罗拉多州美里迪安，2014 年的收入约为 146 亿美元，拥有约 19 000 名员工，为 3 580 万用户提供卫星电视、卫星网络、音频录制、高清电视、交互电视服务等。

弗若斯特沙利文公司

英文名称：Frost & Sullivan

网　　址：http：//ww2. frost. com/

机构简介

弗若斯特沙利文公司成立于 1961 年，总部位于美国加州硅谷圣何塞市，以自己独创的"市场工程体系"服务于大量世界顶尖的高科技公司。

多年来，弗若斯特沙利文公司已经为世界 50 多个国家和地区的公司提供了可靠的市场及战略咨询服务，并在 300 多个关键工业领域内赢得了世界性的声誉，包括航空航天与国防，汽车与运输，化学、材料与食品，电子与安全，能源与动力系统，环境、建筑技术，卫生保健，工业自动化与过程控制，信息与通信技术，测量与仪器等。

会议信息

❑ GIL 2015：Indonesia；2015. 10. 01；Jakarta, Indonesia.

❑ GIL 2015：India；2015. 10. 07；Mumbai, India.

❑ Leadership：What it Takes to Get Results – Europe；2015. 10. 07—09；Lodon, UK.

❑ Best Practices Banquets（Award Galas）7th Annual India Healthcare Excellence Awards 2015；2015. 10. 09；Mumbai, India.

❑ Professional Product Management – North America；2015. 10. 12—14；Chicago, USA.

❑ 2015 Singapore Excellence Awards, Singapore；2015. 10. 15；Singapore.

❑ New Product Launch – North America；2015. 10. 15—16；Chicago, USA.

❑ GIL 2015：Asia Pacific；2015. 10. 15；Singapore, Asia Pacific.

❑ 2015 Asia Pacific Best Practices Awards, Singapore；2015. 10. 15；Singapore.

❑ Selling on Value – Europe；2015. 10. 16；Lodon, UK.

❑ 11th Annual Customer Contact 2015 West；2015. 10. 18—21；San Diego, CA, USA.

❑ GIL 2015：Monaco；2015. 10. 22；Monte Carlo, France.

❑ 2015 Excellence in Best Practices Awards Banquet, Monaco；2015. 10. 22；Monte Carlo, France.

❑ Best Practices in Sales Management – North America；2015. 10. 26—27；Chicago, USA.

❑ Professional Product Management – Europe；2015. 10. 26—28；London, Europe.

- ❏ GIL 2015：China；2015. 10. 30；Shanghai, China.
- ❏ GIL 2015：Germany；2015. 11. 17；Jumeirah Frankfurt, Germany.
- ❏ 2015 Excellence in Best Practices Awards Banquet, Frankfurt；2015. 11. 17；Jumeirah Frankfurt, Germany.
- ❏ 2015 Growth, Innovation & Leadership Awards Gala；2015. 12. 01；Alexander, USA.
- ❏ GIL 2015：Miami；2015. 12. 01；Miami, Florida, USA.
- ❏ GIL 2015：Australia；2015. 12. 03；Sydney, Australia.
- ❏ 2015 Australia Excellence Awards, Sydney Australia；2015. 12. 03；Sydney, Australia.
- ❏ India Manufacturing Excellence Awards 2015；2015. 12. 11；Miami, Florida, USA.
- ❏ 10th Anniversary New Product Innovation & Development 2016；2016. 01. 12—13；San Diego, CA, USA.
- ❏ Digital Marketing World 2016, Europe；2016. 01. 25—27；Cascais, Portugal.
- ❏ GIL 2016：Middle East；2016. 02. 10；Dubai, U. A. E.
- ❏ GIL 2016：Mexico；2016. 03. 02；Mexico.
- ❏ 21st Annual Medical Technologies 2016；2016. 03. 14—15；San Diego, CA, USA.
- ❏ GIL 2016：Thailand；2016. 04. 05；Bangkok, Thailand.
- ❏ GIL 2016：Malaysia；2016. 04. 14；Kuala Lumpur, Malaysia.
- ❏ 12th Annual Customer Contact 2016 East；2016. 04. 17—20；Orlando, Florida, USA.
- ❏ GIL 2016：Brazil；2016. 05. 02；Brazil.
- ❏ GIL 2016：Europe；2016. 05. 12；London, Europe.
- ❏ GIL 2016：Japan；2016. 06. 01；Tokyo, Japan.
- ❏ 12th Annual Manufacturing Leadership Summit；2016. 06. 06—09；Carlsbad, CA, USA.
- ❏ 10th Anniversary Customer Contact 2016 Europe；2016. 06. 20—22；Croatia, Europe.
- ❏ 4th Annual CIO Impact！2016；2016. 12. 05—07；Austin, TX, USA.

戈兰研究中心

英文名称：NASA John H. Glenn Research Center，GRC

网　　址：http：//www. nasa. gov/centers/glenn/home/index. html

机构简介

戈兰研究中心于 1941 年作为国家航空资讯委员会（NASA 的前身，National Advisory Committee for Aeronautics，NACA）下属的飞机发动机研究实验室（Aircraft Engine Research Laboratory）而成立，1948 年为纪念乔治·刘易斯而改名为刘易斯研究中心（LeRC），1999 年为纪念 John H. Glenn 改称戈兰研究中心。

戈兰研究中心位于俄亥俄州克利夫兰，是 NASA 的 10 大研究中心之一，拥有 3 200 多名员工。该中心主要的研究工作包括空气推进系统和航天推进系统、燃料与燃烧、输电、摩擦学、发动机计算流体力学、高温发动机仪表和空间通信等，负责设计开发美国空间站发电、蓄电和配电系统等，在航天器和太空探索方面取得了巨大成就。

出版物

简讯

❑ AeroSpace Frontiers，月刊，内部刊物。

轨道阿连特公司

英文名称：Orbital ATK Inc，Orbital ATK

网　　址：http：//www.orbitalatk.com/

机构简介

轨道阿连特公司成立于 2015 年，其历史可追溯至 1982 年成立的轨道科学公司（Orbital Sciences Corporation）。该公司是一家专门制造和发射卫星的美国公司，其卫星发射系统对

美国导弹防御系统有着重要影响。2015 年 2 月，轨道科学公司与阿连特技术系统公司（Alliant Techsystems Inc.）旗下的航空航天与防务业务（Aerospace and Defense Groups）完成合并，成立新的公司——轨道阿连特公司。

轨道阿连特公司总部位于弗吉尼亚州杜勒斯，2014 年的收入约为 44 亿美元，有 12 000 多名员工。

轨道阿连特公司是全球领先的航空航天和防务技术提供商，设计、建造、交付空间和防务及航空相关的系统，如：发射器及相关的推进系统，卫星及相关部件和服务，复合材料航空航天结构、战术导弹、子系统及防务电子、精密武器、武器系统及弹药等。轨道阿连特公司下设三个业务运营小组。

（1）飞行系统小组：世界领先的中小型空间发射器提供商，提供固体火箭推进系统及用于导弹防御应用的拦截器及目标工具，还是商用机军用飞机和发射器的复合材料结构的世界级制造商。

（2）防务系统小组：陆、海、空基战术导弹和导弹防御拦截器的推进和控制系统及战术导弹和弹药的引信弹头的领先制造商，下一代打击武器系统、导弹预警和飞机存活性、特殊任务飞机的先进防务电子提供商，中—大口径弹药、中口径枪支系统和精确弹药制导套件等领先生产商。

（3）空间系统小组：用于全球通信和高清地球成像的商用卫星、政府客户执行科学研究和国家安全任务的中小型航天器、国际空间站的商业货运服务提供商，先进商业太空发射系统开发商，航天器部件和子系统及特殊工程服务的重要提供商。

出版物

1）简讯

❑ Orbital Quarterly Newsletter.

2）报告

❑ Annual Report.

3）资料单

轨道阿连特公司的卫星及发射器、发射台等产品或设备的介绍。

国防系统信息分析中心

英文名称：Defense Systems Information Analysis Center，DSIAC

网　　址：https：//www. dsiac. org/

机构简介

国防系统信息分析中心于 2014 年 1 月 1 日由美国国防部的 6 个信息分析中心合并而成。这 6 个信息分析中心分别是：先进材料制造与测试信息分析中心（Advanced Materials，Manufacturing，and Testing Information Analysis Center，AMMTIAC），化学推进信息分析中心（Chemical Propulsion Information Analysis Center，CPIAC），可靠性信息分析中心（Reliability Information Analysis Center，RIAC），军事传感信息分析中心（Military Sensing Information Analysis Center，SENSIAC），生存能力/易损性信息分析中心（Survivability/Vulnerability Information Analysis Center，SUR-VIAC）和武器系统技术信息分析中心（Weapons Systems Technology Information Analysis Center，WSTIAC）。

国防系统信息分析中心是美国国防部信息分析体系中的一个组成部分，总部位于马里兰州的贝尔坎普，目的是利用其他政府机构、研究实验室、工业界及学术界的专业知识来帮助国防系统领域解决最棘手的科技问题。

国防系统信息分析中心拥有主题专家网络（Subject Matter Experts，SMEs），以及国防部科技信息（Scientific and Technical Information，STI）数据库等，为国防领域提供如下领域的服务：先进材料，自助系统，定向能，热力学，军事遥感，非致命性武器，可靠性、可维修性、质量、可支援性、互通性（RMQSI），生存能力与易损性，以及武器系统等。

出版物

1）期刊与杂志

❑ DSIAC Journal，季刊。

2）标准

❑ Directive – Type Memorandum（DTM）11 – 003，Reliability Analysis，Planning，Tracking，and Reporting.

❑ Endorsement of Next – Generation Performance – Based Logistics Strategies.

会议信息

❑ 86th Shock & Vibration Symposium；2015. 10. 05—08；Orlando，FL.

❑ 2015 Air Armament Symposium；2015. 11. 03—04；Fort Walton Beach，FL.

国家船舶电子协会

英文名称：National Marine Electronics Association，NMEA

网　　址：http：//www. nmea. org/

机构简介

国家船舶电子协会成立于 1957 年，由纽约船展上的电子经销商讨论建立。初衷在于建立电子制造商之间的关系，

其宗旨是：通过标准、教育、培训和认证推动船用电子工业的发展；推进其成员间良好的商贸管理和公平的商贸实践；鼓励工业界雇用高技能和有技术资格的人员；通过会议和出版物等方式提高大众船舶方面的知识，使他们安全恰当地使用船舶电子设备。

出版物

1）会议录

❏ NMEA International Marine Electronics Conference & Expo.

❏ NMEA Conference and Expo Presentations.

2）期刊与杂志

❏ Marine Electronics Journal.

3）标准

标准可以分为以下 5 类。

❏ NMEA 2000 ® Standard.

❏ NMEA 0183 Standard.

❏ Installation Standards.

❏ 2012 Standards Update Status.

❏ Future Standard：OneNet ®.

4）其他出版物

❏ GROL + RADAR Study Manual.

❏ GROL + RADAR with Practice Exam Software.

❏ GMDSS Elements 7 and 9 Question Pool Booklet with Practice Exam Software.

❏ Basic Electronics，主要介绍了电子基础知识。

❏ Basic Digital Electronics，图书，主要介绍了数字系统的功能和如何用电路实现。

- Basic Communications，介绍电子硬件和电路的类似物，主要强调了半导体和集成电路。

会议信息

- National Marine Electronics Association（NMEA）2015 Conference & Expo；2015. 09. 29—10. 01；Baltimore，Maryland.

航空电子协会

英文名称：Aircraft Electronics Association，AEA

网　　址：http://www.aea.net/

机构简介

航空电子协会成立于 1957 年，致力于成为全球性的自我维持的机构。航空电子协会代表着 43 个国家的近 1 300 家航空企业，这些企业的业务包括飞机的航空电子和电子系统的维修、安装、后续服务等。航空电子协

会的会员包括航空电子设备制造商、仪器维修设备制造商、仪器制造商、机身制造商、测试设备制造商及相关的教育机构等。

出版物

1）期刊与杂志

❑ Avionics News，月刊，ISSN：0567 - 2899。

❑ Pilot's Guide To Avionics，年刊。

❑ AEA Wired，电子刊，每月两期。

2）报告

❑ AEA Avionics Market Report.

3）数据库

❑ Stolen Equipment，该数据库由 Aviation Crime Prevention Institute 制作，面向会员提供。

会议信息

❑ AEA Canada Regional Meeting；2015. 10. 01—02；Toronto，Canada.

❑ AEA U. S. East Regional Meeting；2015. 10. 12—13；Tampa，Fla，USA.

❑ AEA South Pacific Regional Meeting；2015. 11. 02—03；Queenstown，New Zealand，USA.

❑ AEA 2016 Europe Regional Meetings；2016. 01. 26—27；Cologne，Germany.

❑ The 59th annual AEA International Convention & Trade Show；2016. 04. 27—30；Orlando，Fla，USA.

❑ The 60th annual AEA International Convention & Trade Show；2017. 03. 13—16；New Orleans，La，USA.

❑ The 61th annual AEA International Convention & Trade Show; 2018.03.26—29; Las Vegas, Nev, USA.

❑ The 62th annual AEA International Convention & Trade Show; 2019.03.25—28; Palm Springs, Calif, USA.

❑ Part 145 Webinars.

航空航天公司

英文名称：Aerospace Corporation，Aerospace

网　址：http：//www. aero. org/index. html

机构简介

航空航天公司于 1960 年 6 月在加利福尼亚成立，是一家独立的非营利性企业，也是美国联邦政府资助的企业（Federally Funded Research and Development Centers，FFRDC）

之一，并受美国空军的资助。航空航天公司致力于空间系统设计、发展、获取和运作方面的技术研究，是美国国家空间安全计划支持者之一，同时也向民用和商业用户提供技术支持。公司业务与研究涉及通信系统、电子工程、标准频率特性、全球定位系统、信息保障、遥感红外成像、传感器系统、软件工程、系统工程、遥感遥测等。

美国国防部认可的美国航空航天公司受联邦资助的 5 项核心能力是：

（1）发射认证（Launch Certification）；

（2）成体系系统工程（System – of – Systems Engineering）；

（3）系统开发与获取（Systems Development and Acquisition）；

（4）过程实施（Process Implementation）；

（5）技术应用（Technology Application）。

出版物

1）期刊与杂志

❏ Crosslink，ISSN：1527 – 5264，半年刊。

2）简讯

❏ Getting It Right，季刊。

3）图书

❏ Advanced Space System Concepts and Technologies：2010—2030.

❏ Applied Orbit Perturbation and Maintenance.

❏ Civil, Commercial, and International Remote Sensing Systems and Geoprocessing.

❏ Communication Satellites, Fifth Edition.

❏ Dynamics of Meteor Outbursts and Satellite Mitigation Strategies.

❏ International Launch Site Guide，Second Edition.

❏ Microengineering Aerospace Systems.

❏ Nickel – Hydrogen Batteries：Principles and Practice.

❏ Nickel – Hydrogen Life Cycle Testing：Review and Analysis.

❑ Rocket Exhaust Plume Phenomenology.

❑ Small Satellites：Past，Present，and Future.

❑ Spacecraft Collision Probability.

❑ Space Modeling and Simulation.

❑ Spacecraft Thermal Control Handbook，Vol. 1：Fundamental Technologies.

❑ Spacecraft Thermal Control Handbook，Vol. 2：Cryogenics.

4）报告

❑ Annual Report.

❑ Laser Direct Write of SiO/sub 2/MEMS and Nano – Scale Devices.

❑ 0. 38 – 2. 5um Spectroscopy and Simultaneous BVR Photometry of DEEP IM-
PACT.

❑ 0. 72 – 1. 35um Spectroscopy of Nova Aquilae.

❑ 0. 72 – 1. 34um Spectrophotometry of Nova Sagittarii o. 2.

❑ 0. 8 – 13. 5 Micron Spectroscopy of IRAS 07077 + 1536：A Dusty Carbon
Star.

❑ 0. 8 – 1. 6 Micron Spectroscopy of the Planetary Nebula NGC 7027.

❑ 0. 8 – 2. 5 Micron Reflectance Spectroscopy of Pluto.

❑ 0. 8 – 2. 5 Micron Spectroscopy of Nova Ophiuchi.

5）数据库

❑ 通过其 Professional Papers 栏目，提供航空航天领域公开发表的期刊与
杂志或者会议的数据库，通过该数据库仅可以获取书目信息，不直接
提供全文。数据收录年限从 1961 年起，可以按出版物名称、主题、出
版年、类型、作者等进行浏览。

会议信息

❑ Manufacturing Problem Prevention Program（MP3）；2015. 10. 06；Segundo，
CA，USA.

❑ NSISC Space INFOSEC Technical Information Exchange；2015. 10. 20—22；
EL SEGUNDO，CA，USA.

❑ Aerospace Testing Seminar；2015. 10. 27—29；Los Angeles，California，USA.

❑ Ground System Architectures Workshop；2016. 02. 29—03. 03；Los Angel-
es，California，USA.

❑ 27 th Spacecraft Thermal Control Workshop；2016. 03. 22—24；EL SEGUN-
DO，CA，USA.

❑ The Space Power Workshop；2016. 04. 18—21；Manhattan，CA，USA.

科技出版社

英文名称： SciTech Publishing, Inc.

网　　址： http://www.scitechpub.com

机构简介

科技出版社于 2012 年成为英国工程技术学会的全资子公司和授权出版商，以出版电子工程领域印刷版和电子版文献为主，涉及雷达、电子战、天线与传播、微波与射频、通信、声学、反潜战、计算机、电路、电磁学、飞机系统测试、生物力学、编程等。

出版物

图书

- [ ] Principles of Underwater Sound, Third Edition.
- [ ] Introduction to Adaptive Arrays, 2nd Edition.
- [ ] Small Antennas: Miniaturization Techniques & Applications.
- [ ] Antenna Design and Visualization Using MATLAB (Version 2.0 with Source Code).
- [ ] Antennas: Fundamentals, Design, Measurement, Third Edition.
- [ ] Antennas: Fundamentals, Design, Measurement, Third Edition – Deluxe Edition.
- [ ] Microstrip and Printed Antenna Design, Second Edition.
- [ ] Narrowband Direction Of Arrival Estimation For Antenna Arrays.
- [ ] Introduction to Smart Antennas.
- [ ] Reconfigurable Antennas.
- [ ] Multi – Antenna Systems for MIMO Communications.
- [ ] Advanced Antenna Considerations I.
- [ ] Introduction to Antenna Fundamentals.
- [ ] Performance of Fundamental Antenna Elements.
- [ ] Introduction to Antennas.
- [ ] Introduction to the Smith Chart.
- [ ] Introduction to Adaptive Arrays, 2nd Edition.
- [ ] Phased – Array Radar Design: Application of Radar Fundamentals.
- [ ] Test and Evaluation of Aircraft Avionics and Weapons Systems.
- [ ] Introduction to Biomechatronics.
- [ ] Designing Amplifier Circuits (Volume 1: Analog Circuit Design Series).

❑ Designing Dynamic Circuit Response (Volume 2: Analog Circuit Design Series) .

❑ Designing High Performance Amplifiers (Volume 3: Analog Circuit Design Series) .

❑ Designing Waveform – Processing Circuits (Volume 4: Analog Circuit Design Series) .

❑ Analog Circuit Design Series (Four Volume Set) .

❑ Multifunctional Adaptive Microwave Circuits and Systems.

❑ Resistor Theory and Technology.

❑ HF Radio Systems and Circuits——A comprehensive reference for the design of high frequency communications systems and equipment.

❑ Advanced Digital Communications: Systems and Signal Processing Techniques.

❑ Introduction to Broadband Communication Systems.

❑ HERALD 3. 1 Radio Link Design Software.

❑ Principles of Satellite Communications.

❑ The Advanced Communications Technology Satellite: An Insider's Account of the Emergence of Interactive Broadband Technology in Space.

❑ Telecommunications Measurements: Analysis & Instrumentation.

❑ Chasing Moore's Law: Information Technology Policy in the United States.

❑ Radar Essentials: A Concise Handbook for Radar Design and Performance Analysis.

❑ Radar Essentials: A Concise Handbook for Radar Design and Performance Analysis E – Book.

❑ Electronic Warfare Pocket Guide.

❑ Principles of Modern Radar: Basic Principles.

❑ Microwave and RF Design: A Systems Approach.

❑ Pocket Radar Guide: Key Radar Facts, Equations, and Data.

❑ Antennas: Fundamentals, Design, Measurement, Third Edition.

❑ Fundamentals of Electromagnetics with MATLAB, 2nd Edition.

❑ Fundamentals of Electromagnetics with MATLAB, Second Edition.

❑ Integral Equation Methods for Electromagnetics.

❑ Electromagnetic Measurements in the Near Field, 2nd Edition.

❑ Designing Electronic Systems for EMC.

❑ Numerical Methods for Engineering: An Introduction Using MATLAB and Computational Electromagnetics.

- ❑ Fundamentals of Wave Phenomena, 2nd Edition.
- ❑ Solutions Manual——The Finite Difference Time Domain Method for Electromagnetics.
- ❑ Introduction to Modern CMOS Digital Electronics: Preliminary Edition.
- ❑ The Finite Difference Time Domain Method for Electromagnetics: With MATLAB Simulations.
- ❑ A Guide to MATLAB Object – Oriented Programming.
- ❑ Fundamentals of Electromagnetics with MATLAB, 2nd Edition.
- ❑ 2008 + Solved Problems in Electromagnetics.
- ❑ Fundamentals of Electromagnetics with MATLAB, Second Edition.
- ❑ Fundamentals of the Physical Theory of Diffraction.
- ❑ Fundamentals of Electromagnetics with MATLAB: Student CD.
- ❑ Fundamentals of Electromagnetics, 1st Edition.
- ❑ Return of the Ether.
- ❑ Electronic Warfare Pocket Guide.
- ❑ Communications, Radar and Electronic Warfare.
- ❑ Battlespace Technologies: Network – Enabled Information Dominance.
- ❑ EW 103: Tactical Battlefield Communications Electronic Warfare.
- ❑ Electronic Warfare – 4 Book Set.
- ❑ Information Operations Planning.
- ❑ Statistical Multisource – Multitarget Information Fusion.
- ❑ Introduction to Electronic Warfare Modeling and Simulation.
- ❑ Introduction to Electronic Defense Systems, Second Edition.
- ❑ Advances in Direction – of – Arrival Estimation.
- ❑ Microwave Receivers With Electronic Warfare Applications.
- ❑ Target Acquisition in Communication Electronic Warfare.
- ❑ Digital Techniques for Wideband Receivers, Second Edition.
- ❑ EW102: A Second Course in Electronic Warfare.
- ❑ Mathematical Techniquesin Multisensor Data Fusion.
- ❑ Microwave Passive Direction Finding.
- ❑ Modern Communications Jamming Principles and Techniques.
- ❑ The Missile Defense Equation: Factors for Decision Making.
- ❑ Curbing Innovation: How Command Technology Limits Network Centric Warfare.
- ❑ Modern Communications Jamming Principles and Techniques.
- ❑ Tactical Communications for the Digitized Battlefield.

- ❏ Professional Expression: To Organize, Write, and Manage for Technical Communication.
- ❏ Electron – Gated Ion Channels.
- ❏ Hazardous Gas Monitors: A Practical Guide to Selection, Operation and Applications.
- ❏ Wireless Receiver Design for Digital Communications, 2nd Edition.
- ❏ Microwave and RF Design: A Systems Approach.
- ❏ RF and Microwave Modeling and Measurement Techniques for Field Effect Transistors.
- ❏ Multifunctional Adaptive Microwave Circuits and Systems.
- ❏ Transceiver and System Design for Digital Communications, Third Edition.
- ❏ Microwave and RF Design: A Systems Approach (BETA Edition).
- ❏ Essentials of Radio Wave Propagation.
- ❏ Wideband Amplifier Design.
- ❏ Fiber Optic Technology: Applications to Commercial, Industrial, Military, and Space Optical Systems.
- ❏ The RF/Microwave Library.
- ❏ Optical Fibers and RF: A Natural Combination.
- ❏ Applied Microwave & Wireless Magazine Archive.
- ❏ Distributed Circuits and Loss.
- ❏ Examples, Unloaded Q, & Tuning.
- ❏ Filter Design by Transmission Zeros.
- ❏ Filter Techniques.
- ❏ High Frequency Oscillator Design.
- ❏ Introduction to Practical Issues and Modeling.
- ❏ Lumped – Element Transforms.
- ❏ Microwave Filters, Couplers, and Matching Networks.
- ❏ Microwave Transmission Lines and Their Physical Realizations.
- ❏ Pulse Doppler Radar.
- ❏ Radar Essentials: A Concise Handbook for Radar Design and Performance Analysis.
- ❏ Waveform Design and Diversity for Advanced Radar Systems.
- ❏ Through – the – Wall Radar Imaging.
- ❏ Foliage Penetration Radar: Detection and Characterization of Objects Under Trees.
- ❏ Principles of Waveform Diversity and Design.

- ❑ Communications, Radar and Electronic Warfare.
- ❑ Principles of Modern Radar: Basic Principles.
- ❑ Pocket Radar Guide: Key Radar Facts, Equations, and Data.
- ❑ Cognitive Radar: The Knowledge – Aided Fully Adaptive Approach.
- ❑ Handbook on Array Processing and Sensor Networks.
- ❑ Phased – Array Radar Design: Application of Radar Fundamentals.
- ❑ Polarimetric Radar Imaging: From Basics to Applications.
- ❑ MIMO Radar Signal Processing.
- ❑ Fundamentals of Ground Radar for Air Traffic Control Engineers and Technicians.
- ❑ Introduction to Sensors for Ranging and Imaging.
- ❑ Understanding Radar: The ABCs of How Radar Systems Work.
- ❑ Theory of Edge Diffraction in Electromagnetics: Origination and Validation of the Physical Theory of Diffraction, Revised Printing.
- ❑ Remote Sensing from Space.
- ❑ Radar System Analysis, Design and Simulation.
- ❑ Knowledge Based Radar Detection, Tracking and Classification.
- ❑ MIMO Radar Signal Processing.
- ❑ Radar Signal Analysis and Processing Using MATLAB.
- ❑ Robust Adaptive Beamforming.
- ❑ Modern Filter Design: Active RC and Switched Capacitor.
- ❑ Signal Processing First, Second Edition.
- ❑ Detection Theory: Applications and Digital Signal Processing.
- ❑ Wavelet Applications in Engineering Electromagnetics.
- ❑ Broadband Communications and Home Networking.
- ❑ Kalman Filtering: Theory and Practice Using MATLAB, 2nd Edition.
- ❑ Spectrum and Network Measurements.
- ❑ Handbook of Multisensor Data Fusion.
- ❑ Advanced Digital Communications: Systems and Signal Processing Techniques.
- ❑ Digital Communications: Microwave Applications, Second Edition.
- ❑ Digital Communications: Satellite/Earth Station Engineering, Second Edition.
- ❑ Digital Communications: 3 Volume Set.
- ❑ Detection of Signals in Noise, Second Edition.
- ❑ Introduction to Biomechatronics.

❏ Numerical Methods for Engineering: An Introduction Using MATLAB and Computational Electromagnetics.

❏ Introduction to Adaptive Arrays, 2nd Edition.

❏ Principles of Modern Radar: Basic Principles.

❏ Fundamentals of Wave Phenomena, 2nd Edition.

❏ Microwave and RF Design: A Systems Approach.

❏ Test and Evaluation of Aircraft Avionics and Weapons Systems.

❏ Introduction to Modern CMOS Digital Electronics: Preliminary Edition.

❏ Antennas: Fundamentals, Design, Measurement, Third Edition.

❏ Fundamentals of Electromagnetics with MATLAB, 2nd Edition.

❏ Fundamentals of Electromagnetics with MATLAB, Second Edition.

❏ Radar Principles for the Non – Specialist, Third Edition.

❏ Introduction to Airborne Radar, Second Edition.

❏ The RF/Microwave Library.

❏ Advanced Antenna Considerations I.

❏ Introduction to Antenna Fundamentals.

❏ Performance of Fundamental Antenna Elements.

❏ Introduction to Antennas.

❏ Introduction to the Smith Chart.

❏ Distributed Circuits and Loss.

❏ Examples, Unloaded Q, & Tuning.

❏ Filter Design by Transmission Zeros.

❏ Filter Techniques.

❏ High Frequency Oscillator Design.

❏ Introduction to Practical Issues and Modeling.

❏ Lumped – Element Transforms.

❏ Microwave Filters, Couplers, and Matching Networks.

❏ Microwave Transmission Lines and Their Physical Realizations.

❏ Noise Concepts and Design.

❏ Practical Issues in RF Design.

❏ Q From A to Z.

❏ RF Circuit Fundamentals I.

❏ RF Circuit Fundamentals II.

❏ RF/Microwave Transistor Amplifier Design.

❏ Theory and Practice of Transmission Line Transformers.

洛克希德·马丁公司

英文名称： Lockheed Martin Corporation，LMC

网　　址： http：//www.lockheedmartin.com/

机构简介

美国洛克希德·马丁公司由洛克希德公司与马丁·玛丽埃塔公司于1995年合并成立。总部位于马里兰州的贝塞斯达，2014年净销售额达456亿美元，有员工约112 000人，其中约一半的员工是科学家、工程师和IT专家。

洛克希德·马丁公司是全球领先的航空航天、安全、信息技术公司和全球最大的军火商，是美国国防部的最大防务承包商，也是美国政府在信息技术、系统一体化和培训领域的最大供应商，近年来一直占据各大军工企业排行榜的榜首，如斯德哥尔摩百强军工企业的榜首，防务新闻百强军工企业榜首等。

洛克希德·马丁公司在全球75个国家和地区开展业务，在美国的50个州的500个城市设有572个办事处，其知名的子公司和分公司如下。

（1）洛克希德·马丁航空公司，总部位于德克萨斯州的福特沃斯，拥有先进的激光超声检测和激光直接制造技术，致力于战术飞机、空运、航空研究和商业航线的发展。2014年，洛克希德·马丁航空公司的销售收入约141亿美元，有员工约30 000人。

（2）臭鼬工厂成立于1943年，最初是洛克希德公司为满足美国陆军空中战术服务司令部应对德国飞机威胁的需求而设立的一个喷气式战斗机项目。洛克希德公司的工程师最初提交的设计方案是XP-80流星喷气式战斗机，于1943年6月被采用并开始由洛克希德公司生产，标志着臭鼬工厂的诞生。臭鼬工厂以担任秘密研究计划为主，承载着先进技术的基础研究，并创造了多项突破性的技术、研发了多型里程碑式的飞机，以隐形飞机和侦察机闻名，如U-2侦察机、SR-71"黑鸟"侦察机以及F-117"夜鹰"战斗机、F-35"闪电Ⅱ"战斗机、F-22"猛禽"战斗机等。臭鼬工厂的高度自治的管理创新模式也是其他军工企业及一般企业学习的样本。2013年6月，臭鼬工厂在其70周年纪念宣传片中曝光了第六代战机和全球打击系统等未来概念武器。

（3）洛克希德·马丁信息系统和全球解决方案公司是联邦服务和信息技术的重要承包商，业务覆盖民用和国防领域，在信息技术解决方案、管理服务及先进技术专业知识等方面提升洛克希德·马丁公司的竞争力。2013年，洛克希德·马丁信息系统和全球解决方案公司实现销售收入约84亿美元，有约26 000名员工。

（4）洛克希德·马丁导弹和火控公司，以为美国及其盟国军队设计、开发及制造精确交战航空航天和防务系统而著称，提供空中和导弹防御系统、战术导弹、空—地精确打击武器系统、物流及其他技术服务、火控系统、任务操作支持、准备、工程支持、载人和无人地面车辆、工程服务、全球飞行解决方案、自动化指挥系统（C⁴ISR）产品支持、威胁应对服务等，同时也为全球的民用核能源产业及军队的绿色能源计划提供产品和服务。该公司知名度较高的产品和项目有："爱国者先进能力－3"导弹，终端高空区域防御空中和导弹防御项目；多管火箭发射系统，地狱火导弹，联合空对地距外导弹，"标枪"战术导弹项目；阿帕奇、狙击手、夜间低空导航暨红外线瞄准夹舱（也叫"蓝盾"）火控系统项目；特种作战部队承包商后勤支持服务项目等。2013年，洛克希德·马丁导弹和火控公司销售收入约78亿美元，其中67%来自美国政府客户，主要有美国陆军、美国海军、美国空军、美国海军陆战队、美国航空航天局等。

（5）洛克希德·马丁信息系统和全球解决方案公司是联邦服务和信息技术的重要承包商，业务覆盖民用和国防领域，在信息技术解决方案、管理服务及先进技术专业知识等方面提升洛克希德·马丁公司的竞争力。2014年，洛克希德·马丁信息系统和全球解决方案公司实现销售收入约78亿美元，有约24 000名员工。洛克希德·马丁信息系统和全球解决方案公司旗下的下一代网络创新与技术中心是世界级的技术中心，为网络研发及客户与合作伙伴间的合作与创新活动而设，是可以有效辅助洛克希德·马丁公司的研发、测试设备的最新机构。该中心的活动集中在7大领域的合作：可重构的空间、全球网络靶场、云计算平台、绿色IT数据中心、远程监控、高清晰度可视电话会议、全球站点连接等。该中心是洛克希德·马丁公司全球靶场的盖瑟斯堡结点，与全世界的实验室和开发中心联接，该网络的安全性通过高速连接到互联网、本地管理接口、HiWAE、GVNet及密级网络等来确保。

（6）洛克希德·马丁任务系统和培训公司，成立于2012年，由之前的海洋系统和传感器业务单元与全球培训和物流业务单元以及电子系统业务单元等联合组成，主要提供系统工程、软件开发、综合项目管理、供应链解决方案和物流、全球安全的训练和模拟技术以及民用和商业市场服务。2014年，洛克希德·马丁任务系统和培训公司的销售收入约71亿美元，有员工18 000多人，大部分员工是计算机系统、软件和硬件工程专家。

（7）洛克希德·马丁空间系统公司主要为国家安全领域客户、民用和商用客户设计、开发、测试、生产、运营全方位的先进系统等，专注于以下业务：载人航天、全球通信系统、商业航天、传感与探索系统、导弹防御系统、战略导弹、商业发射系统、监视与导航系统及特别项目等。该公司的主要产品包括载人航天系统以及一系列的遥感、导航、气象和通信卫星及设备等，空间观测和行星际飞船、激光雷达、舰队弹道导弹以及导弹防御系统等。比较知名的产品和项目有：用潜艇发射的"三叉戟Ⅱ"D5型舰载弹道导弹、空基红外系统、先进极高频卫星、为美国航空航天局设计的猎户座多用途载人飞船、全球定位系统Ⅲ、同步运行环境卫星R系列、美国海军的新一代窄波段卫星通信系统—移动用户目标系统。2014年，洛克希德·马丁空间系统公司的销售收入约81亿美元，97%的收入来自美国政府客户。

（8）洛克希德·马丁全球公司成立于1975年，是洛克希德·马丁公司的全资子公司，是一个专注于研究、设计、开发、制造高科技产品和服务的全球型企业，主要业务是将洛克希德·马丁公司的产品运送给美国以外的客户，有3 000多名员工。

洛克希德·马丁公司在所经营的业务领域有丰富的产品，具体如下。

（1）航空航天和防务领域的产品涉及飞机、地面车辆、导弹和制导武器、导弹防御、海军系统、雷达系统、传感器和飞行感知、战术通信、培训和物流、运输和安全管理以及无人系统。著名的产品有F-16战隼，F-22猛禽，F-35 Lightning Ⅱ，多任务地面作战车辆Havoc，高机动性炮兵火箭系统（High Mobility Artillery Rocket System，HIMARS）等。

（2）信息技术领域的产品涉及生物信息、云计算、网络安全和信息管理等。

（3）空间领域的产品涉及气候监测、卫星和太空探索等，如A2100、Geo-Eye-2等。

（4）新兴业务领域涉及的产品有纳米复合材料、可再生能源等。

出版物

报告

❑ Annual Report.

美国 TriQuint 半导体公司

英文名称：TriQuint Semiconductor Inc，TriQuint

网　　址：http：//www. triquint. com/

机构简介

美国 TriQuint 半导体公司成立于 1985 年。1991 年，TriQuint 与砷化镓（GaAs）先驱 Gazelle Microcircuits、Gigabit Logic 合并。美国 TriQuint 半

导体公司主要进行高性能射频零组件、部件的设计、生产和供应并提供铸造服务，是世界上最大的商用砷化镓铸造服务提供者，也是世界第三大砷化镓设备生产商，是研发氮化镓[1]（GaN）的先驱。该公司专门为移动设备、3G 和 4G 蜂窝基站、WLAN、WiMAX、GPS、国防与航空等领域的客户提供各种服务，采用砷化镓（GaAs）、氮化镓（GaN）、声表面波（SAW）和体声波（BAW）技术设计、开发和生产先进的高性能射频解决方案，满足全球客户需求，其产品广泛应用于国防航空、移动设备、网络设备等。

美国 TriQuint 半导体公司创造了很多个"第一"，它是第一个将砷化镓集成电路（GaAs IC）转换成 100mm 晶片的生产商，是第一个采用塑料封装的砷化镓集成电路（GaAs IC）生产商，第一个将航空产品应用到商业通信卫星，推出业界第一个 7mm × 7mm 和 6mm × 6mm 的功率放大（PA）模块和 6mm × 6mm 四频段功率放大器（PA），推出业界第一个高功率射频晶体管半导体 PowerBandTM。

美国 TriQuint 半导体公司在发展过程中，收购了多家公司，不断扩展自己的业务实力。

1998 年，美国 TriQuint 半导体公司收购了得克萨斯仪器公司（Texas Instruments Inc）的 GaAs MMIC 业务，并承诺支持商业和军事应用，建立了从事砷化镓（GaAs）、磷化铟（InP）、氮化镓（GaN）以及其他先进半导体技术和材料的研发部门。

2001 年，美国 TriQuint 半导体公司收购了 Sawtek Inc.，增加了基于 SAW（声表面波）的信号处理元器件业务。

2002 年，美国 TriQuint 半导体公司收购了英飞凌公司（Infineon，1999 年 5 月 1 日，西门子半导体公司正式更名为 Infineon）砷化镓半导体业务，在慕

---

① 氮化镓（Gallium Nitride，GaN）是一种半导体化合物，它可以使无线转发器小型化、高功率。这些转发器可以与灵敏接收器相结合，并接入到能够直接访问通信卫星的电话机上。氮化镓这种化合物还可以用在发光二极管以及其他半导体设备中。氮化镓设备的优势还包括：①在小体积环境下有较高的输出功率；②在超高频率以及微波无线频率下的功率放大器中有较高的效率。

尼黑成立了一个设计中心，并签署了合作伙伴协议进行开发和生产用于定制无线系统方案中的高集成度射频、元器件和模块。

2013年，美国TriQuint半导体公司收购了CAP Wireless（网址：www.capwireless.com/）公司及其Spatium™技术，主要生产防务电子（Defense Electronics）、电子战（Electronic Warfare）产品和Spatium SATCOM产品等。

美国TriQuint半导体公司与波音公司、通用动力公司、洛克希德·马丁公司、诺斯罗普·格鲁曼公司、雷神公司等建立了合作关系，并与美国空军（US Air Force）、美国陆军研究实验室（US Army Research Laboratory）、美国海军研究局（Office of Naval Research）、美国国防高级研究计划局（DARPA）等有密切合作。

美国TriQuint半导体公司的砷化镓（GaAs）微波单片集成电路（MMICs）产品用于洛克希德·马丁公司的雷达系统EQ-36反火炮目标数据采集雷达系统，其功率放大器、砷化镓（GaAs）器件以及体声波（BAW）滤波器用于F-35战斗机闪电Ⅱ火控雷达系统和相控阵雷达系统。

美国TriQuint半导体公司还将为美国陆军研究实验室（ARL）提供采用美国TriQuint公司的增强/耗尽型（E/D）氮化镓（GaN）技术的新型高频和混合信号集成电路（IC）。

2013年，美国TriQuint半导体公司继续为混合信号设备（数字和射频）创建基准性能标准，其氮化镓技术也使其作为微型电源转换项目（MPC）的主承包商之一，为集成RF放大器开发超高速高功率DC-DC开关调制器技术。

美国电缆电信工程师协会

英文名称：Society of Cable Telecommunications Engineers，SCTE

网　址：http：//www. scte. org/

机构简介

美国电缆电信工程师协会成立于 1969 年，是一个非营利性的专业组织，是电缆电信产业领域技术与应用科学的领导者，旨在推动电缆通信工程相关技术的进步，现有会员12 000多个。

出版物

SCTE 面向会员提供如下出版物。

1）期刊与杂志

❏ CED.

❏ Cable Learning Review，季刊。

❏ Field Focus，季刊。

❏ Broadband Library，季刊。

2）简讯

❏ SCTE Interval，季刊。

❏ SCTE Monthly，季刊。

❏ Light Reading Cable's Weekly Newsletter，周刊。

3）简报

❏ SCTE NewsBrief.

4）公告

❏ SCTE Standards Bulletin，季刊。

5）报告

❏ Heavy Reading Research Reports.

6）标准

❏ ANSI/SCTE 104 2012 Automation System to Compression System Communications Applications Program Interface（API）.

❏ ANSI/SCTE 35 2013 Digital Program Insertion Cueing Message for Cable.

❏ ANSI/SCTE 135 – 2 2013 DOCSIS 3. 0 Part 2：MAC and Upper Layer Protocols.

❏ ANSI/SCTE 135 – 4 2013 DOCSIS 3. 0 Part 4：Operations Support Systems Interface.

❏ ANSI/SCTE 135 – 3 2013 DOCSIS 3. 0 Part 3：Security Services.

❏ ANSI/SCTE 135 – 1 2013 DOCSIS 3. 0 Part 1：Physical Layer Specification.

❏ ANSI/SCTE 130 – 3 2010 Digital Program Insertion—Advertising Systems

Interfaces Part 3：Ad Management Service（ADM）Interface.

❑ ANSI/SCTE 40 2011 Digital Cable Network Interface Standard.

❑ ANSI/SCTE 77 2013 Specification for Underground Enclosure Integrity.

❑ ANSI/SCTE 28 2012 Host – POD Interface Standard.

会议信息

❑ SCTE EXPO；2015. 10. 13—16；New Orleans，LA，USA.

美国电信行业协会

英文名称：Telecommunications Industry Association，TIA

网　　址：http：//www. tiaonline. org/

机构简介

美国电信行业协会于 1988 年由美国电信
供应商协会（United States Telecommunications
Suppliers Association，USTSA）和电子工业协
会（Electronic Industries Association，EIA）的
信息与电信技术小组（Information and Telecommunications Technologies Group）合并成立，2000 年又将多媒体电信协会
（MultiMedia Telecommunications Association，MMTA）合并。

　　美国电信行业协会是一个会员运营的机构，从会员公司中挑选会员，设置
的部门有标准与技术部门、市场情报部门、营销与会员部门、活动与会议部
门，还有用户处设备、无线通信、光纤、网络与卫星通信等部门，另外还设置
有通信研究部门。

　　另外，该协会还是经美国标准协会（American National Standards Intstitute，
ANSI）认证的组织，可制定信息与通信技术领域产品的行业标准。

出版物

1）报告

❑ Market Intelligence：TIA's 2013 ICT Market Review and Forecast.

❑ Industry Standards for ICT Products：The Standards and Technology Annual
Report.

❑ Understanding ICT Policies：The 2013 Industry Playbook.

2）其他出版物

❑ The Telecommunications Glossary，定义了 6 000 多个信息通信技术的技
术术语。

会议信息

❑ TIA CTO Council Meeting；2015. 10. 18—19；Austin，TX，USA.

❑ Women in High – Tech Dinner；2015. 10. 20；Washington，DC.

❑ TIA Wireless and Cellular Workshop #4：Microwave Backhaul and Design；
2015. 10. 21；Arlington，VA，USA.

❑ TIA Board Meeting；2015. 11. 11；Arlington，VA，USA.

❑ DAS and Small Cell Workshop；2015. 11. 11—12；Arlington，VA，USA.

❑ TIA Wireless and Cellular Workshop #5：Understanding LTE and LTE – Ad-
vanced；2015. 12. 02；Arlington，VA.

美国电气与电子工程师学会

英文名称：Institute of Electrical and Electronics Engineers, Inc. , IEEE

网　　址：http：//www. ieee. org/index. html

机构简介

美国电气与电子工程师学会成立于 1963 年，由美国电气工程师学会（AIEE，1884 年成立）和无线电工程师学会（IRE，1912 年成立）合并而成。

美国电气与电子工程师学会拥有分布于 140 多个国家和地区的会员 32 万余人，是世界上最大的技术团体，主要从事电气、电子、计算机工程和计算机科学的研究，每年独家或合办 300 多个国际会议和展览会，其出版物占世界该领域文献的 20% 以上，主要有期刊与杂志、图书、会议录和报道计算技术、电子学及电气工程的期刊与杂志。

出版物

1）会议录

❑ Proceedings of the IEEE.

2）期刊与杂志

❑ IEEE Spectrum Magazine.

❑ Women in Engineering Magazine, IEEE.

❑ Signal Processing, IEEE Transactions on.

❑ Broadcasting, IEEE Transactions on.

❑ Consumer Electronics, IEEE Transactions on.

❑ Antennas and Propagation, IEEE Transactions on.

❑ Nuclear Science, IEEE Transactions on.

❑ Plasma Science, IEEE Transactions on.

❑ Vehicular Technology, IEEE Transactions on.

❑ Reliability, IEEE Transactions on.

❑ Instrumentation and Measurement Subscription, IEEE Transactions on.

❑ Aerospace and Electronic Systems, IEEE Transactions on.

❑ Information Theory, IEEE Transactions on.

❑ Industrial Electronics, IEEE Transactions on.

❑ Engineering Management, IEEE Transactions on.

❑ Electron Devices, IEEE Transactions on.

❑ Computers, IEEE Transactions on.

❑ Software Engineering, IEEE Transactions on.

❑ Microwave Theory and Techniques, IEEE Transactions on.

- ❏ Biomedical Engineering, IEEE Transactions on.
- ❏ Communications, IEEE Transactions on.
- ❏ Ultrasonics, Ferroelectrics, and Frequency Control, IEEE Transactions on.
- ❏ Automatic Control, IEEE Transactions on.
- ❏ Education, IEEE Transactions on.
- ❏ Professional Communication, IEEE Transactions on.
- ❏ Electromagnetic Compatibility, IEEE Transactions on.
- ❏ Systems, Man, and Cybernetics: Systems, IEEE Trans on.
- ❏ Geoscience and Remote Sensing, IEEE Transactions on.
- ❏ Dielectrics and Electrical Insulation, IEEE Transactions on.
- ❏ Magnetics, IEEE Transactions on.
- ❏ Industry Applications, IEEE Transactions on.
- ❏ Quantum Electronics, IEEE Journal of.
- ❏ Pattern Analysis and Machine Intelligence, IEEE Transactions on (Online Plus).
- ❏ Pattern Analysis and Machine Intelligence, IEEE Transactions on.
- ❏ Medical Imaging, IEEE Transactions on.
- ❏ Computer – Aided Design of Integrated Circuits and Systems, IEEE Transactions on.
- ❏ Technology and Society Magazine, IEEE.
- ❏ Selected Areas in Communications, IEEE Journal of.
- ❏ Energy Conversion, IEEE Transactions on.
- ❏ Power Delivery, IEEE Transactions on.
- ❏ Power Systems, IEEE Transactions on.
- ❏ Semiconductor Manufacturing, IEEE Transactions on.
- ❏ Robotics, IEEE Transactions on.
- ❏ Knowledge and Data Engineering, IEEE Transactions on.
- ❏ Photonics Technology Letters, IEEE.
- ❏ Neural Networks and Learning Systems, IEEE Transactions on.
- ❏ Parallel and Distributed Systems, IEEE Transactions on.
- ❏ Microwave and Wireless Components Letters, IEEE.
- ❏ Applied Superconductivity, IEEE Transactions on.
- ❏ Circuits and Systems for Video Technology, IEEE Transactions on.
- ❏ Image Processing, IEEE Transactions on.
- ❏ Fuzzy Systems, IEEE Transactions on.
- ❏ Networking, IEEE/ACM Transactions on.

- Audio, Speech and Language Processing, IEEE/ACM Transactions on.
- Control Systems Technology, IEEE Transactions on.
- Very Large Scale Integration Systems, IEEE Transactions on.
- Neural Systems and Rehabilitation Engineering, IEEE Transactions on.
- Visualization and Computer Graphics, IEEE Transactions on.
- Mechatronics, IEEE/ASME Transactions on.
- Cybernetics, IEEE Transactions on.
- Evolutionary Computation, IEEE Transactions on.
- Biomedical and Health Informatics, IEEE Journal of.
- Communications Letters, IEEE.
- Internet Computing Magazine, IEEE.
- Emerging and Selected Topics in Circuits and Systems, IEEE Journal on.
- Photonics Society DVD Collection, IEEE.
- Photovoltaics, IEEE Journal of.
- Human – Machine Systems, IEEE Transactions on.
- Multimedia, IEEE Transactions on.
- IT Professional.
- Intelligent Transportation Systems, IEEE Transactions on.
- Sensors Journal, IEEE.
- Device and Materials Reliability, IEEE Transactions on.
- Antennas and Wireless Propagation Letters, IEEE.
- Mobile Computing, IEEE Transactions on (OnlinePlus).
- NanoBioscience, IEEE Transactions on.
- Nanotechnology, IEEE Transactions on.
- Wireless Communications, IEEE Transactions on.
- Terahertz Science and Technology, IEEE Transactions on.
- Geoscience and Remote Sensing Letters, IEEE.
- Computational Biology and Bioinformatics, IEEE/ACM Transactions on.
- Dependable and Secure Computing, IEEE Transactions on.
- Automation Science and Engineering, IEEE Transactions on.
- Circuits and Systems, Part I: Regular Papers, IEEE Transactions on.
- Circuits and Systems, Part II: Express Briefs, IEEE Transactions on.
- Display Technology, Journal of.
- Industrial Informatics, IEEE Transactions on.
- Information Forensics and Security, IEEE Transactions on.
- Computer Architecture Letters, IEEE.

- Biomedical Circuits and Systems, IEEE Transactions on.
- Industrial Electronics Magazine, IEEE.
- Nanotechnology Magazine, IEEE.
- Network and Service Management, IEEE Transactions on.
- Selected Topics in Signal Processing, IEEE Journal of.
- Systems Journal, IEEE.
- Haptics, IEEE Transactions on.
- Reviews in Biomedical Engineering, IEEE.
- Selected Topics in Applied Earth Observations and Remote Sensing, IEEE Journal of.
- Services Computing, IEEE Transactions on.
- Intelligent Transportation Systems Magazine, IEEE.
- Learning Technologies, IEEE Transactions on.
- Technology Management Package, IEEE.
- Autonomous Mental Development, IEEE Transactions on.
- Solid – State Circuits Magazine, IEEE.
- Embedded Systems Letters, IEEE.
- Computational Intelligence and AI in Games, IEEE Transactions on.
- Communications Surveys & Tutorials, IEEE.
- Optical Communications and Networking, IEEE/OSA Journal of.
- Affective Computing, IEEE Transactions on.
- Sustainable Energy, IEEE Transactions on.
- Smart Grid, IEEE Transactions on.
- Magnetics Letters, IEEE.
- Components, Packaging and Manufacturing Technology, IEEE Transactions on.
- China Communications Magazine.
- Wireless Communications Letters, IEEE.
- Electromagnetic Compatibility Magazine, IEEE.
- Consumer Electronics Magazine, IEEE.
- Iberoamericana de Tecnologias del Aprendizaje, IEEE Revista.
- Geoscience and Remote Sensing Magazine, IEEE.
- Electrification Magazine, IEEE.
- Cloud Computing, IEEE Transactions on.
- Emerging and Selected Topics in Power Electronics, IEEE Journal of.
- Cloud Computing, IEEE.
- Network Science and Engineering, IEEE Transactions on.

- ❏ Control of Network Systems, IEEE Transactions on.
- ❏ Power Electronics Magazine, IEEE.
- ❏ Computational Social Systems, IEEE Transactions on.
- ❏ Journal of Automatica Sinica, IEEE/CAA.
- ❏ Internet of Things Journal, IEEE.
- ❏ Computer Magazine, IEEE.
- ❏ Engineering Management Review, IEEE.
- ❏ Communications Magazine, IEEE.
- ❏ Electron Device Letters, IEEE.
- ❏ Control Systems Magazine, IEEE.
- ❏ Computer Graphics and Applications Magazine, IEEE.
- ❏ Micro Magazine, IEEE.
- ❏ PULSE, IEEE: A Magazine published by the IEEE Engineering in Medicine and Biology Society.
- ❏ Signal Processing Magazine, IEEE.
- ❏ Design and Test, IEEE.
- ❏ Software Magazine, IEEE.
- ❏ Electrical Insulation Magazine, IEEE.
- ❏ Intelligent Systems Magazine, IEEE.
- ❏ Aerospace and Electronic Systems Magazine, IEEE.
- ❏ Network Magazine, IEEE.
- ❏ Antennas and Propagation Magazine, IEEE.
- ❏ Annals of the History of Computing, IEEE.
- ❏ Computing in Science & Engineering.
- ❏ MultiMedia Magazine, IEEE.
- ❏ Signal Processing Letters, IEEE.
- ❏ Robotics and Automation Magazine, IEEE.
- ❏ Wireless Communications Magazine, IEEE.
- ❏ Industry Applications Magazine, IEEE.
- ❏ Instrumentation and Measurement Magazine, IEEE.
- ❏ Microwave Magazine, IEEE.
- ❏ Circuits and Systems Magazine, IEEE.
- ❏ Pervasive Computing Magazine, IEEE.
- ❏ Power and Energy Magazine, IEEE.
- ❏ Security & Privacy Magazine, IEEE.
- ❏ Computational Intelligence Magazine, IEEE.

- ❑ Vehicular Technology Magazine, IEEE.
- ❑ Solid – State Circuits, IEEE Journal of.
- ❑ Oceanic Engineering, IEEE Journal of.
- ❑ Lightwave Technology, Journal of.
- ❑ Computational Intelligence Periodical Package, IEEE.
- ❑ Robotics and Automation Transactions Package, IEEE.
- ❑ Power Electronics, IEEE Transactions on.
- ❑ Signal Processing Periodical Package, IEEE.
- ❑ Instrumentation and Measurement, IEEE Transactions on.
- ❑ Electronic Materials, IEEE/TMS Journal of.
- ❑ Microelectromechanical Systems, Journal of.
- ❑ Selected Topics in Quantum Electronics, IEEE Journal of.
- ❑ Microwave Theory and Techniques Periodical Package, IEEE.
- ❑ Spectrum, IEEE.
- ❑ Proceedings of the IEEE.
- ❑ Potentials Magazine, IEEE.

3）简讯

- ❑ The Institute.

4）标准

- ❑ IEEE Standards.

5）数据库（Digital Library）

- ❑ IEL 数据库：IEEE Xplore® Digital Library.

会议信息

- ❑ 2015 Integrated Nonlinear Microwave and Millimetre – wave Circuits Workshop（INMMiC）；2015. 10. 01—02；Taormina, Italy.
- ❑ 2015 Fourth Berkeley Symposium on Energy Efficient Electronic Systems（E3S）；2015. 10. 01—02；Berkeley, CA, USA.
- ❑ 2015 IEEE 3rd International Conference on MOOCs, Innovation and Technology in Education（MITE）；2015. 10. 01—02；Amritsar, India.
- ❑ 2015 Latin American Network Operations and Management Symposium（LANOMS）；2015. 10. 01—03；João Pessoa, Brazil.
- ❑ 2015 IEEE 7th International Workshop on Managing Technical Debt（MTD）；2015. 10. 02；Bremen, Germany.
- ❑ 2015 IEEE 9th International Symposium on the Maintenance and Evolution of Service – Oriented and Cloud – Based Environments（MESOCA）；2015. 10. 02；

Bremen, Germany.

❏ 2015 North American Power Symposium (NAPS); 2015. 10. 04—06; Charlotte, NC, USA.

❏ 2015 IEEE International Symposium on Workload Characterization (IISWC); 2015. 10. 04—06; Atlanta, GA, USA.

❏ 2015 IEEE International Conference on Ubiquitous Wireless Broadband (ICUWB); 2015. 10. 04—07; QC, Canada.

❏ 2015 IEEE Photonics Conference (IPC); 2015. 10. 04—08; Reston, VA, USA.

❏ 2015 7th International Workshop on Reliable Networks Design and Modeling (RNDM); 2015. 10. 05—07; Germany.

❏ 2015 International Conference on Computer, Control, Informatics and its Applications (IC3INA); 2015. 10. 05—07; Bandung, Indonesia.

❏ 2015 IEEE 23rd International Symposium on Modeling, Analysis and Simulation of Computer and Telecommunication Systems (MASCOTS); 2015. 10. 05—07; Atlanta, GA, USA.

❏ 2015 International Conference on Sustainable Energy Engineering and Application (ICSEEA); 2015. 10. 05—07; Bandung, Indonesia.

❏ 2015 IEEE Petroleum and Chemical Industry Committee Conference (PCIC); 2015. 10. 05—07; Houston, TX, USA.

❏ 2015 IEEE PES Innovative Smart Grid Technologies Latin America (ISGT LATAM); 2015. 10. 05—07; Montevideo, Uruguay.

❏ 2015 IFIP/IEEE International Conference on Very Large Scale Integration (VLSI – SoC); 2015. 10. 05—07; Daejeon, Korea.

❏ 2015 8th IFIP Wireless and Mobile Networking Conference (WMNC); 2015. 10. 05—07; Serbia.

❏ 2015 International Conference on Radar, Antenna, Microwave, Electronics and Telecommunications (ICRAMET); 2015. 10. 05—07; Bandung, Indonesia.

❏ 2015 IEEE SOI-3D-Subthreshold Microelectronics Technology Unified Conference (S3S); 2015. 10. 05—08; Rohnert Park, CA, USA.

❏ 2015 26th European Symposium on Reliability of Electron Devices, Failure Physics and Analysis (ESREF); 2015. 10. 05—09; TOULOUSE, France.

❏ 2015 International Conference on Embedded Software (EMSOFT); 2015. 10. 05—09; Amsterdam, Netherlands.

❏ 2015 International Conference "Stability and Control Processes" in Memory of V. I. Zubov (SCP); 2015. 10. 05—09; Saint Petersburg, Russia.

❏ 2015 International Workshop on Fiber Optics in Access Network (FOAN); 2015. 10. 06—07; Brno, Czech Republic.

❏ 2015 Fifth International Conference on e − Learning (econf); 2015. 10. 06—08; Manama, Bahrain.

❏ 2015 7th International Congress on Ultra Modern Telecommunications and Control Systems and Workshops (ICUMT); 2015. 10. 06—08; Brno, Czech Republic.

❏ 2015 IEEE International Test Conference (ITC); 2015. 10. 06—08; Anaheim, CA, USA.

❏ 2015 Sensor Data Fusion: Trends, Solutions, Applications (SDF); 2015. 10. 06—08; Bonn, Germany.

❏ 2015 International Conference on Man − Machine Interactions (ICMMI); 2015. 10. 06—09; Andrychów, Poland.

❏ 2015 18th CSI International Symposium on Computer Architecture and Digital Systems (CADS); 2015. 10. 07—08; Tehran, Iran.

❏ 2015 IEEE Brasil RFID; 2015. 10. 07—08; Sao Paulo, Brazil.

❏ 2015 CSI Symposium on Real − Time and Embedded Systems and Technologies (RTEST); 2015. 10. 07—08; Tehran, Iran.

❏ 2015 Information Technologies in Innovation Business Conference (ITIB); 2015. 10. 07—09; Kharkiv, Ukraine.

❏ 2015 3rd RSI International Conference on Robotics and Mechatronics (ICROM); 2015. 10. 07—09; Tehran, Iran.

❏ 2015 IEEE 9th International Conference on Standardization and Innovation in Information Technology (SIIT); 2015. 10. 07—09; CA, USA.

❏ 2015 15th International Symposium on Communications and Information Technologies (ISCIT); 2015. 10. 07—09; Nara, Japan.

❏ 2015 Fifth International Conference on Digital Information Processing and Communications (ICDIPC); 2015. 10. 07—09; Sierre, Switzerland.

❏ 2015 International Symposium on Rapid System Prototyping (RSP); 2015. 10. 08—09; Amsterdam, Netherlands.

❏ 2015 13th IEEE Symposium on Embedded Systems For Real − time Multimedia (ESTIMedia); 2015. 10. 08—09; Amsterdam, Netherlands.

❏ 2015 Seventh International Conference on Knowledge and Systems Engineering (KSE); 2015. 10. 08—10; Ho Chi Minh, Vietnam.

❏ 2015 International Conference on Soft Computing Techniques and Implementations（ICSCTI）；2015. 10. 08—10；Faridabad，India.

❏ 2015 International Conference on Green Computing and Internet of Things（ICGCIoT）；2015. 10. 08—10；Noida，Delhi，India.

❏ 2015 International Conference on Advanced Computer Science and Information Systems（ICACSIS）；2015. 10. 10—11；West Java，Indonesia.

❏ 2015 IEEE 61st Holm Conference on Electrical Contacts（Holm）；2015. 10. 11—14；San Diego，CA，USA.

❏ 2015 IEEE Compound Semiconductor Integrated Circuit Symposium（CSICS）；2015. 10. 11—14；New Orleans，LA，USA.

❏ 2015 IEEE International Integrated Reliability Workshop（IIRW）；2015. 10. 11—15；South Lake Tahoe，CA，USA.

❏ 2015 IEEE Information Theory Workshop – Fall（ITW）；2015. 10. 11—15；Jeju Island，Korea.

❏ 2015 IEEE International Symposium on Precision Clock Synchronization for Measurement，Control，and Communication（ISPCS）；2015. 10. 11—16；Beijing，China.

❏ 2015 IEEE Dallas Circuits and Systems Conference（DCAS）；2015. 10. 12—13；Dallas，TX，USA.

❏ 2015 IEEE International Workshop on Measurements and Networking（M&N）；2015. 10. 12—13；Coimbra，Portugal.

❏ 2015 International Semiconductor Conference（CAS）；2015. 10. 12—14；Sinaia，Romania.

❏ 2015 IEEE International Symposium on Defect and Fault Tolerance in VLSI and Nanotechnology Systems（DFTS）；2015. 10. 12—14；Amherst，MA，USA.

❏ 2015 15th Non-Volatile Memory Technology Symposium（NVMTS）；2015. 10. 12—14；Beijing，China.

❏ 2015 IEEE 27th Annual Software Technology Conference（STC）；2015. 10. 12—15；Long Beach，CA，USA.

❏ 2015 IEEE Rock Stars of SDx（SDx）；2015. 10. 13；Seattle，WA，USA.

❏ 2015 56th International Scientific Conference on Power and Electrical Engineering of Riga Technical University（RTUCON）；2015. 10. 14；Riga，Latvia.

❏ 2015 International Conference on Enterprise Systems（ES）；2015. 10. 14—15；Basel，Switzerland.

❏ 2015 IEEE Workshop on Signal Processing Systems（SiPS）；2015. 10. 14—16；Hangzhou，China.

❏ 2015 21st Asia-Pacific Conference on Communications（APCC）；2015. 10. 14—16；Kyoto, Japan.

❏ 2015 IET International Radar Conference（IET Radar）；2015. 10. 14—16；Hangzhou, China.

❏ 2015 8th International Congress on Image and Signal Processing（CISP）；2015. 10. 14—16；Shenyang, China.

❏ 2015 IEEE 2nd Colombian Conference on Automatic Control（CCAC）；2015. 10. 14—16；Manizales, Colombia.

❏ 2015 AEIT Annual Conference（AEIT）；2015. 10. 14—16；Milano, Italy.

❏ 2015 IEEE High Power Diode Lasers and Systems Conference（HPD）；2015. 10. 14—16；Coventry, United Kingdom .

❏ 2015 International Conference on Advanced Technologies for Communications（ATC）；2015. 10. 14—16；Ho Chi Minh, Vietnam.

❏ 2015 International Conference on Mechanical Engineering, Automation and Control Systems（MEACS）；2015. 10. 14—16；Tomsk, Russia.

❏ 2015 Asia – Pacific Conference on Emerging Technologies（APCET）；2015. 10. 14—16；Singapore.

❏ 2015 IEEE Games Entertainment Media Conference（GEM）；2015. 10. 14—16；Toronto, ON, Canada.

❏ 2015 19th International Conference on System Theory, Control and Computing（ICSTCC）；2015. 10. 14—16；Cheile Gradistei, Romania.

❏ 2015 8th International Conference on Biomedical Engineering and Informatics（BMEI）；2015. 10. 14—16；Shenyang, China.

❏ 2015 IEEE/ACM 19th International Symposium on Distributed Simulation and Real Time Applications（DS – RT）；2015. 10. 14—16；China.

❏ 2015 9th International Conference on Application of Information and Communication Technologies（AICT）；2015. 10. 14—16；Rostov – on – Don, Russia.

❏ 2015 IEEE Underwater Acoustic Signal Processing Workshop（UASP）；2015. 10. 14—16；West Greenwich, RI, USA.

❏ 2015 International Symposium on Bioelectronics and Bioinformatics（ISBB）；2015. 10. 14—17；Beijing, China.

❏ 2015 17th International Conference on E – health Networking, Application & Services（HealthCom）；2015. 10. 14—17；Boston, MA, USA.

❏ 2015 12th International Conference on Telecommunication in Modern Satellite, Cable and Broadcasting Services（TELSIKS）；2015. 10. 14—17；Nis,

Serbia.

❑ 2015 International Conference on Speech Technology and Human – Computer Dialogue (SpeD); 2015. 10. 14—17; Bucharest, Romania.

❑ 2015 Medical Technologies National Conference (TIPTEKNO); 2015. 10. 15—17; Mugla, Turkey.

❑ 2015 IEEE Conference on Sustainable Utilization And Development In Engineering and Technology (CSUDET); 2015. 10. 15—17; Malaysia.

❑ 2015 IEEE Power, Communication and Information Technology Conference (PCITC); 2015. 10. 15—17; BHUBANESWAR, India.

❑ 2015 International Conference on Advanced Mechatronics, Intelligent Manufacture, and Industrial Automation (ICAMIMIA); 2015. 10. 15—17; Surabaya, Indonesia.

❑ 2015 International Conference on Wireless Communications & Signal Processing (WCSP); 2015. 10. 15—17; Nanjing, China.

❑ 2015 International Conference and Workshop on Computing and Communication (IEMCON); 2015. 10. 15—17; Vancouver, BC, Canada.

❑ 2015 12th International Symposium on Neural Networks (ISNN); 2015. 10. 15—18; Jeju, Korea.

❑ 2015 2nd International Conference on Opto – Electronics and Applied Optics (IEM OPTRONIX); 2015. 10. 16—17; Vancouver, BC, Canada.

❑ 2015 Fourth International Congress of Telecomunications (TELCON UNI); 2015. 10. 16—17; Lima, Peru.

❑ 2015 IEEE International Conference on Communication Problem – Solving (ICCP); 2015. 10. 16—18; Guilin, China.

❑ 2015 2nd International Conference on Information Technology, Computer, and Electrical Engineering (ICITACEE); 2015. 10. 16—18; Semarang, Indonesia.

❑ 2015 IEEE International Conference of Energy Storage Technology and Materials (ICESTM); 2015. 10. 16—18; Beijing, China.

❑ 2015 IEEE PES Insulated Conductors Committee Fall Meeting (PES ICC); 2015. 10. 16—24; Las Vegas, NV, USA.

❑ 2015 International Conference on Virtual Reality and Visualization (ICVRV); 2015. 10. 17—18; Fujian, China.

❑ 2015 27th International Symposium on Computer Architecture and High Performance Computing (SBAC – PAD); 2015. 10. 17—21; Florianopolis, Brazil.

❑ 2015 IEEE International Symposium on Safety, Security, and Rescue Robotics (SSRR); 2015. 10. 18—20; West Lafayette, IN, USA.

❑ 2015 IEEE International Symposium on Robotics and Intelligent Sensors (IRIS); 2015. 10. 18—20; Malaysia.

❑ 2015 IEEE 16th International Conference on Communication Technology (ICCT); 2015. 10. 18—21; Hangzhou, China.

❑ 2015 International Conference on Parallel Architecture and Compilation (PACT); 2015. 10. 18—21; San Francisco, CA, USA.

❑ 2015 IEEE Workshop on Applications of Signal Processing to Audio and Acoustics (WASPAA); 2015. 10. 18—21; New Paltz, NY, USA.

❑ 2015 IEEE Conference on Electrical Insulation and Dielectric Phenomena (CEIDP); 2015. 10. 18—21; Ann Arbor, MI, USA.

❑ 2015 IEEE Symposium on Visual Languages and Human – Centric Computing (VL/HCC); 2015. 10. 18—22; Atlanta, GA, USA.

❑ OCEANS 2015 – MTS/IEEE Washington; 2015. 10. 18—22; Washington, DC, USA.

❑ INTELEC 2015 IEEE International Telecommunications Energy Conference; 2015. 10. 18—22; Osaka, Japan.

❑ 2015 IEEE Industry Applications Society Annual Meeting; 2015. 10. 18—22; Addison, TX, USA.

❑ 2015 Symposium on Recent Advances in Electrical Engineering (RAEE); 2015. 10. 19—20; Islamabad, Pakistan.

❑ 2015 12th International Conference & Expo on Emerging Technologies for a Smarter World (CEWIT); 2015. 10. 19—20; Melville, NY, USA.

❑ 2015 IEEE International Conference on Data Science and Advanced Analytics (DSAA); 2015. 10. 19—21; Paris, France.

❑ 2015 IEEE Conference on Energy Conversion (CENCON); 2015. 10. 19—21; JOHOR, Malaysia.

❑ 2015 IEEE 17th International Workshop on Multimedia Signal Processing (MMSP); 2015. 10. 19—21; Xiamen, China.

❑ 2015 World Congress on Internet Security (WorldCIS); 2015. 10. 19—21; Dublin, Ireland.

❑ 2015 IEEE 8th International Conference on Service – Oriented Computing and Applications (SOCA); 2015. 10. 19—21; Roma, Italy.

❑ 2015 IEEE 11th International Conference on Wireless and Mobile Computing, Networking and Communications (WiMob); 2015. 10. 19—21; Abu

Dhabi, United Arab Emirates.

❏ 2015 6th IEEE International Conference on Cognitive Infocommunications (CogInfoCom); 2015. 10. 19—21; Gyor, Hungary.

❏ 2015 IEEE International Conference on Signal and Image Processing Applications (ICSIPA); 2015. 10. 19—21; Kuala Lumpur, Malaysia.

❏ 2015 IEEE International Conference on Space Optical Systems and Applications (ICSOS); 2015. 10. 20—21; CA, USA.

❏ 2015 10th International Conference on Intelligent Systems: Theories and Applications (SITA); 2015. 10. 20—21; Rabat, Morocco.

❏ 2015 International Conference on Management Science and Engineering (ICMSE); 2015. 10. 19—22; Dubai, United Arab Emirates.

❏ 2015 IEEE 12th International Conference on Mobile Ad Hoc and Sensor Systems (MASS); 2015. 10. 19—22; Richardson, TX, USA.

❏ 2015 IEEE Vehicle Power and Propulsion Conference (VPPC); 2015. 10. 19—22; Montreal, QC, Canada.

❏ 2015 33rd IEEE International Conference on Computer Design (ICCD); 2015. 10. 19—22; New York City, NY, USA.

❏ 2015 XLI Latin American Computing Conference (CLEI); 2015. 10. 19—23; Arequipa, Peru.

❏ 2015 International Conference on Wireless Networks and Mobile Communications (WINCOM); 2015. 10. 20—23; Marrakech, Morocco.

❏ 2015 International Conference on Smart Grid and Clean Energy Technologies (ICSGCE); 2015. 10. 20—23; Offenburg, Germany.

❏ 2015 International Association of Institutes of Navigation World Congress (IAIN); 2015. 10. 20—23; Prague, Czech Republic.

❏ 2015 IEEE 18th International Conference on Computational Science and Engineering (CSE); 2015. 10. 21—23; Porto, Portugal.

❏ 2015 IEEE 13th International Conference on Embedded and Ubiquitous Computing (EUC); 2015. 10. 21—23; Porto, Portugal.

❏ 2015 First International Conference on Reliability Systems Engineering (ICRSE); 2015. 10. 21—23; Beijing, China.

❏ 2015 Tenth International Conference on Digital Information Management (ICDIM); 2015. 10. 21—23; Jeju Island, Korea.

❏ 2015 International Workshop on High Mobility Wireless Communications (HMWC); 2015. 10. 21—23; Xi'an, China.

❏ 2015 International Conference on Industrial Engineering and Systems Management (IESM); 2015. 10. 21—23; Seville, Spain.

❑ 2015 Prognostics and System Health Management Conference (PHM); 2015. 10. 21—23; Beijing, China.

❑ 2015 10th International Microsystems, Packaging, Assembly and Circuits Technology Conference (IMPACT); 2015. 10. 21—23; Taipei, Taiwan.

❑ 2015 IEEE Frontiers in Education Conference (FIE); 2015. 10. 21—24; El Paso, TX, USA.

❑ 2015 IEEE International Ultrasonics Symposium (IUS); 2015. 10. 21—24; Taipei, Taiwan.

❑ 2015 ACM/IEEE International Symposium on Empirical Software Engineering and Measurement (ESEM); 2015. 10. 22—23; Beijing, China.

❑ 2015 International EURASIP Workshop on RFID Technology (EURFID); 2015. 10. 22—23; Oberaudorf, Germany.

❑ 2015 IEEE Biomedical Circuits and Systems Conference (BioCAS); 2015. 10. 22—24; GA, USA.

❑ 2015 IEEE 21st International Symposium for Design and Technology in Electronic Packaging (SIITME); 2015. 10. 22—25; Brasov, Romania.

❑ 2015 IEEE MetroCon; 2015. 10. 22—25; Arlington, TX, USA.

❑ 2015 IEEE International Conference on the Edges of Innovation for Smarter Cities, Tech Expo, Career Fair, and Industry Forum (IICE – ISC); 2015. 10. 22—25; Burlington, VT, USA.

❑ 2015 24th Wireless and Optical Communication Conference (WOCC); 2015. 10. 23—24; Taipei, Taiwan.

❑ 2015 IEEE 12th International Conference on e-Business Engineering (ICEBE); 2015. 10. 23—25; Beijing, China.

❑ 2015 25th International Conference on Computer Theory and Applications (ICCTA); 2015. 10. 24—26; Alexandria, Egypt.

❑ 2015 IEEE 5th Symposium on Large Data Analysis and Visualization (LDAV); 2015. 10. 25—26; Chicago, IL, USA.

❑ 2015 IEEE First International Smart Cities Conference (ISC2); 2015. 10. 25—28; Guadalajara, Mexico.

❑ 2015 3rd International Conference on Electric Power Equipment – Switching Technology (ICEPE – ST); 2015. 10. 25—28; Busan, Korea.

❑ 2015 18th International Conference on Electrical Machines and Systems (ICEMS); 2015. 10. 25—28; Pattaya, Thailand.

❑ 2015 IEEE 24th Electrical Performance of Electronic Packaging and Systems

（EPEPS）；2015. 10. 25—28；San Jose，CA，USA.

❑ 2015 20th Microoptics Conference（MOC）；2015. 10. 25—28；Fukuoka，Japan.

❑ 2015 IEEE Bipolar/BiCMOS Circuits and Technology Meeting（BCTM）；2015. 10. 25—28；Boston，MA，USA.

❑ 2015 IEEE Visualization Conference（VIS）；2015. 10. 25—30；Chicago，IL，USA.

❑ 2015 IEEE Symposium on Visualization for Cyber Security（VizSec）；2015. 10. 26；Chicago，IL，USA.

❑ MILCOM 2015 – 2015 IEEE Military Communications Conference；2015. 10. 26—28；Tampa，FL，USA.

❑ 2015 Nordic Circuits and Systems Conference（NORCAS）：NORCHIP & International Symposium on System – on – Chip（SoC）；2015. 10. 26—28；Oslo，Norway.

❑ 2015 5th International Conference on the Internet of Things（IOT）；2015. 10. 26—28；Seoul，Korea.

❑ 2015 IEEE Electrical Power and Energy Conference（EPEC）；2015. 10. 26—28；London，ON，Canada.

❑ 2015 International Topical Meeting on Microwave Photonics（MWP）；2015. 10. 26—29；Paphos，Cyprus.

❑ 2015 IEEE 40th Conference on Local Computer Networks（LCN 2015）；2015. 10. 26—29；Clearwater Beach，FL，USA.

❑ 2015 IEEE 40th Local Computer Networks Conference Workshops（LCN Workshops）；2015. 10. 26—29；Clearwater Beach，FL，USA.

❑ 2015 IEEE Rock Stars of Cybersecurity（RSC）；2015. 10. 27；San Jose，CA，USA.

❑ 2015 International Conference on Science in Information Technology（ICSITech）；2015. 10. 27—28；Yogyakarta，Indonesia.

❑ 2015 IEEE 4th Global Conference on Consumer Electronics（GCCE）；2015. 10. 27—30；Osaka City，Japan.

❑ 2015 IEEE Radar Conference；2015. 10. 27—30；Johannesburg，South Africa.

❑ 2015 IEEE Conference on Collaboration and Internet Computing（CIC）；2015. 10. 27—30；Hangzhou，China.

❑ 2015 Global Information Infrastructure and Networking Symposium（GIIS）；2015. 10. 28—30；Guadalajara，Mexico.

❑ 2015 IEEE 6th International Symposium on Microwave，Antenna，Propagation, and EMC Technologies (MAPE); 2015. 10. 28—30; Shanghai, China.

❏ 2015 Conference "Grid, Cloud & High Performance Computing in Science" (ROLCG); 2015. 10. 28—30; Cluj – Napoca, Romania.

❏ 2015 12th International Conference on Electrical Engineering, Computing Science and Automatic Control (CCE); 2015. 10. 28—30; Mexico City, Mexico.

❏ 2015 International Conference on Information and Communication Technology Convergence (ICTC); 2015. 10. 28—30; Jeju Island, Korea.

❏ 2015 12th International Conference on Ubiquitous Robots and Ambient Intelligence (URAI); 2015. 10. 28—30; Korea.

❏ 2015 International Conference on Biomedical Engineering and Computational Technologies (SIBIRCON); 2015. 10. 28—30; Novosibirsk, Russia.

❏ 2015 IEEE Conference on Standards for Communications and Networking (CSCN); 2015. 10. 28—30; Tokyo, Japan.

❏ 2015 International Conference on Computing Systems and Telematics (ICCSAT); 2015. 10. 28—30; Xalapa, Mexico.

❏ 2015 International Conference on Healthcare Informatics (ICHI); 2015. 10. 28—30; Dallas, TX, USA.

❏ 2015 5th International Conference on Computer and Knowledge Engineering (ICCKE); 2015. 10. 29—30; Mashhad, Iran.

❏ 2015 International Conference on Automation, Cognitive Science, Optics, Micro Electro – Mechanical System, and Information Technology (ICACOMIT); 2015. 10. 29—30; West Java, Indonesia.

❏ 2015 7th International Conference on Information Technology and Electrical Engineering; 2015. 10. 29—30; Chiang Mai, Thailand.

❏ 2015 International Conference on Applied and Theoretical Computing and Communication Technology (iCATccT); 2015. 10. 29—31; DAVANGERE, India.

❏ 2015 International Conference on Control, Automation and Information Sciences (ICCAIS); 2015. 10. 29—31; Changshu, China.

❏ 2015 IDEATOPOS Conference: "Bridging the technological excellence and social innovation for democracy"; 2015. 10. 29—31; Athens, Greece.

❏ 2015 XXV International Conference on Information, Communication and Automation Technologies (ICAT); 2015. 10. 29—31; Sarajevo, Bosnia and Herzegovina.

❏ 2015 12th Latin American Robotics Symposium (LARS) and 2015 3rd Brazilian Symposium on Robotics (LARS – SBR); 2015. 10. 29—31; Uberlândia, Brazil.

❑ 2015 IEEE International Conference on Big Data (Big Data); 2015. 10. 29—11. 01; Santa Clara, CA, USA.

❑ 2015 International Conference on Behavioral, Economic and Socio – cultural Computing (BESC); 2015. 10. 30—11. 01; Nanjing, China.

❑ 2015 Symposium on Piezoelectricity, Acoustic Waves, and Device Applications (SPAWDA); 2015. 10. 30—11. 01; Jinan, China.

❑ 2015 International Conference on Energy Systems and Applications; 2015. 10. 30—11. 01; PUNE, India.

❑ 2015 IEEE Nuclear Science Symposium and Medical Imaging Conference (NSS/MIC); 2015. 10. 30—11. 08; San Diego, CA, USA.

❑ 2015 11th International Conference on Innovations in Information Technology (IIT); 2015. 11. 01—03; Dubai, United Arab Emirates.

❑ 2015 IEEE SENSORS; 2015. 11. 01—04; Busan, Korea.

❑ TENCON 2015 IEEE Region 10 Conference; 2015. 11. 01—04; Macao, China.

❑ 2015 IEEE 2nd International Future Energy Electronics Conference (IFEEC); 2015. 11. 01—04; Taipei, Taiwan.

❑ 2015 IEEE International Conference on Computer Graphics, Vision and Information Security (CGVIS); 2015. 11. 02—03; Bhubaneshwar, India.

❑ 2015 4th International Conference on Instrumentation, Communications, Information Technology, and Biomedical Engineering (ICICI – BME); 2015. 11. 02—03; Bandung, Indonesia.

❑ 2015 International Conference on Computers, Communications, and Systems (ICCCS); 2015. 11. 02—03; Kanyakumari, India.

❑ 2015 Loughborough Antennas & Propagation Conference (LAPC); 2015. 11. 02—03; Leicestershire, United Kingdom.

❑ 2015 IEEE/CIC International Conference on Communications in China – Workshops (CIC/ICCC); 2015. 11. 02—04; Shenzhen, China.

❑ 2015 IEEE International Conference on Microwaves, Communications, Antennas and Electronic Systems (COMCAS); 2015. 11. 02—04; Tel – Aviv, Israel.

❑ 2015 IEEE 3rd Workshop on Wide Bandgap Power Devices and Applications (WiPDA); 2015. 11. 02—04; Blacksburg, VA, USA.

❑ 2015 IEEE/CIC International Conference on Communications in China (IC-

CC）；2015. 11. 02—04；Shenzhen, China.

❑ 2015 IEEE 26th International Symposium on Software Reliability Engineering（ISSRE）；2015. 11. 02—05；Gaithersburg, MD, USA.

❑ 2015 IEEE AUTOTESTCON；2015. 11. 02—05；MD, USA.

❑ 2015 IEEE 15th International Conference on Bioinformatics and Bioengineering（BIBE）；2015. 11. 02—05；Belgrade, Serbia.

❑ 2015 International SoC Design Conference（ISOCC）；2015. 11. 02—05；Gyungju, Korea.

❑ 2015 IEEE International Conference on Smart Grid Communications（SmartGridComm）；2015. 11. 02—05；miami, FL, USA.

❑ 2015 3rd IAPR Asian Conference on Pattern Recognition（ACPR）；2015. 11. 03—11. 04；Kuala Lumpur, Malaysia.

❑ 2015 IEEE 2nd International Conference on Cyber Security and Cloud Computing（CSCloud）；2015. 11. 03—05；New York, NY, USA.

❑ 2015 IEEE – RAS 15th International Conference on Humanoid Robots（Humanoids）；2015. 11. 03—05；Seoul, Korea.

❑ 2015 IEEE Jordan Conference on Applied Electrical Engineering and Computing Technologies（AEECT）；2015. 11. 03—05；Amman, Jordan.

❑ 2015 IEEE 11th International Conference on ASIC（ASICON）；2015. 11. 03—06；Chengdu, China.

❑ 2015 SBMO/IEEE MTT – S International Microwave and Optoelectronics Conference（IMOC）；2015. 11. 03—06；Porto de Galinhas, Brazil.

❑ 2015 IEEE Student Symposium in Biomedical Engineering & Sciences（ISSBES）；2015. 11. 04；Shah Alam, Malaysia.

❑ 2015 IEEE International Autumn Meeting on Power, Electronics and Computing（ROPEC）；2015. 11. 04—06；Ixtapa, Mexico.

❑ IEEE Innovative Smart Grid Technologies – Asia（ISGT ASIA）；2015. 11. 04—06；Bangkok, Thailand.

❑ 2015 International Conference on Electrical & Electronic Engineering（ICEEE）；2015. 11. 04—06；Rajshahi, Bangladesh.

❑ 2015 7th IEEE Latin – American Conference on Communications（LATINCOM）；2015. 11. 04—06；Arequipa, Peru.

❑ 2015 International Conference on Science and Technology（TICST）；2015. 11. 04—06；Pathum Thani, Thailand.

❑ 2015 7th Asia – Pacific Conference on Environmental Electromagnetics（CEEM）；2015. 11. 04—07；Hangzhou, China.

- 2015 International Conference on Cyberspace (CYBER – Abuja); 2015. 11. 04—07; Abuja, Nigeria.
- 2015 IEEE – Chicago Section Technical Symposium and Exhibition; 2015. 11. 05; Schaumburg, IL, USA.
- 2015 5th Australian Control Conference (AUCC); 2015. 11. 05—06; Gold Coast, Australia.
- 2015 Advances in Wireless and Optical Communications (RTUWO); 2015. 11. 05—06; Riga, Latvia.
- 2015 10th International Workshop on Semantic and Social Media Adaptation and Personalization (SMAP); 2015. 11. 05—06; Trento, Italy.
- 2015 2nd International Conference on Knowledge – Based Engineering and Innovation (KBEI); 2015. 11. 05—06; Tehran, Iran.
- 2015 IEEE International Conference on Vehicular Electronics and Safety (ICVES); 2015. 11. 05—07; Yokohama, Japan.
- 2015 IEEE 8th International Workshop on Computational Intelligence and Applications (IWCIA); 2015. 11. 06—07; Hiroshima, Japan.
- 2015 IEEE Students Conference on Engineering and Systems (SCES); 2015. 11. 06—08; Allahabad, India.
- 2015 IEEE EMBS Quinquennial International Student Conference (Q – ISC); 2015. 11. 06—08; Orlando, FL, USA.
- 2015 IEEE Women in Engineering (WIE) Summit USA East; 2015. 11. 06—08; Philadelphia, PA, USA.
- 2015 Communication, Control and Intelligent Systems (CCIS); 2015. 11. 07—08; Mathura, India.
- 2015 First International Conference on New Technologies of Information and Communication (NTIC); 2015. 11. 08—09; Mila, Algeria.
- 2015 International Conference on Memristive Systems (MEMRISYS); 2015. 11. 08—10; Paphos, Cyprus.
- 2015 IEEE Green Energy and Systems Conference (IGESC); 2015. 11. 09; Long Beach, CA, USA.
- 2015 Healthcare Innovation Point – Of – Care Technologies Conference (HI – POCT); 2015. 11. 09—10; Bethesda, MD, USA.
- 2015 Conference of Telecommunication, Media and Internet Techno – Economics (CTTE); 2015. 11. 09—10; München, Germany.
- 2015 IEEE 27th International Conference on Tools with Artificial Intelligence (ICTAI); 2015. 11. 09—11; Vietri sul Mare, Italy.

❑ 2015 IEEE CPMT Symposium Japan（ICSJ）；2015. 11. 09—11；Kyoto，Japan.

❑ 2015 International Conference on Information Society（i – Society）；2015. 11. 09—11；London，United Kingdom.

❑ 2015 International Conference on Complex Systems Engineering（ICCSE）；2015. 11. 09—11；Storrs，CT，USA.

❑ 2015 IEEE Asian Solid – State Circuits Conference（A – SSCC）；2015. 11. 09—11；Fujian Province，China.

❑ 2015 IEEE/ACM International Conference on Computer – Aided Design（IC-CAD）；2015. 11. 09—12；TBD，CA，USA.

❑ 2015 International Symposium on Antennas and Propagation（ISAP）；2015. 11. 09—12；Tasmania，Australia.

❑ 2015 International Symposium on Intelligent Signal Processing and Communication Systems（ISPACS）；2015. 11. 09—12；Bali，Indonesia.

❑ 2015 IEEE International Conference on Bioinformatics and Biomedicine（BIBM）；2015. 11. 09—12；Washington，DC，USA.

❑ IECON 2015 – 41st Annual Conference of the IEEE Industrial Electronics Society；2015. 11. 09—12；Yokohama，Japan.

❑ 2015 30th IEEE/ACM International Conference on Automated Software Engineering（ASE）；2015. 11. 09—13；Lincoln，NE，USA.

❑ 2015 11th International Conference on Network and Service Management（CNSM）；2015. 11. 09—13；Barcelona，Spain.

❑ 2015 SAI Intelligent Systems Conference（IntelliSys）；2015. 11. 10—11；United Kingdom.

❑ 2015 IEEE Global Electromagnetic Compatibility Conference（GEMCCON）；2015. 11. 10—12；West Lakes，Australia.

❑ 2015 First International Conference on Anti – Cybercrime（ICACC）；2015. 11. 10—12；Riyadh，Saudi Arabia.

❑ 2015 IEEE Online Conference on Green Communications（OnlineGreenComm）；2015. 11. 10—12；Piscataway，NJ，USA.

❑ 2015 Military Communications and Information Systems Conference（MilCIS）；2015. 11. 10—12；Canberra，Australia.

❑ 2015 IEEE Avionics and Vehicle Fiber – Optics and Photonics Conference（AVFOP）；2015. 11. 10—12；Santa Barbara，CA，USA.

❑ 2015 IEEE 23rd International Conference on Network Protocols（ICNP）；2015. 11. 10—13；San Francisco，CA，USA.

- 2015 International Conference on Image Processing Theory, Tools and Applications (IPTA); 2015. 11. 10—13; Orléans, France.
- 2015 10th International Workshop on the Electromagnetic Compatibility of Integrated Circuits (EMC Compo); 2015. 11. 10—13; Edinburgh, United Kingdom.
- 2015 IEEE International Symposium on Technology and Society (ISTAS); 2015. 11. 11—12; Malahide, Ireland.
- 2015 IEEE Thirty Fifth Central American and Panama Convention (CONCAPAN XXXV); 2015. 11. 11—13; Tegucigalpa, Honduras.
- 2015 IEEE PES PowerAfrica; 2015. 11. 11—14; Gammarth, Tunisia.
- 2015 International Energy and Sustainability Conference (IESC); 2015. 11. 12—13; Farmingdale, NY, USA.
- 2015 7th International Joint Conference on Knowledge Discovery, Knowledge Engineering and Knowledge Management (IC3K); 2015. 11. 12—14; Lisbon, Portugal.
- 2015 7th International Joint Conference on Computational Intelligence (IJCCI); 2015. 11. 12—14; Lisbon, Portugal.
- 2015 IEEE 3rd Workshop on Advances in Information, Electronic and Electrical Engineering; 2015. 11. 13—14; Riga, Latvia.
- 2015 7th International Conference of Soft Computing and Pattern Recognition (SoCPaR); 2015. 11. 13—15; Fukuoka, Japan.
- 2015 7th International Conference on Information Technology in Medicine and Education (ITME); 2015. 11. 13—15; China.
- 2015 IEEE International Conference on Data Mining (ICDM); 2015. 11. 14—17; Atlantic City, NJ, USA.
- 2015 Second International Conference on Information Security and Cyber Forensics (InfoSec); 2015. 11. 15—17; Cape Town, South Africa.
- 2015 IEEE PES Asia – Pacific Power and Energy Engineering Conference (APPEEC); 2015. 11. 15—18; TBD, Australia.
- 2015 SC – International Conference for High Performance Computing, Networking, Storage and Analysis; 2015. 11. 15—20; Austin, TX, USA.
- 2015 IEEE International Workshop on Information Forensics and Security (WIFS); 2015. 11. 16—17; Roma, Italy.
- 2015 2nd International Symposium on Dependable Computing and Internet of Things (DICT); 2015. 11. 16—18; Wuhan, China.
- 2015 International Workshop on Electromagnetics: Applications and Student

Innovation Competition (iWEM); 2015. 11. 16—18; Hsin – Chu, Taiwan.

❏ 2015 International Conference on Information Technology Systems and Innovation (ICITSI); 2015. 11. 16—19; Bandung, Indonesia.

❏ 2015 Annual Meeting on Innovation, Technology and Engineering (AMITE); 2015. 11. 16—20; Veracruz, Mexico.

❏ 2015 IEEE 7th International Conference on Engineering Education (ICEED); 2015. 11. 17—18; TBD, Japan.

❏ 2015 IEEE/ACS 12th International Conference of Computer Systems and Applications (AICCSA); 2015. 11. 17—20; Marrakech, Morocco.

❏ 2015 IEEE 21st Pacific Rim International Symposium on Dependable Computing (PRDC); 2015. 11. 18—20; Zhangjiajie, China.

❏ 2015 IEEE International Conference on Cloud Computing in Emerging Markets (CCEM); 2015. 11. 18—20; Bangalore, India.

❏ 2015 International Telecommunication Networks and Applications Conference (ITNAC); 2015. 11. 18—20; Kensington, Australia.

❏ 2015 16th International Conference on Research and Education in Mechatronics (REM); 2015. 11. 18—20; Bochum, Germany.

❏ 2015 13th International Conference on ICT and Knowledge Engineering (ICT & Knowledge Engineering 2015); 2015. 11. 18—20; Bangkok, Thailand.

❏ 2015 7th International Conference on Emerging Trends in Engineering & Technology (ICETET); 2015. 11. 18—20; Kobe, Japan.

❏ 2015 International Automatic Control Conference (CACS); 2015. 11. 18—20; Yilan, Taiwan.

❏ 2015 International Conference on Fuzzy Theory and Its Applications (iFUZZY); 2015. 11. 18—20; Yilan, Taiwan.

❏ 2015 International Symposium on Ocean Electronics (SYMPOL); 2015. 11. 18—20; Kochi, India.

❏ 2015 IEEE Conference on Network Function Virtualization and Software Defined Network (NFV – SDN); 2015. 11. 18—21; TBD, CA, USA.

❏ 2015 International Conference on Interactive Mobile Communication Technologies and Learning (IMCL); 2015. 11. 19—20; Thessaloniki, Greece.

❏ 2015 IEEE IAS Joint Industrial and Commercial Power Systems / Petroleum and Chemical Industry Conference Acronym (ICPSPCIC); 2015. 11. 19—21; HYDERABAD, India.

❏ 2015 International Conference on Control Communication & Computing India (ICCC); 2015. 11. 19—21; Kerala, India.

❑ 2015 E – Health and Bioengineering Conference (EHB); 2015. 11. 19—21; IASI, Romania.

❑ 2015 International Conference on Communication Networks (ICCN); 2015. 11. 19—21; Gwalior, India.

❑ 2015 IEEE International Conference on Research in Computational Intelligence and Communication Networks (ICRCICN); 2015. 11. 20—22; Kolkata, India.

❑ 2015 Conference on Technologies and Applications of Artificial Intelligence (TAAI); 2015. 11. 20—22; Tainan, Taiwan.

❑ 2015 IEEE International Conference on Applied Superconductivity and Electromagnetic Devices (ASEMD); 2015. 11. 20—23; Shanghai, China.

❑ 2015 International Conference on Renewable Energy Research and Applications (ICRERA); 2015. 11. 22—25; Palermo, Italy.

❑ 2015 Third World Conference on Complex Systems (WCCS); 2015. 11. 23—25; Marrakech, Morocco.

❑ 2015 Workshop on Research, Education and Development of Unmanned Aerial Systems (RED – UAS); 2015. 11. 23—25; Cancun, Mexico.

❑ 2015 International Symposium on Micro – Nano Mechatronics and Human Science (MHS); 2015. 11. 23—25; Nagoya, Japan.

❑ 2015 IEEE 12th Malaysia International Conference on Communications (MICC); 2015. 11. 23—25; Kuching, Malaysia.

❑ 2015 International Conference on Digital Image Computing: Techniques and Applications (DICTA); 2015. 11. 23—25; Adelaide, Australia.

❑ 2015 International Computer Science and Engineering Conference (ICSEC); 2015. 11. 23—26; Chiang Mai, Thailand.

❑ 2015 IEEE Symposium on Communications and Vehicular Technology in the Benelux (SCVT); 2015. 11. 24; Luxembourg, Luxembourg.

❑ 2015 8th International Conference on Multimedia Communications, Services and Security (MCSS); 2015. 11. 24; Krakow, Poland.

❑ 2015 IEEE 3rd International Conference on Smart Instrumentation, Measurement and Applications (ICSIMA); 2015. 11. 24—25; Putrajaya, Malaysia.

❑ 2015 23rd Telecommunications Forum Telfor (TELFOR); 2015. 11. 24—26; Belgrade, Serbia.

❑ 2015 4th International Conference on Electric Power and Energy Conversion Systems (EPECS); 2015. 11. 24—26; Sharjah, United Arab Emirates.

❑ 2015 10th International Conference on Intelligent Systems and Knowledge

Engineering (ISKE); 2015.11.24—27; Taipei, Taiwan.

❏ 2015 38th Symposium on Information Theory and its Applications (SITA); 2015.11.24—27; Kurashiki, Japan.

❏ 2015 International Conference on Data and Software Engineering (ICoDSE); 2015.11.25—26; Yogyakarta, Indonesia.

❏ 2015 3rd International Conference on New Media (CONMEDIA); 2015.11.25—27; TANGERANG, Indonesia.

❏ 2015 International Symposium on Computers in Education (SIIE); 2015.11.25—27; Setúbal, Portugal.

❏ 2015 Conference on Design of Circuits and Integrated Systems (DCIS); 2015.11.25—27; Portugal.

❏ 2015 8th Biomedical Engineering International Conference (BMEiCON); 2015.11.25—27; Chonburi, Thailand.

❏ 2015 22nd Iranian Conference on Biomedical Engineering (ICBME); 2015.11.25—27; Iran.

❏ eChallenges e – 2015 Conference; 2015.11.25—27; Vilnius, Lithuania.

❏ 2015 9th International Conference on Electrical and Electronics Engineering (ELECO); 2015.11.26—28; Bursa, Turkey.

❏ 2015 13th International Conference on Emerging eLearning Technologies and Applications (ICETA); 2015.11.26—27; Starý Smokovec, Slovakia.

❏ 2015 Pattern Recognition Association of South Africa and Robotics and Mechatronics International Conference (PRASA – RobMech); 2015.11.26—27; Port Elizabeth, South Africa.

❏ 2015 5th Nirma University International Conference on Engineering (NUiCONE); 2015.11.26—28; Ahmedabad, India.

❏ 2015 Sixth International Conference on Intelligent Control and Information Processing (ICICIP); 2015.11.26—28; Wuhan, China.

❏ 2015 IEEE Asia Pacific Conference on Postgraduate Research in Microelectronics and Electronics (PrimeAsia); 2015.11.26—28; Hyderabad, India.

❏ 2015 5th International Conference on Electric Utility Deregulation and Restructuring and Power Technologies (DRPT); 2015.11.26—29; Changsha, China.

❏ 2015 IEEE International Conference on Control System, Computing and Engineering (ICCSCE); 2015.11.27—29; Penang, Malaysia.

❏ 2015 Chinese Automation Congress (CAC); 2015.11.27—29; Wuhan, China.

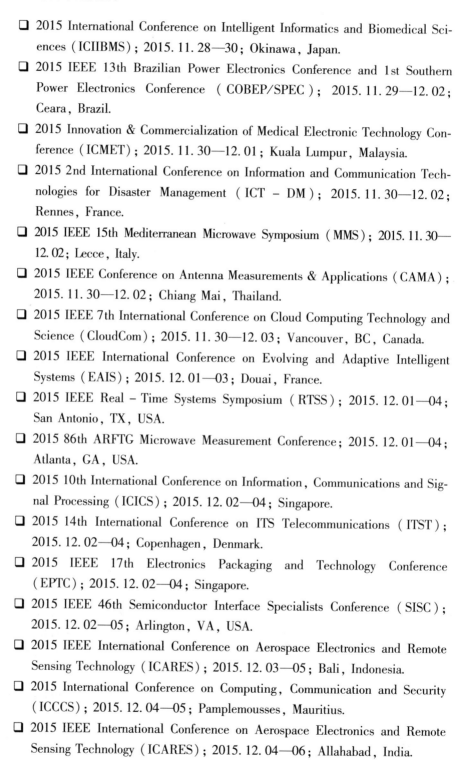

- 2015 International Conference on Intelligent Informatics and Biomedical Sciences (ICIIBMS); 2015. 11. 28—30; Okinawa, Japan.

- 2015 IEEE 13th Brazilian Power Electronics Conference and 1st Southern Power Electronics Conference (COBEP/SPEC); 2015. 11. 29—12. 02; Ceara, Brazil.

- 2015 Innovation & Commercialization of Medical Electronic Technology Conference (ICMET); 2015. 11. 30—12. 01; Kuala Lumpur, Malaysia.

- 2015 2nd International Conference on Information and Communication Technologies for Disaster Management (ICT – DM); 2015. 11. 30—12. 02; Rennes, France.

- 2015 IEEE 15th Mediterranean Microwave Symposium (MMS); 2015. 11. 30—12. 02; Lecce, Italy.

- 2015 IEEE Conference on Antenna Measurements & Applications (CAMA); 2015. 11. 30—12. 02; Chiang Mai, Thailand.

- 2015 IEEE 7th International Conference on Cloud Computing Technology and Science (CloudCom); 2015. 11. 30—12. 03; Vancouver, BC, Canada.

- 2015 IEEE International Conference on Evolving and Adaptive Intelligent Systems (EAIS); 2015. 12. 01—03; Douai, France.

- 2015 IEEE Real – Time Systems Symposium (RTSS); 2015. 12. 01—04; San Antonio, TX, USA.

- 2015 86th ARFTG Microwave Measurement Conference; 2015. 12. 01—04; Atlanta, GA, USA.

- 2015 10th International Conference on Information, Communications and Signal Processing (ICICS); 2015. 12. 02—04; Singapore.

- 2015 14th International Conference on ITS Telecommunications (ITST); 2015. 12. 02—04; Copenhagen, Denmark.

- 2015 IEEE 17th Electronics Packaging and Technology Conference (EPTC); 2015. 12. 02—04; Singapore.

- 2015 IEEE 46th Semiconductor Interface Specialists Conference (SISC); 2015. 12. 02—05; Arlington, VA, USA.

- 2015 IEEE International Conference on Aerospace Electronics and Remote Sensing Technology (ICARES); 2015. 12. 03—05; Bali, Indonesia.

- 2015 International Conference on Computing, Communication and Security (ICCCS); 2015. 12. 04—05; Pamplemousses, Mauritius.

- 2015 IEEE International Conference on Aerospace Electronics and Remote Sensing Technology (ICARES); 2015. 12. 04—06; Allahabad, India.

❑ 2015 IEEE International Conference on Industrial Engineering and Engineering Management（IEEM）；2015.12.06—09；Suntec，Singapore.

❑ IEEE International Conference on Electronics，Circuitss，and Systems；2015.12.06—09；Cairo，Egypt.

❑ 2015 IEEE International Conference on Robotics and Biomimetics（ROBIO）；2015.12.06—09；Zhuhai，China.

❑ 2015 Asia – Pacific Microwave Conference（APMC）；2015.12.06—09；Nanjing，China.

❑ 2015 IEEE Global Communications Conference（GLOBECOM 2015）；2015.12.06—10；San Diego，CA，USA.

❑ 2015 IEEE Globecom Workshops（GC Wkshps）；2015.12.06—10；San Diego，CA，USA.

❑ 2015 Fourth International Conference on Eco – friendly Computing and Communication Systems（ICECCS）；2015.12.07—08；Kurukshetra，India.

❑ 2015 International Conference on ReConFigurable Computing and FPGAs（ReConFig）；2015.12.07—09；Cancun，Mexico.

❑ 2015 International Conference on Field Programmable Technology（FPT）；2015.12.07—09；Queenstown，New Zealand.

❑ 2015 Saudi Arabia Smart Grid（SASG）；2015.12.07—09；Jeddah，Saudi Arabia.

❑ 2015 IEEE International Electron Devices Meeting（IEDM）；2015.12.07—09；Washington，DC，USA.

❑ 2015 IEEE Symposium Series on Computational Intelligence（SSCI）；2015.12.07—10；Cape Town，South Africa.

❑ 2015 IEEE International Conference on Computer Vision（ICCV）；2015.12.07—13；Chile.

❑ 2015 9th International Conference on Sensing Technology（ICST）；2015.12.08—10；Auckland，New Zealand.

❑ 2015 10th International Symposium on Mechatronics and its Applications（ISMA）；2015.12.08—10；Sharjah，United Arab Emirates.

❑ 2015 International Conference on Power，Instrumentation，Control and Computing（PICC）；2015.12.09—11；Thrissur，India.

❑ 2015 International Conference on Machine Learning and Applications（ICMLA）；2015.12.09—11；FL，USA.

❑ 2015 ITU Kaleidoscope：Trust in the Information Society（K – 2015）；2015.12.09—11；Barcelona，Spain.

❑ 2015 TRON Symposium（TRONSHOW）；2015. 12. 09—11；Tokyo, Japan.

❑ 2015 International Conference on Humanoid, Nanotechnology, Information Technology, Communication and Control, Environment and Management（HNICEM）；2015. 12. 09—12；Cebu City, Philippines.

❑ 2015 IEEE Region 10 Humanitarian Technology Conference（R10 – HTC）；2015. 12. 09—12；Cebu, Philippines.

❑ 2015 International Conference on Condition Assessment Techniques in Electrical Systems（CATCON）；2015. 12. 10—12；Bengaluru, India.

❑ 2015 IEEE Recent Advances in Intelligent Computational Systems（RAICS）；2015. 12. 10—12；Thirvananthapuram, India.

❑ 2015 2nd International Conference on Electrical Information and Communication Technologies（EICT）；2015. 12. 10—12；Khulna, Bangladesh.

❑ 2015 IEEE International Conference on Communication, Networks and Satellite（COMNESTAT）；2015. 12. 10—12；Bandung, Indonesia.

❑ 2015 IEEE International Conference on Computational Intelligence and Computing Research（ICCIC）；2015. 12. 10—12；Madurai, India.

❑ 2015 IEEE Seventh International Conference on Technology for Education（T4E）；2015. 12. 10—12；Telangana, India.

❑ 2015 IEEE International Conference on Teaching, Assessment, and Learning for Engineering（TALE）；2015. 12. 10—12；Zhuhai, China.

❑ 2015 3rd International Renewable and Sustainable Energy Conference（IRSEC）；2015. 12. 10—13；Marrakech, Morocco.

❑ 2015 Third International Conference on Image Information Processing（ICIIP）；2015. 12. 10—13；Solan, India.

❑ 2015 Conference on Power, Control, Communication and Computational Technologies for Sustainable Growth（PCCCTSG）；2015. 12. 11—12；Kurnool, India.

❑ 2015 International Conference on Smart Grid（ICSG）；2015. 12. 11—13；Bhopal, India.

❑ 2015 International Conference on Microwave and Photonics（ICMAP）；2015. 12. 11—13；Dhanbad, India.

❑ 2015 IEEE/SICE International Symposium on System Integration（SII）；2015. 12. 11—13；Nagoya, Japan.

❑ 2015 Computational Imaging, Speech, and Language Processing（CISLP）；2015. 12. 12—13；Allahabad, India.

❑ 2015 International Conference on Information and Communication Technolo-

美　国 111

gies（ICICT）; 2015. 12. 12—13; Karachi, Pakistan.

❏ 2015 8th International Symposium on Computational Intelligence and Design （ISCID）; 2015. 12. 12—13; Hangzhou, China.

❏ 2015 International Conference on Computational Intelligence and Communication Networks（CICN）; 2015. 12. 12—14; Jabalpur, India.

❏ 2015 IEEE Seventh International Conference on Intelligent Computing and Information Systems（ICICIS）; 2015. 12. 12—14; Cairo, Egypt.

❏ 2015 IEEE Student Conference on Research and Development（SCOReD）; 2015. 12. 13—14; Kuala Lumpur, Malaysia.

❏ 2015 4th International Conference on Electrical Engineering（ICEE）; 2015. 12. 13—15; Boumerdes, Algeria.

❏ 2015 5th International Conference on Wireless Communications, Vehicular Technology, Information Theory and Aerospace & Electronic Systems（VITAE）; 2015. 12. 13—16; Hyderabad, India.

❏ 2015 IEEE 6th International Workshop on Computational Advances in Multi – Sensor Adaptive Processing（CAMSAP）; 2015. 12. 13—16; Cancun, Mexico.

❏ 2015 18th International Symposium on Wireless Personal Multimedia Communications（WPMC）; 2015. 12. 13—16; Hyderabad, India.

❏ 2015 Visual Communications and Image Processing（VCIP）; 2015. 12. 13—16; Nanyang, Singapore.

❏ 2015 IEEE Workshop on Automatic Speech Recognition and Understanding （ASRU）; 2015. 12. 13—17; Scottsdale, AZ, USA.

❏ 2015 International Conference on 3D Imaging（IC3D）; 2015. 12. 14—15; Liège, Belgium.

❏ 2015 7th International Conference Intelligent Human Computer Interaction （IHCI）; 2015. 12. 14—16; Allahabad, India.

❏ 2015 IEEE International Symposium on Multimedia（ISM）; 2015. 12. 14—16; Miami Beach, FL, USA.

❏ 2015 13th International Conference on Frontiers of Information Technology （FIT）; 2015. 12. 14—16; Islamabad, Pakistan.

❏ 2015 IEEE International Conference on Wireless for Space and Extreme Environments（WiSEE）; 2015. 12. 14—16; Orlando, FL, USA.

❏ 2015 9th International Conference on Signal Processing and Communication Systems（ICSPCS）; 2015. 12. 14—16; Cairns, Australia.

❏ 2015 IEEE International RF and Microwave Conference（RFM）; 2015. 12. 14—16; Kuching, Malaysia.

- 2015 IEEE Electrical Design of Advanced Packaging and Systems Symposium (EDAPS); 2015. 12. 14—16; Seoul, Korea.
- 2015 IEEE 2nd World Forum on Internet of Things (WF – IoT); 2015. 12. 14—16; Milan, Italy.
- 2015 IEEE MTT – S International Microwave and RF Conference (IMaRC); 2015. 12. 14—16; TBD, India.
- 2015 World Congress on Sustainable Technologies (WCST); 2015. 12. 14—16; London, United Kingdom.
- 2015 World Congress on Sustainable Technologies (WCST); 2015. 12. 14—16; Nanjing, China.
- 2015 39th National Systems Conference (NSC); 2015. 12. 14—16; Greater Noida, India.
- 2015 10th International Conference for Internet Technology and Secured Transactions (ICITST); 2015. 12. 14—16; London, United Kingdom.
- 2015 IEEE Workshop on Computational Intelligence: Theories, Applications and Future Directions (WCI); 2015. 12. 14—17; Kanpur, India.
- 2015 IEEE Global Conference on Signal and Information Processing (GlobalSIP); 2015. 12. 14—17; Orlando, FL, USA.
- 2015 IEEE 21st International Conference on Parallel and Distributed Systems (ICPADS); 2015. 12. 14—17; Melbourne, Australia.
- 2015 9th International Conference on Software, Knowledge, Information Management and Applications (SKIMA); 2015. 12. 15—17; Kathmandu, Nepal.
- 2015 6th International Conference on Power Electronics Systems and Applications (PESA) – Advancement in Electric Transportation – Automotive, Vessel & Aircraft; 2015. 12. 15—17; Kowloon, Hong Kong.
- 2015 54th IEEE Conference on Decision and Control (CDC); 2015. 12. 15—18; Osaka, Japan.
- 2015 10th International Conference for Internet Technology and Secured Transactions (ICITST); 2015. 12. 15—18; Kolkata, India.
- 2015 9th Malaysian Software Engineering Conference (MySEC); 2015. 12. 16—17; Seri Kembangan, Malaysia.
- 2015 Workshop on Recent Advances in Photonics (WRAP); 2015. 12. 16—17; Bangalore, India.
- 2015 IEEE Vehicular Networking Conference (VNC); 2015. 12. 16—18; Kyoto, Japan.
- 2015 IEEE 22nd International Conference on High Performance Computing

（HiPC）；2015. 12. 16—19；Bengaluru，India.

❑ 2015 Asia – Pacific Signal and Information Processing Association Annual Summit and Conference（APSIPA）；2015. 12. 16—19；Kowloon，Hong Kong.

❑ 2015 Fifth National Conference on Computer Vision，Pattern Recognition，Image Processing and Graphics（NCVPRIPG）；2015. 12. 16—19；Patna，India.

❑ 2015 International Conference on Information Processing（ICIP）；2015. 12. 16—19；Pune，India.

❑ 2015 National Software Engineering Conference（NSEC）；2015. 12. 17；Rawalpindi，Pakistan.

❑ 2015 International Conference on Advances in Electrical Engineering（ICAEE）；2015. 12. 17—19；Dhaka，Bangladesh.

❑ 2015 Annual IEEE India Conference（INDICON）；2015. 12. 17—19；New Delhi，India.

❑ 2015 International Conference on Open Source Systems & Technologies（ICOSST）；2015. 12. 17—19；Lahore，Pakistan.

❑ 2015 International Conference on Emerging Research in Electronics，Computer Science and Technology（ICERECT）；2015. 12. 17—19；Mandya，India.

❑ 2015 International Conference on Information Processing（ICIP）；2015. 12. 17—20；Peradeniya，Sri Lanka.

❑ 2015 Conference on Information Assurance and Cyber Security（CIACS）；2015. 12. 18；Rawalpindi，Pakistan.

❑ 2015 International Conference on Microwave，Optical and Communication Engineering（ICMOCE）；2015. 12. 18—20；Bhubaneswar，India.

❑ 2015 7th International Conference on Modelling，Identification and Control（ICMIC）；2015. 12. 18—20；Sousse，Tunisia.

❑ 2015 IEEE Conference on Systems，Process and Control（ICSPC）；2015. 12. 18—20；Kuala Lumpur，Malaysia.

❑ 2015 IEEE International Conference on Progress in Informatics and Computing（PIC）；2015. 12. 18—20；Nanjing，China.

❑ 2015 IEEE Advanced Information Technology，Electronic and Automation Control Conference（IAEAC）；2015. 12. 19—20；Chongqing，China.

❑ 2015 4th International Conference on Computer Science and Network Technology (ICCSNT); 2015. 12. 19—20; Harbin, China.

❏ 2015 IEEE International WIE Conference on Electrical and Computer Engineering (WIECON – ECE); 2015. 12. 19—20; Dhaka, Bangladesh.

❏ 2015 International Conference on Emerging Technologies (ICET); 2015. 12. 19—20; Peshawar, Pakistan.

❏ 2015 International Conference on Orange Technologies (ICOT); 2015. 12. 19—22; Kowloon, Hong Kong.

❏ 2015 International Conference on "Trends in Automation, Communications and Computing Technology" (I – TACT – 15); 2015. 12. 21—22; BANGALORE, India.

❏ 2015 12th IEEE International Conference on Control and Automation (ICCA); 2015. 12. 21—23; Kathmandu, Nepal.

❏ 2015 16th International Conference on Sciences and Techniques of Automatic Control and Computer Engineering (STA); 2015. 12. 21—23; Monastir, Tunisia.

❏ 2015 International Conference on Information Technology (ICIT); 2015. 12. 21—23; Bhubaneswar, India.

❏ 2015 International Conference on Smart Sensors and Systems (IC – SSS); 2015. 12. 21—23; Bangalore, India.

❏ 2015 IEEE International Symposium on Nanoelectronic and Information Systems (iNIS); 2015. 12. 21—23; Indore, India.

❏ 2015 12th International Conference on High – capacity Optical Networks and Enabling/Emerging Technologies (HONET); 2015. 12. 21—23; Islamabad, Pakistan.

❏ 2015 18th International Conference on Computer and Information Technology (ICCIT); 2015. 12. 22—23; Dhaka, Bangladesh.

❏ 2015 Tenth International Conference on Computer Engineering & Systems (ICCES); 2015. 12. 23—24; Cairo, Egypt.

❏ 2015 Seventh International Symposium on Parallel Architectures, Algorithms and Programming (PAAP); 2015. 12. 26—28; Nanjing, China.

❏ 2015 International Conference on Communications, Management and Telecommunications (ComManTel); 2015. 12. 28—30; DaNang, Vietnam.

❏ 2015 11th International Computer Engineering Conference (ICENCO); 2015. 12. 29—30; Cairo, Egypt.

美国分析技术公司

英文名称：Analysis Tech Inc.，Analysis Tech

网 址：http：//www. analysistech. com/

机构简介

美国分析技术公司成立于1983年，位于马萨诸塞州波士顿，是用于电子包装可靠性测试的电子仪器的全球顶级设计商、制造商和供应商。主要的产品与服务包括：

（1）事件检测器，用于焊接点、电连接器和电连接体的可靠性测试；

（2）半导体热分析器，用于测试半导体热阻抗和电阻；

（3）热介面材料检测器，用于对材料进行热阻抗、电阻和电导率测试。

美国光电产业发展协会

英文名称：Optoelectronics Industry Development Association，OIDA

网　　址：http：//www.osa.org/zh－cn/corporate_ gateway/

机构简介

美国光电产业发展协会成立于 1991 年，位于美国华盛顿，是一个代表光电团体的非营利组织，会员包括光电部件和系统的领先供应商，以及大学和研究机构。协会为会员提供报告、行业资料，召开行业会议，并为行业内的机构提供交流信息的平

台。2011 年，美国光电产业发展协会被美国光学协会（The Optical Society，OSA）兼并。2014 年 10 月，美国光学协会宣布美国光学协会企业协会（OSA Corporate Associates）和美国光电产业发展协会合并到美国光学协会产业发展协会（OSA Industry Development Associates，OIDA）中，同时两个机构的 250 多个会员也自动享有美国光学协会产业发展协会提供的服务。

出版物

1）报告

❑ OIDA Market Update（Annual Market Report）.

❑ OIDA Roadmap Report：Future Needs of Scale－Out Data Centers（OIDA Workshop Report）.

2）会议录

❑ OIDA 召开的会议的会议录。

会议信息

❑ International Symposium on Optical Memory 2015；2015.10.04—08；Toyama，Japan.

❑ Advanced Solid State Lasers Conference and Exhibition（ASSL）；2015.10.04—09；Berlin，Germany.

❑ Adaptive Optics and Wavefront Control in Microscopy and Ophthalmology；2015.10.05—07；Paris，France.

❑ International Workshop on Fiber Optics in Access Network；2015.10.06—07；Brno，Czech Republic.

❑ OSA 2015 International Workshop on Compact EUV & X－ray Light Sources；2015.10.08—09；Maastricht，Netherlands.

❑ Semiconductor Overview：Technology，Manufacturing，Business；2015.10.13；Towcester，UK.

- 2nd International Conference on Opto – Electronics and Applied Optics, 2015; 2015. 10. 16—17; Vancouver, Canada.
- OSA Vision Meeting; 2015. 10. 16—18; San Jose, US.
- Frontiers in Optics: The 99th OSA Annual Meeting and Exhibit/Laser Science XXXI; 2015. 10. 18—22; San Jose, US.
- Day of Photonics; 2015. 10. 21; Brussels, Belgium.
- EPIC Workshop on Adverse Atmospheric Conditions on the Battlefield; 2015. 10. 22; Veurey – Voroize, France.
- The 20th Microoptics Conference; 2015. 10. 25—28; Fukuoka, Japan.
- The 5th Advances in Optoelectronics and Micro/nano – optics; 2015. 10. 29—31; Hangzhou, China.
- Solid – State and Organic Lighting (SOLED); 2015. 11. 02—05; Suzhou, China.
- Optics for Solar Energy (SOLAR); 2015. 11. 02—05; Suzhou, China.
- Optical Nanostructures and Advanced Materials for Photovoltaics (PV); 2015. 11. 02—05; Suzhou, China.
- Optics and Photonics for Energy & the Environment (E2); 2015. 11. 02—05; Suzhou, China.
- OIDA Workshop on State of the Art Integrated Photonics; 2015. 11. 03; Washington DC, US.
- Workshop on Specialty Optical Fibers and Their Applications; 2015. 11. 04—06; Hong Kong, China.
- Adaptive Structure Illumination Incubator; 2015. 11. 04—06; Washington DC, US.
- Optical Biosensors Incubator; 2015. 11. 08—10; Washington DC, US.
- 2da Escuela Andina en Óptica, Espectrosocpia, Fotónica y Láseres; 2015. 11. 09—13; Pichincha, Ecuador.
- 16th International Feofilov Symposium on spectroscopy of crystals doped with rare earth and transition metal ions; 2015. 11. 09—13; St. Petersburg, Russia.
- EPIC Workshop on Photonic Systems for Life Sciences Applications; 2015. 11. 18—19; Cork, Ireland.
- Optical Computing Incubator; 2015. 11. 18—20; Washington DC, US.
- Asia Communications and Photonics Conference (ACP); 2015. 11. 19—23; Hong Kong, China.
- IONS KOALA 2015; 2015. 11. 23—25; Auckland, New Zealand.

❑ EPIC Biophotonics Symposium and Exhibition; 2015. 11. 26—27; Berlin, Germany.

❑ The 2nd Israeli Biophotonics Conference; 2015. 12. 01—02; Ramat Gan, Israel.

❑ Extreme Events in Complex Optical Systems; 2015. 12. 01—04; Buenos Aires, Argentina.

❑ Levitated Optomechanics; 2015. 12. 02—04.

❑ International Conference on Nanoscience and Nanotechnology 2016; 2016. 02. 07—11; Canberra, Australia.

❑ 10th International Conference on Optics – Photonics Design and Fabrication; 2016. 02. 28—03. 02; Ravensburg, Germany.

❑ High – Intensity Lasers and High – Field Phenomena (HILAS); 2016. 03. 20—22; Long Beach, US.

❑ Mid – Infrared Coherence Sources (MICS); 2016. 03. 20—22; Long Beach, US.

❑ Compact (EUV & X – ray) Light Sources (XRAY); 2016. 03. 20—22; Long Beach, US.

❑ Optical Fiber Communications Conference and Exposition; 2016. 03. 20—24; Anaheim, US.

❑ OIDA Workshop on Integrated Photonics High Volume Packaging; 2016. 03. 20; Anaheim, US.

❑ 2016 OSA Executive Forum; 2016. 03. 21; Anaheim, US.

❑ 2016 ASLMS Annual Conference; 2016. 03. 30—04. 03; Boston, US.

❑ Clinical and Translational Biophotonics; 2016. 04. 24—28; Fort Lauderdale, US.

❑ Cancer Imaging and Therapy; 2016. 04. 24—28; Fort Lauderdale, US.

❑ Neuroimaging, Optics, and the Brain; 2016. 04. 24—28; Fort Lauderdale, US.

❑ Optical Tomography and Spectroscopy; 2016. 04. 24—28; Fort Lauderdale, US.

❑ ARVO 2016 Annual Meeting; 2016. 05. 01—05; Washington DC, US.

❑ CLEO: 2016; 2016. 06. 05—10; San Jose, US.

❑ Gordon Research Conference on Image Science; 2016. 06. 05—10; Easton, US.

❑ Optical Interference Coatings (OIC); 2016. 06. 19—24; Tuscon, US.

❑ 21th OptoElectronics and Communications Conference/International Conference on Photonics in Switching 2016; 2016. 07. 04—07; Niigata, Japan.

❑ International Conference on Ultrafast Phenomena; 2016. 07. 17—22; Santa

Fe, US.

❑ Visual and Physiological Optics 2016; 2016. 08. 22—26; Antwerp, Belgium.

❑ European Conference on Optical Communications; 2016. 09. 18—22; Dusseldorf, Germany.

❑ 35th International Congress on Applications of Lasers & Electro – Optics; 2016. 10. 16—22; San Diego, US.

❑ Frontiers in Optics: The 100th OSA Annual Meeting and Exhibit/Laser Science XXXII; 2016. 10. 17—21; New York, US.

❑ ARVO 2017 Annual Meeting; 2017. 05. 07—11; Baltimore, US.

❑ CLEO: 2017; 2017. 05. 14—19; San Jose, US.

❑ European Conference on Optical Communications; 2017. 09. 17—21; Gothenburg, Sweden.

❑ ARVO 2018 Annual Meeting; 2018. 04. 29—05. 02; Honolulu, US.

❑ ARVO 2019 Annual Meeting; 2019. 04. 28—05. 02; Vancouver, Canada.

❑ ARVO 2020 Annual Meeting; 2020. 05. 03—07; Baltimore, US.

❑ ARVO 2021 Annual Meeting; 2021. 05. 02—06; San Francisco, US.

美国国家地理空间情报局

英文名称：National Geospatial – Intelligence Agency，NGA

网　　址：https：//www1. nga. mil/Pages/default. aspx

机构简介

美国国家地理空间情报局成立于 2003 年，其前身是成立于 1996 年美国国家影像与制图局（The National Imagery and Mapping Agency，NIMA），后改为现名。此次更名，反映美国测绘科技从传统影像制图发展到对地理空间信息的快速获取与监测。

美国国家地理空间情报局总部位于弗吉尼亚州斯普林菲尔德，在密苏里州阿诺德和圣路易斯两地设有办事机构，为美国军队、外交提供服务，有员工约 14 500 人。

美国国家地理空间情报局隶属于美国国防部，受美国国防部、美国国家情报主任和国会的指导和监督，是地理空间情报界的领先者，首要任务是协助情报部门挑选、分析和发布地理空间信息。它既是情报机构也是作战支持机构，为决策者、作战人员、情报专家和第一响应人提供世界级的地理空间情报，增强他们的决策优势，为美国的国防和外交（如美国情报界和美国国防部等）提供可靠的情报。

美国国家地理空间情报局的主管既是地理空间情报国家系统的领导，也是全球地理空间情报联盟系统的协调员。

卫星侦察是美国国家地理空间情报局的重要情报来源，该局出色的战场情况判断力都得益于美国全天候的全球地理空间数据采集能力。美军掌握着全世界数量最多、种类最全的遥感、侦察卫星。目前，在轨的军用侦察卫星主要有"长曲棍球"、"锁眼"等。其中，"锁眼 – 12"是目前世界上分辨率最高的侦察卫星，其影像分辨率达 0.1m。

在 2004 年 12 月发生的印度洋海啸中，国家地理空间情报局利用间谍卫星，测定海啸受灾情况，并指挥美国救援人员的行动。2005 年 8 月"卡特里娜"飓风席卷美国，该局向联邦救援人员提供了约 100 幅由间谍卫星拍摄的受灾地区图片。飓风袭击过后，情报部门还为市政当局提供了新奥尔良市中心的卫星实拍图像，为规划灾后重建提供了帮助。

出版物

期刊与杂志

❑ PATHFINDER，每 2 个月一期。

美国海军研究局

英文名称：Office of Naval Research，ONR

网　　址：http：//www. onr. navy. mil

机构简介

　　海军研究局成立于 1946 年，历史可追溯至成立于 1923 年的海军研究实验室，是美国海军第一个现代化的研究机构。海军研究局是美国国防部的执行机构之一，也是为美国海军部长提供技术建议支持的机构。该机构除行政管理部门外，还设有 6 个主要工作部门，分别是：信息、电子与侦察科技部；海洋、大气与太空科技部；工程、材料与物理科学部；人力系统科技部；海军远征部；工业合作部等。各部门分别担负不同学科的科研工作。属该局管辖范围的还有海军研究部、国际区域办公室。

　　海军研究局主要负责美国海军基础科学和长远发展计划的研究工作，并通过下属的研究所，向高等院校和非营利机构拨款资助以及与各应用企业签订合同执行计划。自 2011 年起，海军研究局开始对其科技部门正在进行的基础研究项目进行同行评审。

　　海军研究局的研究领域主要包括：

（1）确保顺利进入海上作战场（Assure Access to the Maritime Battlespace）；

（2）自动化和无人系统（Autonomy and Unmanned Systems）；

（3）战争和非常规战（Expeditionary and Irregular Warfar）；

（4）信息主导（Information Dominance）；

（5）平台设计和耐用性（Platform Design and Survivability）；

（6）动力与能源（Power and Energy）；

（7）力量投射和综合防务（Power Projection and Integrated Defense）；

（8）所有权总成本（Total Ownership Cost）；

（9）战士表现（Warfighter Performance）。

出版物

1）战略规划

❏ 2015 Naval Science and Technology Strategic Plan.

❏ 2012 Marine Corps Strategic Plan.

2）资料单

❏ Adaptive Expert System.

❏ Adaptive Wide Area Clusters for Surveillance.

❏ Advanced Computational Microscopy.

- Advanced Electronics for Active Aperture Array Architectures.
- Affordable Modular Panoramic Photonics.
- Aircraft Structural Parts via Direct Digital Manufacturing.
- Anti – Tamper Protection of Critical System Elements.
- Automated Image Understanding.
- Automated Shipboard Weather Observation System.
- Autonomous Patient Care.
- Autonomous Persistent Tactical Surveillance.
- Autonomy for Large Teams of Collaborating Unmanned Systems.
- Biofouling Prevention Coatings.
- Bio – Inspired Autonomous Systems.
- Combat Safe Insensitive Munitions.
- Combat Tactical Vehicle.
- Combat/C2 Systems Data Exchange Technology Development and Experimentation.
- Command and Control Rapid Prototyping Capability.
- Command and Control, Computers and Communications.
- Command Decision – Making Program.
- Communications and Networks.
- Computational Methods in Decision Making.
- Counter Air Defense Improvements.
- Counter Directed Energy Weapons.
- Direct Attack Seeker Head.
- Distributed Electronic Warfare.
- Dynamically Reconfigurable Data Architectures.
- Electromagnetic Railgun.
- Electronic Warfare Battle Management for Surface Defense.
- Electronic Warfare Technologies for Navy and Marine Corps Aircraft.
- Energetic Materials.
- Expeditionary Communications.
- Fast Tint Protective Eyewear.
- Fires Thrust.
- Force Protection.
- Free Electron Laser.
- Fuel Cell Program.
- Fuel Cell Vehicle.

❑ Game – Based Training and Education.

❑ Graphene and the Future of Nanoelectronics.

❑ Ground Renewable Expeditionary Energy System.

❑ High – Bandwidth, Free – Space Optical Communications.

❑ High – Energy Dense Oxidizers.

❑ High – Energy Fiber Laser System.

❑ High – Energy Laser.

❑ High – Performance, Low – Cost Communications.

❑ High – Speed Components.

❑ Human Performance, Training and Education: Warrior Resilience.

❑ Human Social Cultural Behavioral Sciences.

❑ Human Systems Integration.

❑ Humanitarian Assistance and Disaster Relief Tools, Maps and Models.

❑ Hybrid Neurocognitive Architectures for Human Systems Design.

❑ Hypervelocity Projectile.

❑ Image Enhancement Unit for the Driver's Vision Enhancer.

❑ Improved Performance Assessment and Readiness Training System.

❑ Information Dominance and Cybersecurity.

❑ Information Processing, Discovery and Integration.

❑ Innovative Naval Prototype: Integrated Topside.

❑ Integrated Topside Innovative Naval Prototype.

❑ Intelligence, Surveillance and Reconnaissance.

❑ Intelligence, Surveillance and Reconnaissance to Command and Control.

❑ Intelligent and Autonomous Systems.

❑ Ion Tiger.

❑ ISR Knowledge Generation.

❑ Jet Noise Reduction.

❑ Laser – Based Helicopter Landing Aids.

❑ Logistic Transport Concepts.

❑ Logistics Thrust.

❑ Machine Reasoning and Learning.

❑ Maneuver Thrust.

❑ Manpower, Personnel, Training and Education.

❑ Marine Mammal Science.

❑ Maritime Weapons of Mass Destruction Detection Program.

❑ Mission – Focused Autonomy.

- Mobile Cleaning Reclaim and Recovery System.
- Mobile Security Architecture.
- Multi – Mode Sensor Seeker.
- Multiple Weapon Control Sight.
- Naval Expeditionary Dog Program.
- Navigation and Timekeeping.
- Navy Small Business Innovation Research/Small Business Technology Transfer Program.
- Next – Generation Airborne Electronic Attack.
- Optimization – Based UAV Planning.
- Persistent Intelligence, Surveillance and Reconnaissance.
- Power Management Kit.
- Precision Urban Mortar Attack (PUMA).
- RADAR.
- Renewable Sustainable Expeditionary Power.
- Robotic Hull Bio – Mimetic Underwater Grooming.
- Scalable Explosive Neutralization.
- Science of Autonomy.
- Sciences Addressing Asymmetric Explosive Threats.
- Sea – Based Automated Launch and Recovery System.
- Sea – Based Aviation National Naval Responsibility.
- Sea – Based Aviation National Naval Responsibility——Air Vehicle Technology.
- Sea – Based Aviation National Naval Responsibility——Airframe Structures and Materials.
- Sea – Based Aviation National Naval Responsibility——Propulsion.
- SeaPerch.
- Sense and Response Logistics.
- Shipboard Autonomous Firefighting Robot (SAFFiR).
- Sidewinder Mission Optimized Kinematic Enhancement.
- Social, Cultural and Behavioral Sciences.
- Socio – Cognitive Architectures for Adaptable Autonomous Systems.
- Software Reprogrammable Payload.
- Solid – State Fiber Laser.
- Solid – State Laser Technology Maturation Program.
- Solid – State Lighting for Submarines.

- ❏ Solid – State Power Amplifiers.
- ❏ Strike Accelerator.
- ❏ Structural Reliability Program.
- ❏ Submarine Piloting and Navigation Training.
- ❏ SwampWorks.
- ❏ Techsolutions.
- ❏ Training Science and Technology.
- ❏ UAS Autonomous Collision Avoidance System.
- ❏ Ultra Endurance Unmanned Aerial Vehicle Heavy Fuel Engine Program.
- ❏ Ultra High Frequency and Very High Frequency Circulators.
- ❏ Undersea Warfare Autonomy in Anti – Submarine Warfare and Mine Warfare.
- ❏ Variable Cycle Advanced Technology.
- ❏ Weapons of Mass Destruction Protection.

美国航空航天学会

英文名称：American Institute of Aeronautics & Astronautics，AIAA

网　　址：http：//www. aiaa. org/

机构简介

美国航空航天学会于 1963 年由美国火箭协会（American Rocket Society）和航空航天科学研究所（Institute of the Aerospace Sciences）合并成立。美国火箭协会可追溯至 1930 年成立的原美国星际协会（American Interplanetary Society）。美国航空航天科学研究所可追溯至成立于 1933 年的原航空科学研究所（Institute of the Aeronautical Sciences）。

美国航空航天学会是世界上最大的致力于全球航空航天发展的技术协会，有来自约 88 个国家的 30 000 多名个人会员和约 95 家企业会员，总部位于弗吉尼亚州雷斯顿。

美国航空航天学会涉及的专业技术领域包括自适应结构、空气声学、气动减速器系统、气动测量技术、吸气式推进系统集成、飞机操作、应用空气动力学、天文动力学、大气与空间环境、大气飞行力学、气球系统、通信系统、计算机系统、数字化航空电子、含能部件与系统、飞行测试、流体动力学、燃气轮机发动机、通用航空、地面测试、制导导航与控制、高速吸气式推进、航空航天历史、混合火箭、信息与指挥控制系统、信息系统组合、智能系统、航空航天法律问题、轻于空气的系统、相关材料、啮合可视化与计算环境、微重力与空间过程、导弹系统、建模与仿真、非确定性方法、核与未来飞行推进、等离子体动力学与激光器、推进剂与燃烧、推进与能源、传感器系统与信息融合、小型卫星、软件、空间建筑、空间自动化与机器人、太空移民、太空物流、太空操作与支持、空间系统、空天通链、太空运输、结构动力学、结构、存活性、地面能源系统、垂直/短距起降飞机系统、武器系统效能等。

美国航空航天学会还是世界领先的航空航天科学出版商，出版物包括图书、期刊、杂志、标准、会议录、电子书等，至今已经出版了 300 多本图书和近 200 000 篇技术文章。

出版物

美国航空航天学会建有电子图书馆（AIAA Electronic Library），通过该图书馆可以获得大多出版物。

1）期刊与杂志

❑ AIAA Journal，月刊，ISSN：0001 - 1452，eISSN：1533 - 385X。

❑ Journal of Aerospace Information Systems，月刊，2327 - 3097。

❑ Journal of Aircraft，双月刊，ISSN：0021 – 8669，eISSN：1533 – 3868。
❑ Journal of Guidance，Control，and Dynamics，双月刊，ISSN：0731 – 5090，eISSN：1533 – 3884。
❑ Journal of Propulsion and Power，双月刊，ISSN：0748 – 4658，eISSN：1533 – 3876。
❑ Journal of Spacecraft and Rockets，双月刊，ISSN：0022 – 4650，eISSN：1533 – 6794。
❑ Journal of Thermophysics and Heat Transfer，季刊，ISSN：0887 – 8722，eISSN：1533 – 6808。

2）图书与电子书

3）会议录

4）标准

❑ Low Earth Orbit Spacecraft Charging Design Standard Requirement and Associated Handbook（ANSI/AIAA S – 115 – 2013）.
❑ Space Plug – and – Play Architecture：Package Set.
❑ Qualification and Quality Requirements for Electrical Components on Space Solar Panels（AIAA S – 112A – 2013）.

会议信息

❑ 54th Structures，Structural Dynamics，and Materials and Co – located Conferences.
❑ The 22nd St. Petersburg International Conference on Integrated Navigation Systems；2015. 05. 25—27；St. Petersburg，Russia.
❑ 66th International Astronautical Congress；2015. 10. 12—15；Jerusalem，Israel.
❑ International Telemetering Conference USA；2015. 10. 26—29；Las Vegas，Nevada，US.
❑ Flight Software Workshop；2015. 10. 27—29；Laurel，Maryland，USA.
❑ 2nd Symposium of the Committee on Space Research（COSPAR）：Water and Life in the Universe；2015. 11. 09—13；Foz do Iguacu，Brazil.
❑ 51st AIAA/SAE/ASEE Joint Propulsion Conference；2015. 07. 27—29；Orlando，Florida.
❑ International Energy Conversion Engineering Conference；2015. 07. 27—29；Orlando，Florida.
❑ AIAA Missile Sciences Conference；2016. 03. 08—10；Laurel，Maryland，USA.
❑ AIAA Science and Technology Forum and Exposition（SciTech 2016）；

2016. 01. 04—08; San Diego, California, USA.

❏ 15th Dynamics Specialists Conference; 2016. 01. 04—08; San Diego, California, USA.

❏ 18th AIAA Non – Deterministic Approaches Conference; 2016. 01. 04—08; San Diego, California, USA.

❏ 24th AIAA/AHS Adaptive Structures Conference; 2016. 01. 04—08; San Diego, California, USA.

❏ 34th Wind Energy Symposium; 2016. 01. 04—08; San Diego, California, USA.

❏ 3rd AIAA Spacecraft Structures Conference; 2016. 01. 04—08; San Diego, California, USA.

❏ 54th AIAA Aerospace Sciences Meeting; 2016. 01. 04—08; San Diego, California, USA.

❏ 57th AIAA/ASCE/AHS/ASC Structures, Structural Dynamics, and Materials Conference; 2016. 01. 04—08; San Diego, California, USA.

❏ 8th Symposium on Space Resource Utilization; 2016. 01. 04—08; San Diego, California, USA.

❏ AIAA Atmospheric Flight Mechanics Conference; 2016. 01. 04—08; San Diego, California, USA.

❏ AIAA Guidance, Navigation, and Control Conference; 2016. 01. 04—08; San Diego, California, USA.

❏ AIAA Information Systems – AIAA Infotech @ Aerospace; 2016. 01. 04—08; San Diego, California, USA.

❏ AIAA Modeling and Simulation Technologies Conference; 2016. 01. 04—08; San Diego, California, USA.

❏ Annual Reliability and Maintainability Symposium (RAMS); 2016. 01. 25—28; Tucson. USA.

❏ 26th AAS/AIAA Space Flight Mechanics Meeting; 2016. 02. 14—18; Napa, USA.

❏ 2016 IEEE Aerospace Conference; 2016. 03. 05—12; Big Sky, USA.

❏ AIAA Defense and Security Forum (AIAA DEFENSE 2016); 2016. 03. 08—10; Laurel, Maryland, USA.

❏ Missile Sciences Conference; 2016. 03. 08—10; Laurel, Maryland, USA.

❏ 14th International Conference on Space Operations (Space Ops 2016); 2016. 05. 16—20; Daejeon, Korea.

❏ 23rd Saint Petersburg International Conference on Integrated Navigation Systems; 2016. 05. 30—06. 01; Saint Petersburg, Russia.

❑ AIAA Aviation and Aeronautics Forum and Exposition（AIAA AVIATION 2016）；2016. 06. 13—17；Washington, DC, USA.

❑ ICNPAA 2016 Mathematical Problems in Engineering, Aerospace and Sciences；2016. 07. 05—08；La Rochelle, France.

❑ AIAA Propulsion and Energy Forum and Exposition（Propulsion and Energy 2016）；2016. 07. 25—27；Salt Lake City, USA.

❑ 41st Scientific Assembly of the Committee on Space Research（COSPAR）and Associated Events；2016. 07. 30—08. 07；Istanbul, Turkey.

❑ AIAA Space and Astronautics Forum and Exposition（SPACE 2016）；2016. 09. 12—15；Long Beach, USA.

❑ 30th Congress of the International Council of the Aeronautical Sciences；2016. 09. 25—30；Daejeon, Korea.

❑ 2016 Joint Conference 22nd Ka and 34th ICSSC；2016. 10. 04；Cleveland, USA.

❑ AIAA Science and Technology Forum and Exposition（SciTech 2017）；2017. 01. 09—13；Grapevine, USA.

❑ AIAA Propulsion and Energy Forum and Exposition（Propulsion and Energy 2017）；2017. 07. 10—12；Atlanta, USA.

❑ AIAA Science and Technology Forum and Exposition（SciTech 2018）；2018. 01. 08—12；Orlando, USA.

美国航空无线电委员会

英文名称：Radio Technical Commission for Aeronautics，RTCA

网　　址：http：//www. rtca. org

机构简介

美国航空无线电技术委员会成立于1935年，位于华盛顿特区，是一个私人的非营利性组织。

作为一个联邦咨询机构，该委员会致力于回应美国联邦航空管理局（Federal Aviation Administration，FAA）的要求，并为联邦政府提供关于从技术性能标准到航空运输的操作概念等建议，以改进空中运输系统的安全性和效率。

美国航空无线电技术委员有490多家会员机构，其会员来自学术界、航空公司、机场、航空服务提供者、美国国防部、通用航空领域、政府机构、工会、制造商、研发机构及自动化和航空电子供应商等。

美国航空无线电技术委员会由董事会进行管理，董事会成员来自会员公司，下属委员会有：

（1）下一代咨询委员会（NextGen Advisory Committee）；

（2）项目管理委员会（Program Management Committee，PMC）；

（3）战术操作委员会（Tactical Operations Committee，TOC）；

（4）航空软件论坛（Forum on Aeronautical Software，FAS）；

（5）特殊委员会（Special Committees，SCs）包括以下委员会。

● 手持电子设备（SC – 234 Portable Electronic Devices）

● 航空电子的人因/飞行员交互问题（SC – 233 Addressing Human Factors/Pilot Interface Issues for Avionics）

● 机载选择性呼叫设备（SC – 232 Airborne Selective Calling Equipment）

● 地形提示和警告系统（SC – 231 Terrain Awareness Warning Systems，TAWS）

● 机载天气探测系统（SC – 230 Airborne Weather Detection Systems）

● 406兆赫兹应急定位发射器（SC – 229 406 MHz Emergency Locator Transmitters，ELTs）

● 无人机系统的毫米操作性能标准（SC – 228 Minimum Operational Performance Standards for Unmanned Aircraft Systems）

● 导航性能标准（SC – 227 Standards of Navigation Performance）

● 可充电锂电池和电池系统（SC – 225 Rechargeable Lithium Batteries and Battery Systems）

- 机场安全接入控制系统（SC – 224 Airport Security Access Control Systems）
- 航空移动机场通信系统（SC – 223 Aeronautical Mobile Airport Communication System）
- 航空移动卫星服务（SC – 222 Aeronautical Mobile – Satellite（R）Service, AMS（R）S）
- 航空数据库（SC – 217 Aeronautical Databases）
- 航空系统安全（SC – 216 Aeronautical Systems Security）
- 空中交通数据通信服务标准（SC – 214 Standards for Air Traffic Data Communication Services）
- 增强型飞行视觉系统与综合视觉系统（SC – 213 Enhanced Flight Vision Systems & Synthetic Vision Systems）
- 空中交通控制雷达塔台系统/模式可选发射机应答器（SC – 209 Air Traffic Control Radar Beacon System/Mode Select, ATCRBS & Mode S Transponder）
- 航空信息服务数据链（SC – 206 Aeronautical Information Services Data Link）
- 广播式自动相关监视系统（SC – 186 Automatic Dependent Surveillance – Broadcast）
- 全球定位系统（SC – 159 Global Positioning System）
- 交通预警与碰撞避免系统（SC – 147 Traffic Alert & Collision Avoidance System）
- 环境测试（SC – 135 Environmental Testing）
- 已废止的委员会（Sunsetted Committees）

出版物

1）会议录
2）报告
☐ Task Force Reports.
☐ Annual Report.
3）标准与指导文件
☐ Operational Services and Environment Definition（OSED）.
☐ Operational, Safety & Performance Requirements（SPR）.
☐ Interoperability Requirements（IRR）.
☐ Minimum Aviation System Performance Standards（MASPS）.
☐ Minimum Operational Performance Standards（MOPS）.

4）其他出版物

❑ Digest，两月出版一次。

会议信息

❑ RTCA 2016 Annual Global Aviation Symposium.

❑ SC – 234 Portable Electronic Devices；2015. 10. 07—09；Cologne，Germany.

❑ SC – 135 Environmental Testing；2015. 10. 27—29；Washington DC，US.

❑ SC – 186 Automatic Dependent Surveillance – Broadcast；2015. 10. 30；Washington DC，US.

❑ DO – 178C Training Bundle；2015. 12. 01—04；Washington DC，US.

❑ Supplements to DO – 178C Training；2015. 12. 04；Washington DC，US.

❑ DO – 160G Training：Track A&B；2015. 12. 14—17；Washington DC，US.

❑ DO – 160G Training：Track A Only；2015. 12. 14—15；Washington DC，US.

❑ DO – 160G Training：Track B Only；2015. 12. 16—17；Washington DC，US.

美国陆军通信电子司令部

英文名称：Communications – Electronics Command，CECOM

网　　址：http：//cecom. army. mil/

机构简介

美国陆军通信电子司令部的前身是成立于 1962 年的电子司令部（Electronics Command, ECOM）。1981 年，美国陆军装备司令部通信与电子装备备战司令部（Communications and Electronics Materiel Readiness Command, CERCOM）和通信研发司令部（the Communications Research and Development Command, CORADCOM）合并成立了通信电子司令部。

美国陆军通信电子司令部隶属于美国陆军装备司令部，总部位于阿伯丁试验场，有约 13 000 名员工。其业务涉及现场支持，对外军事援助，互通性认证，信息技术系统工程与集成，软件维护，供应链管理，后勤、保障规划与执行等，设有 7 个下属机构。

（1）中央技术支持办公室。中央技术支持办公室（Central Technical Support Facility, CTSF）位于得克萨斯州胡德堡（Fort Hood），是美国陆军的战略与中央测试机构，负责互通性工程、执行美国陆军的互通性认证测试、通过战术层面的信息技术/国家安全系统维护认证控制的操作、支持部署士兵的电子需求，是美国陆军唯一一个在网络中心环境下测试战场层面系统之系统产品的机构。

（2）后勤与备战中心。后勤与备战中心（Logisitics and Readiness Center, LRC）的使命是为士兵和联合部队提供及时的、高效的、全球性的 C4ISR 后勤支持，并为美国陆军提供能够使坦克、飞机、直升机、舰船、卫星和导弹等进行对话和获得战场优势的通信与电子系统。

除在本土的阿伯丁试验场等地设有办事机构外，后勤与备战中心还在 8 个国家设有后勤协助代表处。

（3）软件工程中心。软件工程中心（CECOM Software Engineering Center, SEC）的历史可追溯至 1983 年 10 月正式成立的软件开发与支持中心（Software Development and Support Center, SDSC），该中心主要为战场自动化系统开发、维护软件。1996 年，信息系统软件司令部（Information Systems Software Command, ISSC）、产业物流系

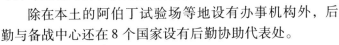

统中心（Industrial Logistics Systems Center, ILSC）、物流系统软件中心（Logistics Systems Software Center, LSSC）合并成立陆军通信电子司令部软件工程中心。

美国陆军软件工程中心是美国国防部内部最富有经验、最全面的软件支持中心，是美国陆军一站式的软件提供商，其使命是通过开发、提供、集成及维护美国陆军的 C^4ISR、物流及业务软件来确保作战准备，提供相关技术与服务，如系统构架、采办、软件开发、测试、变化管理、信息保障、认证、保障及支持服务等。

该中心的信息技术工程委员会（Information Technology Engineering Directorate, ITED）是软件工程中心、陆军及美国国防部和其他美国政府部门的信息技术产品和服务的重要提供商，为美国陆军和联合作战部队提供 IT 基础服务及软件解决方案，为陆军指挥、控制、通信、计算机、情报、电子战和传感器系统（Army Command, Control, Communications, Computer, Intelligence/Electronic Warfare and Sensor, C^4IEWS）提供支持。

（4）托比哈那补给站。托比哈那补给站（Tobyhanna Army Depot, TYAD）位于宾夕法尼亚州托比哈那，是美国国防部的一个全服务电子维修站，其使命是负责卫星终端、无线电和雷达系统、电话、电光、夜视与防入侵设备、机载监视设备、导航仪器、电子战与战术导弹的制导控制系统等在内的电子系统设计、制造、修理、大修等全面保障。

托比哈那补给站是美国国防部承认的自动化测试装备、系统集成、电子系统精简等领域的领先者。美国陆军将托比哈那补给站视为其 C^4ISR 和电子、航空电子与导弹制导控制的工业与技术卓越中心（Center of Industrial and Technical Excellence for C^4ISR and Electronics, Avionics and Missile Guidance and Control），美国空军也将托比哈那补给站视为其指挥控制通信与情报系统修理的技术来源。

（5）美国陆军信息系统工程司令部。美国陆军信息系统工程司令部（U. S. Army Informations Systems Engineering Command, USAISEC）为世界范围内的通信与信息技术系统提供系统工程、安装、集成实施、评估支持等，以保证美国陆军机构、作战指挥官、美国国防部及联邦机构等为作战士兵提供支持，其使命是对信息系统进行

设计、策划、集成、开发、维护、安装、测试、验收等，在指定的信息系统的系统工程与集成上为项目执行官和项目经理提供矩阵支持。

（6）美国陆军通信电子司令部历史办公室。美国陆军通信电子司令部历

史办公室（CECOM Historian）是历史资料收藏的中央知识库，该办公室职员负责收集、审核、保存文献，维护司令部档案，为项目提供参考与教育服务。此外，该办公室还根据陆军870-5条令（Army Regulation 870-5）编写年度历史评论（Annual Historical Review）。

（7）美国陆军通信电子司令部安全委员会。美国陆军通信司令部安全委员会（CECOM Directorate for Safety）的职责是将安全风险管理融入到为作战士兵提供较高的 C⁴ISR 系统作战能力的设计、开发、投入战场和维护上，为客户提供世界级的辐射安全支持。

出版物

1）期刊与杂志

❏ The LINK，半年一期。

❏ Army iSalute.

2）指南

❏ Defense Media Activity Guide To Keeping Your Social Media Accounts Secure.

❏ Cyber Security Protecting Operational Information.

❏ Cyber Security Phising Information.

❏ 2015 Antiterrorism Awareness Message.

3）手册

❏ Individual Security Vulnerability Assessment Checklist.

❏ Home and Family Security Tips.

❏ Operations Security Guidance for Family Members.

4）博客

❏ Army Echoes Blog.

5）资源网站

❏ Army OneSource，网址：http：//www. myarmyonesource. com/familyprogramsandservices/iwatchprogram/default. aspx.

❏ Army Policing Portal（APP），网址：https：//army. deps. mil/army/sites/APP/SiteAssets/AppHome. aspx.

❏ Army Antiterrorism Enterprise Portal（ATEP），网址：https：//army. deps. mil/army/sites/PMG/OPMG/OPS/antiterror/ATEP/default. aspx.

美国陆军研发与工程司令部

英文名称：U. S. Army Research, Development and Engineering Command, RDE-COM

网　址：http://www. army. mil/info/organization/unitsandcommands/com-mandstructure /rdecom/

机构简介

美国陆军研发与工程司令部成立于2003年，总部位于马里兰州阿伯丁试验场，拥有超过 14 000 名员工，包括科学家、工程师、研究人员等。

美国陆军研发与工程司令部隶属于美国陆军装备司令部，其下属的6个重要的研发与工程中心以及美国陆军研究实验室几乎承担美国陆军所有的基础研究、应用研究和技术开发工作，为美国战机提供技术解决方案，以满足当前和未来的作战需求。其下属机构包括：

（1）美国陆军研究实验室（Army Research Laboratory，ARL）；

（2）武器研发与工程中心（Armament Research, Development and Engineering Center，ARDEC）；

（3）航空与导弹研发与工程中心（Aviation and Missile Research, Development and Engineering Center，AMRDEC）；

（4）通信电子研发与工程中心（Communications - Electronics Research, Development and Engineering Center，CERDEC）；

（5）埃奇伍德生化中心（Edgewood Chemical Biological Center，ECBC）；

（6）纳蒂克士兵研发与工程中心（Natick Soldier Research, Development and Engineering Center，NSRDEC）；

（7）坦克车辆研发与工程中心（Tank Automotive Research, Development and Engineering Center，TARDEC）。

出版物

❑ RDECOM Strategic Plan FY 2015—2040.

美国陆军夜视与电子传感器委员会

英文名称：Night Vision and Electronic Sensors Directorate，NVESD

网　　址：http：//www. cerdec. army. mil/inside_cerdec/nvesd/

机构简介

美国陆军夜视与电子传感器委员会隶属于美国陆军通信电子研发与工程中心（The Communications – Electronics Research，Development and Engineering Center，CERDEC），历史可追溯至 1954 年成立的美国陆军工程兵团（U. S. Army Corps of Engineers）的工程研发实验室（Engineering Research and Development Laboratories，ERDL）的研究和光度测定部门（Research and Photometric Section）。1958 年，美国陆军夜视与电子传感器委员会召开了第一届图像增强仪会议（Image Intensifier Symposium）。20 世纪 60 年代，美国陆军夜视与电子传感器委员会开发出了星光镜、AN/TVS – 4 夜间观测设备、第一个激光测距仪等。20 世纪 70 年代，美国陆军夜视与电子传感器委员会又开发出了热成像系统、手持热观察仪器、前视红外产品、AN/PVS – 4 单兵武器瞄准镜、AN/PVS – 5 夜视眼睛等。20 世纪 80 年代，美国陆军夜视与电子传感器委员会开发出了 AN/VGS – 2 坦克热瞄准镜、AN/TAS – 6 长距夜间观测设备、AN/GVS – 5 激光测距仪、AN/AAS – 32 机载激光追踪器等，并不断地在夜视和电子传感器领域取得技术上的突破和进步，开发出了夜视综合性能模型（Night Vision Integrated Performance Model，NV – IPM）软件包。

美国陆军夜视与电子传感器委员会提供有关情报、监视、侦察、瞄准领域的技术，以保证士兵可以更好地了解周围环境、更安全有效地执行任务。

美国数字地球公司

英文名称：DigitalGlobe，DG

网　　址：http：//combination. digitalglobe. com/

机构简介

美国数字地球公司由成立于 1992 年的世界观影像公司（WordView Imaging Corporation）发展而来，1995 年改名为地球观察公司（EarthWatch Incorporated），2002 年改名为 DigitalGlobe。2013 年 1 月 31 日，全球最大的两家卫星影像公司——数字地球公司（DigitalGlobe）与地球眼（GeoEye）合并，DigitalGlobe 公司以 4.53 亿美元的价格收购了 GeoEye 公司，新成立的公司名仍为 DigitalGlobe。

数字地球公司是全球著名的高分辨率商业影像数据提供商，总部设在美国科罗拉多州朗蒙特市，分支机构遍布世界各地。

数字地球公司图像对各种行业都具有极其重要的意义，包括能源勘探、地区规划、环境监控、紧急响应规划、情报和 3D 仿真等，客户和合作伙伴包括 Google 以及众多的国际公司、政府机构和新闻媒体。

出版物

1）白皮书

❑ The Benefits of the Eight Spectral Bands of WorldView – 2.

❑ Digital Photogrammetry and Digital Surface Modeling Project.

❑ Digital Photogrammetry Project.

❑ Digital Photogrammetry and Digital Surface Modeling Project.

❑ Geolocation Accuracy of WorldView Products.

❑ High – Resolution Stereo Satellite Elevation Mapping Service.

❑ Tasking the DigitalGlobe Constellation：How To Obtain Current Earth Imagery Wherever You Need It.

2）卫星资料

❑ QuickBird Spacecraft Data Sheet：QuickBird spacecraft information and specifications.

❑ WorldView – 1 Spacecraft Data Sheet：WorldView – 1 spacecraft information and specifications.

❑ WorldView – 2 Spacecraft Data Sheet：WorldView – 2 spacecraft information and specifications.

❑ WorldView – 3 Spacecraft Data Sheet：WorldView – 3 spacecraft information and specifications.

- WorldView - 2 8 - band Applications Whitepaper: The Benefits of the 8 Spectral Bands of WorldView - 2.

3) 技术资料

- DigitalGlobe Imagery Products, Product Guide.
- Imagery Support Data (ISD) Documentation: Supplemental information for the Product Guide.
- DigitalGlobe Satellite Tasking: Information on a flexible and comprehensive set of tasking options.
- DigitalGlobe Spectral Response: Spectral Responses for QuickBird, World-View - 1 and WorldView - 2 Earth Imaging Instruments.
- Radiometric Use of WorldView - 2 Imagery: Technical note on radiometric use of WorldView - 2 imagery.
- Specifications for Customer - Provided Support Data: DigitalGlobe will orthorectify imagery using your support data.
- WorldView Elevation Suite Accuracy Report: Information on accuracy of the WorldView Elevation Suite.

4) 产品数据信息

- Advanced Elevation Series: Information and specifications on Advanced Elevation Series.
- Advanced Ortho Series: Information and specifications on Advanced Ortho Series.
- Analysis Center: Overview of DigitalGlobe's Analysis Center.
- Basic Imagery: Information and specifications on Basic Satellite Imagery.
- Change Indicator: Information on Change Indicator customized maps.
- Cloud Services: Overview of DigitalGlobe's Cloud Services.
- DigitalGlobe Satellite Tasking: Information on a flexible and comprehensive set of tasking options.
- Diplomatic Facilities Support Package: Information and specifications on Diplomatic Facilities Support Package.
- FirstLook: Information and specifications on FirstLook.
- Global Basemap: Overview of DigitalGlobe's Global Basemap.
- Precision Aerial: Information and specifications on Precision Aerial.
- Professional Services: Custom Software & Solutions.
- Information and specifications on Professional Services: Custom Software & Solutions.

- Professional Services: Service Contracts & Subscriptions.
- Information and specifications on Professional Services: Service Contracts & Subscriptions.
- Professional Services: Customer & Reseller Training.
- Information and specifications on Professional Services: Customer & Reseller Training.
- Standard Imagery: Information and specifications on Standard Satellite Imagery.
- Stereo Imagery: Information and specifications on Stereo Imagery.
- WorldView Elevation Suite: Information and specifications on WorldView Elevation Suite.

5）案例分析

- Amazing Real – time Navigation and Search on Your Cell Phone: LocatioNet Systems Ltd.
- DigitalGlobe Central to Bangladesh Cellular Network Expansion: Grameenphone.
- DigitalGlobe Provides Insight into Energy Infrastructure Projects: Genscape.
- DigitalGlobe Imagery Speeds Design of Irrigation Project in Konkan Irrigation Development Corporation.
- An EPA – Wide Solution for Obtaining and Sharing Earth Imagery: Environmental Protection Agency.
- Evaluating Atrocities under the Watchful Eye of Satellite Imagery: American Association for the Advancement of Science.
- A Full View for Real Estate Professionals: e – Neighborhoods, Worldwide.
- Improved Decision Making with DigitalGlobe Imagery: PEMEX SICORI.
- Integrating Imagery with GIS for Controlling Wildfires: Ontario Ministry of Natural Resources.
- Landslide! Satellite Imagery Use in Rescue and Recoveries: County of Ventura, California U. S. A.
- Media Access to Satellite Imagery of Worldwide Breaking News Events: Vizrt.
- A Monitoring Technique for the Springs of the Great Artesian Basin: Australian National Water Commission.
- Multi – Community Big Picture Planning Using Satellite Imagery: Nunavut, Canada.
- OSMRE Streamlines Operations with High Resolution Satellite Imagery: Of-

fice of Surface Mining, Reclamation, and Enforcement.

❑ Record Ten – Day Turnaround in Red Sea Bathymetric Study: Proteus.

❑ Restoring the Right – of – Way Along the 800km TransSakhalin Pipeline, One of the World's Largest Oil and Gas Projects: Sakhalin – 2 Oil & Gas Right – of – Way Restoration Project.

❑ Safeguarding California Communities: Pacific Gas and Electric Company.

❑ Streamlining Workflow at LSA Associates: LSA Associates.

❑ Using Precision Aerial Imagery to Accomplish County – Level Goals: Jackson County, Georgia U. S. A.

❑ Waldo Canyon Fire Demonstrates FirstLook Responsiveness: Colorado Springs, Colorado U. S. A.

❑ Worldwide Rapid 3D Mapping from Saab & DigitalGlobe: Saab Vricon Systems.

❑ Your Tax Dollars at Work: City of Solvang, California U. S. A.

美国武装部队通信与电子协会

英文名称：Armed Forces Communication and Electronic Association，AFCEA

网　　址：http：//www. afcea. org/

机构简介

美国武装部队通信与电子协会成立于1946年，是一个非营利性的协会，为军队、政府、工业、院校提供通信、IT、情报、全球安全领域方面的先进的专业知识和相关联系。该协会有约140个分会，几乎一半的分会每年都会组织年会，其会员、赞助商、合作伙伴都是世界领先的通信、情报、信息系统方面的设计师、策划师、制造商、检测师、系统员。

美国武装部队通信与电子协会一直倡导教育，与该协会的教育专项基金会长年合作，每年为科技专业的学生、情报和国家安全领域相关的研究所、ROTC programs、教育机构等设立1 500万美元的奖学金、津贴、补助等。

美国武装部队通信与电子协会的专家发展中心是由教育基金机构运营，为政府、军方、工业界专家提供涉密和未涉密的通信课程、情报课程、信息系统课程。

美国武装部队通信与电子协会通过展览会、技术专业小组会议、报告为C^4ISR、情报、国家安全、信息技术专家提供了解决疑难问题的机会。

出版物

1）期刊与杂志

❑ SIGNAL Magazine，月刊。

2）索引

AFCEA以在线形式出版了4部可供检索的索引（AFCEA's Directories）。

❑ Source Book Directory.

❑ Cybersecurity Directory.

❑ Health IT Directory.

❑ Intelligence Directory.

3）博客

❑ The MAZZ – INT Blog，http：//www. afcea. org/mission/intel/blog/index. cfm.

❑ Small Business Blog.

4）简讯

❑ AFCEA Weekly Digest.

5）白皮书或特殊报告

会议信息

- ❏ MILCOM 2015; 2015. 10. 26—28; TAMPA, FL.
- ❏ TechNet Europe; 2015. 10. 20—22; Berlin, Germany.
- ❏ TechNet Asia – Pacific; 2015. 11. 17—19; Honolulu, Hawaii.
- ❏ AFCEA International Cyber Symposium; 2015. 12. 08—10; Sofia, Bulgaria.
- ❏ TechNet Europe; 2016. 1st quarter; Berlin, Germany.
- ❏ MILCOM; 2016. 1st quarter; Tampa, FL.
- ❏ West Conference and Exposition; 2016. 02. 17—19; San Diego, CA.
- ❏ Air Force ISR Industry Day; 2016. 02. 25; Chantilly, VA.
- ❏ NGA Industry Day; 2016. 03. 16; Springfield, VA.
- ❏ TechNet Air; 2016. 03. 22—24; San Antonio, TX.
- ❏ Army Singal Ball; 2016. 2nd quarter; Washington, DC.
- ❏ Coast Guard Intelligence Industry Day; 2016. 04. 07; Chantilly, VA.
- ❏ AFCEA Spring Intelligence Symposium; 2016. 04. 20—21; Springfield, VA.
- ❏ Defensive Cyber Operations Symposium; 2016. 04. 20—22; Washington, DC.
- ❏ NRO Industry Day; 2016. 05. 07; Chantilly, VA.
- ❏ NITEC – NCI Agency Conference and AFCEA TechNet Intertional; 2016. 3rd; Europe.
- ❏ AFCEA Solutions Series: George Mason University Symposium; 2016. 05. 24—25 Fairfax, VA.
- ❏ Navy Information Dominance Industry Day; 2016. 06. 14; Chantilly, VA.
- ❏ Army Intelligence Industry Day; 2016; Chantilly, VA.
- ❏ Homeland Security Conference; 2016. 3rd quarter; Washington, DC.
- ❏ TechNet Augusta; 2016. 08. 02—04; Augusta, GA.
- ❏ Intelligence and National Security Summit; 2016. 09. 28—29; Washington, DC.
- ❏ Global Identity Summit; 2016. 4th quarter; Tampa, FL.
- ❏ Army Cyber Ball; 2016. 4th quarter; Alexandria, VA.
- ❏ TechNet Asia – Pacific; 2016. 11. 15—17; Honolulu, Hawaii.
- ❏ AFCEA International Cyber Symposium; 2016. 12. 06—08; US.
- ❏ TechNet Europe; 2017. 1st quarter; Berlin, Germany.
- ❏ MILCOM; 2017. 1st quarter; Tampa, FL.
- ❏ West Conference and Exposition; 2017. 02. 21—23; San Diego, CA.
- ❏ Air Force ISR Industry Day; 2017. 02. 25; Chantilly, VA.
- ❏ NGA Industry; 2017; Springfield, VA.
- ❏ TechNet Air; 2017. 03. 28—30; San Antonio, TX.

- ❑ Coast Guard Intelligence Industry Day; 2017; Chantilly, VA.
- ❑ NRO Industry Day; 2017; Chantilly, VA.
- ❑ Army Singal Ball; 2017. 2nd quarter; Washington, DC.
- ❑ AFCEA Solutions Series: George Mason University Symposium; 2017. 05. 23—24 Fairfax, VA.
- ❑ Navy Information Dominance Industry Day; 2017; Chantilly, VA.
- ❑ Army Intelligence Industry Day; 2017; Chantilly, VA.
- ❑ Homeland Security Conference; 2016. 3rd quarter; Washington, DC.
- ❑ NITEC – NCI Agency Conference and AFCEA TechNet Intertional; 2017. 3rd quarter; Europe.
- ❑ AFCEA Spring Intelligence Symposium; 2017. 3rd quarter; Springfield, VA.
- ❑ Defensive Cyber Operations Symposium; 2017. 3rd quarter; Blatimore, MD.
- ❑ TechNet Augusta; 2017. 08. 08—10; Augusta, GA.
- ❑ Army Cyber Ball; 2017. 4th quarter; Alexandria, VA.
- ❑ Intelligence and National Security Summit; 2017. 4th quarter; Washington, DC.
- ❑ Global Identity Summit; 2017. 4th quarter; Tampa, FL.
- ❑ TechNet Asia – Pacific; 2017. 10. 31—11. 02; Honolulu, Hawaii.
- ❑ AFCEA International Cyber Symposium; 2017. 12. 05—07; Europe.

美国物理声学公司

英文名称：Physical Acoustics Companies，PAC

网　　址：http：//www. physicalacoustics. com/

机构简介

美国物理声学公司于 1968 年由来自贝尔实验室的科学家 Sotirios J. Vahaviolos 博士成立，依靠声发射领域众多卓越的人才  和不断创新的技术而使公司得以迅速发展和壮大，并于 1985 年兼并了当时世界上最著名的声发射技术公司——美国 Dunegan 公司（成立于 1968 年），而使美国物理声学公司成为世界上最大的声发射技术研发公司和公认的世界声发射技术的领导者。正是由于该公司在声发射领域的一次次技术突破和创新，使声发射技术渐渐走出实验室而不断进入一个又一个工程应用领域，成功地解决了一个又一个工程问题，并带领声发射技术向更深、更高和更实用的方向发展。

美国物理声学公司不仅是世界声发射技术的领导者，而且已经发展成为无损检测领域最大的公司之一，其业务涉及科研项目研发、声发射检测、超声 C 扫描检测、振动检测、电阻测量仪等无损检测设备的生产与销售、技术咨询、技术服务及培训认证等多个领域。该公司的研发中心为美国国防、政府部门及大公司等领域完成了数十个项目研发及应用的交钥匙工程。

出版物

简讯

❑ PAC Newsletter.

会议信息

❑ Acoustic Emission Conferences.

❑ Manufacturing Problem Prevention Program 2015；2015. 10. 06；El Segundo，USA.

❑ Deepwater 2015；2015. 11. 03—05；Galveston，USA.

❑ WCAE – 2015；2015. 11. 10—13；Honolulu，Hawaii，USA.

❑ PowerGen 2015；2015. 12. 08—10；Las Vegas，USA.

美国应用计算电磁学学会

英文名称：Applied Computational Electromagnetics Society，ACES

网　址：http：//www. aces – society. org/

机构简介

应用计算电磁学学会源起于 1985 年的计算机建模/电磁学工作小组。该学会是一家国际性的会员  制学会，主要致力于电磁学理论与应用研究，每年举行年度研讨会，为与数字建模在应用电磁学领域的相关议题提供论坛，发行出版物，在会员之间保持较高专业水平的信息交流。

出版物

1）期刊与杂志

❑ The ACES Journal，月刊。

2）简讯

❑ Applied Computational Electromagnetics Society Newsletter，不定期出版，每年 2 期或 3 期。

会议信息

❑ 2016 IEEE International Conference on Wireless Information Technology and Systems（ICWITS）and Applied Computational Electromagnetics（ACES）；2016. 03. 13—17；Honolulu，Hawaii.

情报科学与技术学会

英文名称：Association for Information Science and Technology，ASIS&T

网　　址：http：//www.asis.org/

机构简介

情报科学与技术学会可追溯至 1937 年成立的美国文献学会（American Documentation Institute，ADI）。1968 年，美国文献学会更名为美国情报科学学会

（American Society for Information Science），2000 年加入了"技术"一词而成为情报科学与技术学会（American Society for Information Science and Technology，ASIS&T），2013 年改为现名，以体现其国际性。

　　情报科学与技术学会位于马里兰州银泉市，是一个非营利性的机构，旨在通过为信息专家和机构提供支持来促进信息科学及相关信息技术的发展，关注的领域包括情报科学、计算机科学、语言学、管理学、图书馆学、工程、法律、医学、化学及教育等。该学会的会员覆盖了来自 50 个国家的信息科学与技术领域的科研人员、学生、教授、管理者、开发人员等。

出版物

该机构建有数字图书馆 The ASIS&T Digital Library。其出版物主要如下。

1）期刊与杂志

❑ The Journal of the American Society for Information Science and Technology（JASIST），月刊。

❑ The Bulletin of the American Society for Information Science and Technology，双月刊。

❑ The Annual Review of Information Science and Technology（ARIST），2006—2011。

2）会议录

❑ ASIS&T conference proceedings.

会议信息

❑ 2015 Annual Meeting；2015.11.06—10；St. Louis，MO，USA.

❑ 2016 IA Summit；2016.05.04—08；Atlanta，GA，USA.

❑ 2016 Annual Meeting；2016.10.14—18；Copenhagen，Denmark.

信息显示协会

英文名称：Society for Information Display, SID

网　　址：http：//www. sid. org/

机构简介

信息显示协会成立于 1962 年，由显示领域的顶级科学家、工程师、企业研究者及商业人士组成，

旨在组织各成员共同拓展 21 世纪的信息显示研究成果，并将其运用于通信、医疗、商业、政府、娱乐、消费品等领域。该机构的 6 000 多位成员来自信息显示研究、设计、制造、应用、销售和营销有关的研究技术等领域。

出版物

1）期刊与杂志

❑ Information Display magazine.

2）期刊与杂志

❑ Journal of SID，季刊，会员免费。

3）会议录

❑ Annual Digest of Technical Papers.

❑ Seminar Notes.

❑ IDRC（International Display Research Conference，alternates between Euro-Display and LatinDisplay）.

❑ IDW（International Display Workshops，Japan）.

❑ notes for the Display Week Short Courses.

会议信息

❑ The 22nd International Display Workshop；2015. 12. 09—11；Otsu，Japan.

应用技术联合公司

英文名称：A – Tech Corporation，d. b. a. Applied Technology Associates，ATA

网　　址：http：//www. atacorp. com/

机构简介

应用技术联合公司创建于 1975 年，位于阿拉巴马州亨茨维尔，主要为政

府和商业客户提供用于地面、空中和太空的精密测量、系统测试与评估，以及传感器与系统及控制领域的产品与服务。

应用技术联合公司与其他公司组建的合资公司有：

（1）ATA 航空航天公司，由应用技术联合公司与 ASRC 空间防御公司（ASRC Space and Defense，AS&D，前身是极地斜率研究公司（Arctic Slope Research Corporation，ASRC））于 2006 年联合成立，主要为卫星和高空气球项目等提供综合工程、集成、物流、测试服务等。

（2）ATAMIR – WSMR 是应用技术联合公司与 MIRATEK 公司（MIRATEK Corporation）的合资公司，主要提供工程与分析服务，包括武器系统硬件和软件的测试规划、执行、分析、测试结果报告等。

出版物

1）综述

❑ ATA Company Overview.

❑ Systems Test and Evaluation.

❑ Technical Services.

❑ SBIR Programs.

2）资料单

❑ Angular Rate Sensors：ARS – 06 and 06S MHD Angular Rate Sensor，ARS – 06 and 06S Triaxial Unit，ARS – 14 MHD Angular Rate Sensor – Installation and Operation Manual，ARS – 15 MHD Angular Rate Sensor – Installation and Operation Manual.

❑ Multi – Axis ARS Packages（Dynapak）.

❑ Multi – Axis Accelerometer Packages.

❑ Inertial Measurement Unit.

❑ NorthFinder.

❑ Reconfigurable Wireless Measurement System（RWMS）.

❑ Fast Steering Mirror.

❑ Optical Inertial Reference Units.

应用水动力声学研究公司

英文名称：Applied Hydro – Acoustics Research, Inc. , AHA

网　　址：http：//www. epicos. com/EPCompanyProfileWeb/GeneralInformation. aspx？id＝21892

机构简介

应用水动力声学研究公司创建于 1972 年，在弗吉尼亚州森特维尔、马里兰州洛克威尔、华盛顿特区、加利福尼亚州圣地亚哥等地设有办事机构。

应用水动力声学研究公司是一个私营防务承包商，将系统工程、软件开发、测试评估与创新性的声呐软件系统解决方案等优势联合起来，与联邦政府合作共同为美国海军的反潜战任务提供支持，如提供实时的反潜战系统、声呐/声学、波束成型、信号处理、建模、战术决策支持开发等。

应用研究联合公司

英文名称：Applied Research Associates, Inc. , ARA

网　　址：http：//www. ara. com/

机构简介

应用研究联合公司成立于 1979 年，位于新墨西哥州阿尔布开克，是一个雇员所有企业，致力于为国家安全、基础建设、能源与环境、医疗等领域提供产品和解决方案。该公司的产品涉及 C^4ISR 系统，化武防御，信息与情报，建模与仿真，化学、生物、辐射和核防护，机器人，测试与评估，武器效果、武器系统，无人地面车辆、无人机，远程自动化手持探测，夜视安全，传感器系统等。

约翰·威利国际出版公司

英文名称：John Wiley & Sons，Inc.

网　　址：http：//www. wiley. com

机构简介

约翰·威利父子出版公司已有 180 多年的历史，自成立以来一直是一家出版专业图书、参考工具书、各种期  刊与杂志和有关资料的独立出版社，每年出版新书及新产品 1 000 多种，其中包括大学教科书、科技参考工具书、百科、软件及联机数据库等。此外，该出版社每年还出版 140 多种期刊与杂志，以出版的科技专业图书、贸易行业性图书和电脑图书的高质量而闻名于世。

出版物

出版物有图书、期刊与杂志，涉及化学、计算机、地球、太空与环境科学、工程与材料科学、医学、物理与天文学、心理学、农业、会计、艺术、商业与管理、人文、教育、经济等学科。

会议信息

❑ Annual Meeting of the Japanese Cancer Association；2015. 10. 18—10；Nagoya，Japan.

❑ APME 2015——IUPAC 11th International Conference on Advanced Polymers VIA Macromo；2015. 10. 18—22；Yokohama，Japan.

综合系统咨询公司

英文名称：Integrated System Consultants, Inc. , ICI
网　　址：http：//integratedconsultants. com/

机构简介

综合系统咨询公司成立于 1979 年，1999 年从联邦管理的商业企业转化成美国国防部合同商，是一家面向海军和商业海事以及联邦管理的商业产业的专业的技术服务和物流流程系统整合商，主要承担海军作战系统和  电子系统方面的任务。该公司还是一个 8（a）STARS Ⅱ 合同商，通过了 ISO 9001：2008 认证，并且符合 AS9100C 的质量系统。

综合系统咨询公司的合同大多来自美国海军海上系统司令部（Naval Sea Systems Command, NAVSEA）、美国总务管理局（U. S. General Services Administration）、美国空间和海上作战系统中心太平洋分部（Space and Naval Warfare Systems Center Pacific, SSC Pacific）、陆军通信电子司令部（US Army Communications Electronics Command, CECOM）、空军联合项目办公室（Air Force Joint Program Office, JPO）等部门或机构。

加拿大

加拿大航空电子设备有限公司

英文名称：CAE Inc. , CAE

网　　址：http：//www. cae. com/en/

机构简介

　　加拿大航空电子设备有限公司成立于1947年，总部位于魁北克，是全球领先的为航空公司、飞机制造商和防务客户提供模拟技术、模型技术和综合训练服务的公司，客户遍及全球190多个国家和地区，每年培训的飞行员数量多达100 000人次。

　　加拿大航空电子设备有限公司下设4个分公司：军用飞机模拟器与机载控制系统分公司（Avion Simulator and Plane Control Systems）、民用飞机模拟器与训练分公司（Commerce Plane Simulator and Training）、森林设备系统分公司（Forest Equipment Systems）、CAE电子有限公司（CAE Electronics Ltd.）。

　　加拿大航空电子设备有限公司主要在北美和欧洲的近30个国家开展业务，涉及民用航空、防务和安全、医疗、采矿及企业合作等，有民用业务、防务业务、新的核心市场（主要是医疗和采矿）等3大核心业务领域，其中民用业务和防务业务占总收入的95%。该公司生产的飞行用半导体产量占全球2/3以上。

　　在民用业务领域，加拿大航空电子设备有限公司研制的高水平的民用飞行模拟器处于世界领先地位，在民用目视系统的设计和生产上也处于世界领先地位，并保有全飞行模拟机（Full - Flight Simulators，FFSs）第一的销售量，在商业航空培训上也居首位，在商务航空培训上位居第二，在民用直升机培训上位居世界第一。另外，该公司的牛津航空学院拥有世界上最大的飞行学院网。

　　在防务和安全领域，该公司是全球公认的培训系统集成商，是飞行员军事模拟培训的世界领导者，占有25%的市场份额，为50多个国家的防务力量服务。

　　加拿大航空电子设备有限公司主要设计、生产、销售和维修军用和民营飞机模拟器、路基模拟器、舰船控制系统、防务系统、森林防护和林业机械设备、木材生产与加工机械设备、木材纤维和纸浆工业制造设备、石油与潜水探测仪器设备、反潜巡逻机及固定翼飞机的磁异探测仪系统、舰载与机载控制系统。此外，加拿大航空电子设备有限公司还从事航空电子仪器与设备的安装与维修业务。其主要产品有目视系统，包括 MAXVUE2000、MASVUE 增强型以及最新的 MAXVUE MEDALION 型产品、飞行训练系统（FTD）、敌我识别模拟训练系统、综合战术环境模拟器、皇家海军山猫 Mk8 和"默林"EH101 模拟器等。

出版物

1）报告

❑ Proxy Circular.

2）小册子

❑ CAE Oxford Aviation Academy.

❑ Civil Helicopter Training Solutions.

❑ Simulation Products for Aviation Training.

❑ Customer Services and Update Services.

❑ Rotorsim Training Centre.

❑ Pilot Training.

❑ Honeywell – CAE Technical Training Alliance.

❑ Flightscape.

3）简讯

❑ CAE Newsletter.

4）数据（Datasheet）

❑ CAE Strat3D – Coal.

5）其他出版物

❑ Enbridge Participant Toolkit.

❑ Enbridge Safe Cycling Guide.

会议信息

❑ Pacific 2015；2015. 10. 06；Sydney，Australia.

❑ Council of Ambulance Authorities（CAA）；2015. 10. 14；Melbourne，Australia.

❑ Seoul ADEX 2015；2015. 10. 20；Seoul，South Korea.

❑ EATS；2015. 11. 03；Istanbul，Turkey.

❑ Dubai Airshow；2015. 11. 08；Dubai，UAE.

❑ GATE；2015. 11. 09；Dubai，UAE.

❑ NBAA 2015；2015. 11. 17；Las Vegas，USA.

加拿大通信安全学会

英文名称：Communications and Security Establishment Canada，CSE

网　　址：http：//www. cse－cst. gc. ca

机构简介

加拿大通信安全学会是加拿大国家密码学机构，位于安大略省渥太华市。2007 年 9 月开始，其英文名称加上了"Canada"一词（以前为 Communications and Security Establishment）。该学会向加拿大政府提供两种主要服务：国外国防信号情报支持和国外政策，电子信息和通信保护（信息技术安全）。另外，加拿大通信安全学会还为联邦法律执法和安全机构提供技术和运作帮助。

加拿大通信安全学会的国外信号情报服务为政府在国家安全、国家防务和国外政策领域的决策提供支持，并在加拿大情报优先级政府部门指导下进行，其使命是使政府部门和机构能够有效地保障他们信息系统和网络的安全，是保护加拿大政府电子信息技术安全的技术领导者。

出版物

加拿大通信安全学会的出版物没有明确分类，主要包括：

（1）CSEC's response to media coverage of Commissioner's Report；

（2）CSEC settles pay equity－related complaint with PSAC；

（3）CSEC Information Kit；

（4）Public－private Partnerships and National Security：Myths vs. Reality；

（5）Letter to the Editor－Ottawa Citizen；

（6）Long－Term Accommodation（LTA）Project Backgrounder。

第三部分

欧洲机构

俄罗斯

英　国

法　国

德　国

意大利

荷　兰

挪　威

西班牙

俄罗斯

俄罗斯"火星"康采恩

俄语名称：Россия Марсе Konzern

英文名称：Russia Mars Konzern

机构简介

　　俄罗斯"火星"康采恩的业务涉及无线电综合系统、无线电电子设备及程序的开发，雷达系统，自动化控制系统，空中交通管制系统，无线电导航系统和机场设备，防空系统，微电子产品，水下测量设备和医疗设备等。

俄罗斯导航信息系统公司

俄语名称：ОАО «Навигационно – информационные системы» （ОАО «НИС»）

英文名称：JSC "Navigation Information Systems", JSC "NIS"

网　　址：http：//www. nis – glonass. ru/en/

机构简介

俄罗斯导航信息系统公司成立于 2007 年，是俄罗斯 GLONASS 卫星技术应用项目的重要的系统整合商，主要负责在俄罗斯或国际市场的车辆及商

业化的现代卫星系统上安装基于 GLONASS 卫星技术的设备。该公司由两家公司合资，分别是持有 70.01％ 股份的 JSFC Sistema 和持有 29.99％ 股份的俄罗斯空间系统公司（JSC Russian Space Systems）。

俄罗斯工业与科技集团

俄语名称：Государственная корпорация по содействию разработке, производству и экспорту высокотехнологичной промышленной продукции «Ростехнологии», Госкорпорация Ростех

英文名称：State Corporation for Assistance to Development, Production and Export of Advanced Technology Industrial Product «Russian Technologies», State Corporation Rostec

网　　址：http：//rostec. ru/en/

机构简介

俄罗斯工业与科技集团于 2007 年底成立，主要致力于研发、生产及出口高科技民用及军用工业产品，2014 年的收入达 9 645亿卢布。

俄罗斯工业与科技集团包括700 家分支机构，其中有 14 家控股公司（9 家军工企业，5 家民用企业）。

（1）康采恩无线电电子技术公司（Concern Radioelectronic Technologies, http：//kret. com），主要研制电子战和敌我识别技术、飞机设备、无线电电子设备，以及各种测量仪器等。

（2）俄罗斯直升机公司（Russian Helicopters, http：//www. russianhelicopters. aero/en/），是俄罗斯唯一的直升机开发商和制造商，也是世界上为数不多的能够进行现代军用和民用直升机的设计、制造、测试、维修的公司。

（3）卡拉什尼科夫康采恩公司（Kalashnikov Concern, www. kalashnikovconcern. com），是俄罗斯最大的自动化与狙击武器，制导炮弹以及一系列的民用产品如猎枪、运动步枪、机械及工具的制造商。

（4）Schvabe 公司主要集合了俄罗斯光学电子领域的生产商和制造商，一起开发制造高技术光电系统、军用和民用系统、光学材料、医疗设备以及节能光学技术等。

（5）联合仪器制造公司（United Instrument Manufacturing Corporation, UIMC），是俄罗斯重要的通信工具与系统、自动化控制系统、电子安全系统与机器人系统及产品的开发商和制造商。

（6）联合发动机公司（United Engine Corporation, www. uk – odk. ru），是军用和民用航空、空间项目及各种发电和热能设备、气体压缩机、舰载燃气涡轮机等发动机的制造商。

（7）俄罗斯技术动态公司（Technodinamika, http：//avia – equipment. ru），主要生产供应航空元件、动力供应系统和降落伞系统等。

（8）国家免疫生物公司（National Immunobiological Company, NIC），从事

免疫生物药品的研发和生产。

（9）俄技—化学复合材料控股公司（RT - Chemcomposite，www. rt - chem-composite. ru），是俄罗斯高分子复合材料领域的领导者之一，是由复合材料研发制造企业组成的控股公司，主要生产新型材料、特殊构件及技术，同时批量生产航天、航空、动力、陆路运输和水路运输所需的高科技产品。

（10）RT - Stankoinstrument 机床工具公司（RT - Stankoinstrument，http：//www. rt - stanko. ru/），主要从事机床制造与相关工具的生产。

（11）俄罗斯电子公司（Russian Electronics），主要业务涉及微波工程、半导体设备及材料等。

（12）高精密度系统科学生产企业（High Precision Systems Vysokotochnye Kompleksy，www. npovk. ru），主要进行高精度武器、配件及零件的开发与生产。

（13）Concern Avtomatika（http：//niia. ru/）是俄罗斯联邦从事保密通信系统和密码信息防护设备研发、生产、质保、服务及现代化升级的最大企业，生产含密码信息保护设备的专用通信控制系统及成套设备，开发密码信息防护技术和方法、自控化控制系统以及硬件—软件设施。

（14）机械工程技术公司（Machine Engineering Technologies Holding），主要从事火炮弹药和特殊化学品的研发和生产。

（15）Rostec 汽车公司（RT - Auto），主要从事汽车制造和汽车零部件的生产。

（16）俄罗斯国防工业公司（Oboronprom，http：//www. oboronprom. ru），是一个机械制造和高技术领域中的跨领域工业投资集团，是俄罗斯直升飞机制造企业的综合协调者，为以前出口的军用直升机装备提供备件、服务和维修。

俄罗斯国际卫星组织

俄语名称： Международная организация космической связи «ИНТЕРСПУ ТНИК»

英文名称： The Intersputnik International Organization of Space Communications, Intersputnik

网　址： http：//www. intersputnik. com/

机构简介

俄罗斯国际卫星组织是全球领先的少数卫星运营商之一，成立于 1971 年，总部位于莫斯科，是一个以前苏联为首由 15 个成员国组成的国际性卫星通信联合组织，根据 1971

年 11 月 15 日政府间的协议成立。与国际通信卫星组织（Intelsat）相似，其目的旨在发展和使用卫星通信系统，以满足日益增长的广播、电视、电报、电话、数据传输等信息的国际交换。俄罗斯国际卫星组织曾向世界上许多国家提供国际、国内以及区域性的高质量卫星通信服务，旗下的卫星群有"快车"、"地平线"、"航向"等系列卫星，以及最新一代的 LM1 系列和 Express – A 系列。

如今，俄罗斯国际卫星组织有 26 个会员国，是国际电信联盟的无线电通信分部的成员之一。

出版物

简讯

❑ Corporate Newsletter INTERSPUTNIK TODAY.

俄罗斯科学院无线电工程和电子学研究所

俄语名称：Институт радиотехники и электроники（ИРЭ）имВ. А. Котель
ников РАН

英文名称：Kotel'nikov Institute of Radio – engineering and Electronics of RAS，
IRE

网　　址：http：//www. cplire. ru/

机构简介

俄罗斯科学院无线电工程和电子学研究所成立
于 1953 年，位于莫斯科，主要进行无线电物理，
无线电技术、物理和量子电子，信息情报学等方面
的基础研究，并主导行星雷达和其他行星的无线电
定位探索。该研究所由几个研究部门组成，下设有
一个特殊设计局和两个工程中心。除了位于莫斯科的总部，俄罗斯科学院还在
弗里亚济诺、萨拉托夫和乌里扬诺夫斯克设有研究分部。

出版物

期刊与杂志

❏ Journal of Radio Electronics，ISSN：1684—1719，月刊。

会议信息

❏ 每个月的第一个周二举行莫斯科电动力学研讨会。

俄罗斯自动化和电测法研究所

俄语名称：Институт автоматики и электрометрии Сибирского отделения Российской академии наук

英文名称：Institute of Automation and Electrometry, Siberian Branch of the Russian Academy of Sciences, IA&E, SB RAS

网　　址：http://www.iae.nsk.su/index.php/en

机构简介

俄罗斯科学院西伯利亚分院自动化与电测法研究所建立于 1957 年，是西伯利亚分院成立最早的一批研究所之一。

自动化与电测法研究所是一个研究物理和技术的研究机构，其研究方向包括光学和激光物理中的实际问题，包括：在气态和压缩媒介中由射线引发的物理过程，射线与结构材料交互作用下的非线性现象，激光和光学技术领域内的基础和实用研究，结构、系统方案、数据处理和计算系统识别的数学模型和软件，复杂动态过程的信息和控制系统的分析和代表。

自动化与电测法研究所是新西伯利亚省立大学物理和技术研究自动化、量子光学、信息测量系统三个专业部门的基地，并基于这些部门和研究所的实验室，成立了科学教育中心以便于培养高水平的年轻专业人士，同时与美国、德国、法国、瑞典、中国、朝鲜以及其他国外的大学、机构和研究机构开展合作。

出版物

1）期刊与杂志

❏ Optoelectronics, Instrumentation and Data Processing，双月刊。

2）报告

❏ Annual Report of the Institute.

❏ Annual Review.

会议信息

❏ III International Scientific and Technical Conference "Radio Engineering, Electronics & Communication – 2015"; 2015.10.06—08; Omsk, Russia.

鄂木斯克仪器制造研究院

俄语名称： Омский научно – исследовательский институт приборостроения

英文名称： Omsk Research Institute of Communications and Electronics，ONIIP

网　　址： http：//www. oniip. ru/

机构简介

鄂木斯克仪器制造研究院成立于 1958 年，承担了从电子管接收机到大规模乃至超大规模集成电路计算机通信设备的 5 代无线电设备的研制和开发工作，是俄罗斯联邦长波、中波、短波及超短波通信领域的重要科研机构，是俄罗斯国防部短波通信设备的定点生产厂。其产品广泛应用于国防和民用，覆盖了以下领域：无线电中心和短波无线电系统，专业用全波段（陆基、舰载及机载长波、中波和短波）无线电接受装置，短波和超短波便携式充线电台，大功率激励式和固定式的天线、天线阵和天线交换机，数字式抗干扰无线电通信设备和无线电调制解调器，近距离雷达检测目标设备，星载无线电定位系统，观测和监视设备，指挥用便携式通信设备等。

航空设备科学研究院

俄语名称：OAO "нии авиационного оборудования"

英文名称：JSC Institute of Aircraft Equipment，NIIAO

网　　址：http：//www. niiao. ru

机构简介

航空设备科学研究院组建于 1983 年，主要从事航空机载设备和航天仪器设备的研究工作，涉及研究和设计数字式机载综合电子系统、电子显示系统、飞机引导系统、飞机控制系统、临界状态告警系统、机载检测和技术维护系统、供电和通风系统等，设计机载设备的高空模拟试验设备，对机载设备进行功效鉴定和验证，研究设备失灵的物理原因，研究设备试验演示法和防止外来影响的保护法，研制机载设备的计算机辅助设计系统、计算系统和机载软件系统，设计集成式操纵台、语音识别和综合对话系统、导航测量仪器、超导天线、光纤通信线路、机载电子库、地图数据库以及大气参数和其他参数的激光测量仪器等。航空设备科学研究院拥有现代化的实验基地，能对全套机载设备、系统和飞机座舱进行演示、试验验证和功效验证，可培训飞行人员和技术人员。

圣彼得堡无线电技术设备厂

英文名称：St. Petersburg Radio Technology Equipment Plant

机构简介

圣彼得堡无线电技术设备厂成立于 1965 年，拥有一整套现代化生产设备，主要承担导弹系统零部件的生产任务，并为俄罗斯防空部队提供现代化武器装备的试验用样机模型。此外，该厂还承担着固定式和移动式地空导弹性能指标统计和分析设备以及复杂气候条件下的模型试验设备的研制工作。

圣彼得堡无线电技术设备厂隶属于 2000 年成立的俄罗斯国防出口公司（Open Joint Stock Company Rosoboronexport，Rosoboronexport）。该公司是目前俄罗斯唯一的国家军品进出口商和专门对军品及技术出口进行宏观调控和指导的机构，代表了俄罗斯著名的武器品牌和先进的军事科学与技术基础。

英　国

简氏信息集团

英文名称：IHS Jane's Information Group，Jane's

网　　址：http：//www. janes. com/

机构简介

简氏信息集团创立于 1898 年，通过全球独家的独立分析师网络，向用户提供独具优势的情报以及产品解决方案、顾问解决方案、风险分析报告等，帮助用户做出正确的决定。

随着简氏出版物的连续问世，简氏信息集团的规模亦不断扩大，成为世界出版军事资料同行中的翘楚，在国际上享有很高声望。1981 年，简氏信息集团被加拿大汤姆逊集团收购，但在业务上是完全独立的。2001 年 4 月，伍德布里奇公司从汤姆逊集团手中收购了简氏信息集团。2007 年 6 月，IHS 集团从伍德布里奇公司手中收购了简氏信息集团，简氏信息集团成为 HIS 集团的防务与安全情报和分析中心。

简氏信息集团的业务涉及航空航天、军事和普通航空运输、军用飞机、民航飞机、舰船、军火弹药、火炮、步兵、海上和空中发射的武器、铁路、雷达系统、电子作战系统、水下作战系统、航空电子设备、空间市场以及情报领域。

简氏信息集团的总部位于英国伦敦南郊的科尔斯登小镇，在美国、日本、澳大利亚、中东地区、非洲等地均设有分支机构，并在世界各地派驻数百名记者。简氏集团的雇员分布在 60 多个国家，另外还有一些主动提供资料的业余人员。

出版物

简氏的出版物主要是期刊杂志和年鉴，除了传统的印刷版本，其产品形式还有电子邮件、在线资源、CD、Binder、特刊（Special Reports）、给特定读者定期寄发的时事通讯、单片缩影胶卷（Microfiche）等。

1）期刊与杂志

❑ Jane's Defence Weekly.

❑ Jane's Navy International.

❑ International Defence Review.

- Jane's Defence Industry.
- Jane's Missiles & Rockets.
- Jane's Airport Review.
- Jane's Intelligence Review.
- Islamic Affairs Analyst.
- Terrorism and Insurgency Monitor.

2）年鉴

- Jane's Fighting Ships.
- Jane's Air Traffic Control.
- Jane's Airports and Handling Agents.
- Jane's Airport, Equipments and Services.
- Jane's Urban Transport Systems.
- Jane's World Railways.
- Jane's Defence Industry News.
- Jane's All the World's Aircraft: Development & Production, In Service, Unmanned.
- Jane's Aero Engines.
- Jane's C^{4}ISR & Mission Systems: Air, Joint & Common Equipment, Land, Maritime.
- Jane's EOD & CBRNE Defence Equipment.
- Jane's Flight Avionics.
- Jane's Land Warfare Platforms: Armoured Fighting Vehicles; Artillery & Air Defence; Logistics, Support & Unmanned; System Upgrades.
- Jane's Mines & EOD Operational Guide.
- Jane's Police & Homeland Security Equipment.
- Jane's Simulation & Training Systems.
- Jane's Space Systems & Industry.
- Jane's Unmanned Maritime Vehicles.
- Jane's Weapons: Air – Launched; Ammunition; Infantry; Naval; Strategic.
- Jane's International ABC Aerospace Directory.
- Jane's International Defence Directory.

3）软皮书

- Jane's Helicopter Markets and Systems.
- Jane's World Defence Industry.
- Jane's World Insurgency and Terrorism.
- Jane's Amphibious and Special Forces.

- ❏ Jane's World Air Forces.
- ❏ Jane's World Armies.
- ❏ Jane's World Navies.

会议信息

会议主要包括在线研讨会（Webinar）和简氏信息集团定期举办的在线研讨会，议题涉及国际政治、军事、安全等。此外，还有其他一些行业领域的会议如化学、航空航天等。

- ❏ OSINT Methods & Techniques；2015. 10. 05—08；UK.
- ❏ Pacific 2015 International Maritime Exposition；2015. 10. 06—08；Sydney，Australia.
- ❏ 2015 AUSA Annual Meeting&Exposition；2015. 10. 12—14；Washington DC，US.
- ❏ Social Media Intelligence；2015. 10. 12—14；Dubai，UAE.
- ❏ Airborne ISR；2015. 10. 26—27；London，UK.
- ❏ Defense & Security 2015；2015. 11. 02—05；Muang Thong Thani，Thailand.
- ❏ Global MilSatCom；2015. 11. 03—05；London，UK.
- ❏ Social Media Intelligence；2015. 11. 10—12；Singapore.
- ❏ Milipol Paris；2015. 11. 17—20；Paris，France.
- ❏ SMi presents the 5th annual conference：Social Media within the Defence and Military Sector；2015. 11. 19—20；London，UK.
- ❏ Future Armoured Vehicle Survivability 2015；2015. 11. 23—24；London，UK.
- ❏ Military Airlift & Rapid Reaction Operations；2015. 12. 01—02；Seville，Spain.

萨里卫星技术有限公司

英文名称：Surrey Satellite Technology Ltd. , SSTL

网　　址：http：//www. sstl. co. uk/

机构简介

　　萨里卫星技术有限公司是由英国萨里大学组建的一家私营卫星制造公司，成立于 1985 年，旨在对该大学的小卫星工程研究成果进行商业开发。空中客车防务与航天控股公司（Airbus Defence and Space Holdings BV）持有该公司 99% 的股份，剩余 1% 的股份由萨里大学拥有。

　　萨里卫星技术有限公司是第一家利用先进的地面技术快速提供低成本小卫星的专业机构。通过 20 多年的努力，该公司已建立起可为公司带来利润的小卫星业务，成为世界上最成功和最富有经验的小卫星供应商。该公司有员工 200 多人，已参与进行了 26 项小卫星任务。

　　萨里卫星技术有限公司的业务专长在于能对各种先进地面技术进行适应性改进，使其适应空间环境的要求。无论任务总承包商还是空间段供应商，无论是分系统还是论证服务，该公司都能基于其广泛的经验和先进的研发能力来提供高效的解决方案。

出版物

该公司网站上列出了一些手册和资料单供查看。

- ❑ SSTL Corporate Brochure.
- ❑ SSTL Earth Observation Brochure.
- ❑ SSTL Telecommunications and Navigation Brochure.
- ❑ NovaSAR – S Brochure.
- ❑ SSTL NovaSAR – S Synthetic Aperture Radar Platform datasheet.
- ❑ SSTL 100 Platform datasheet.
- ❑ SSTL 100 v3. 0 datasheet.
- ❑ SSTL 150 Platform datasheet.
- ❑ SSTL 300 Platform datasheet.
- ❑ SSTL 300i Platform datasheet.
- ❑ SSTL Earthmapper datasheet.
- ❑ SSTL GMP – T Platform datasheet.
- ❑ Earth Observation Comparative Resolutions datasheet.
- ❑ Ground Segment datasheet.

- ❑ SSTL Space Missions Training and Development Brochure.
- ❑ SSTL Subsystems datasheets.
- ❑ Changing the economics of space for 25 years（the SSTL story）.
- ❑ Subsystems Products brochure.
- ❑ CHRIS Imager datasheet.
- ❑ VHRI 250 Imager datasheet.
- ❑ DMC MSI Imager datasheet.

苏格兰光电协会

英文名称：Scottish Optoelectronics Association，SOA

网　　址：http：//www. optoelectronics. org. uk/

机构简介

苏格兰光电协会成立于 1994 年，成立的目的是通过光电知识、制造和应用来刺激苏格兰的经济增长。该协会是苏格兰

技术网络（Scottish Technology Network，STN）的一部分，苏格兰技术网络代表的是技术领域（从传感器到医疗设备）的所有公司。

会议信息

❑ Fit for the Future Network：Integrated Energy Systems；2015. 11. 18；Cheshire，UK.

英国超级电子公司

英文名称：Ultra Electronics Holdings Plc，ULE

网　　址：http：//www.ultra – electronics.com

企业概况

英国超级电子公司成立于 1920 年，总部位于英国伦敦，是全球最大的声呐探测装置提供商，在世界范围内为国防、安全和航空应用领域设计并制造电子和机电装置、子系统及相关产品，其业务与服务覆盖了 C^4ISTAR、网络安全、声呐系统、民用运输和能源系统设备、防务安全应用设备、军用飞机及民用飞机设备等。

超级电子有限公司主要的客户包括：空中客车公司，英国宇航系统公司，波音公司，雷神公司，洛克希德·马丁公司，通用动力公司，劳斯莱斯公司，美国国防部，英国国防部，澳大利亚国防部等。

英国超级电子公司设置三个业务部门：飞机与车辆系统部门、信息与动力系统部门、战术与声呐系统部门。其中，战术与声呐系统部门的收入和利润占公司总收入和总利润的一半以上，2014 年的收入达 7.137 亿英镑，在全球有 4 870 多名员工。

出版物

报告

❏ Annual Report.

英国船舶电子电气协会

英文名称：British Marine Electrical and Electronics Association，BMEEA

网　　址：http：//bmeea. org/

机构简介

英国船舶电子电气协会于 2013 年由原英国船舶电子协会（British Marine Electronics Association，BMEA）更名而来，是英国航海联合会（British Marine Federation，BMF）的成员之一。

英国船舶电子电气协会是代表电子电气设备生产商的贸易组织，这些电子电器设备包括船舶使用的雷达、GPS 接收器、无线电、导航辅助及电池充电器等。

英国船舶电子电气协会每年为其会员举办会议，并邀请业内外的专家参会。

会议信息

❏ BMEEA Annual Conference.

英国工程技术学会

英文名称: The Institution of Engineering and Technology, IET

网　　址: http: //www. theiet. org/

机构简介

英国工程技术学会由英国电气工程师学会 (Institute of Electrical Engineers, IEE) 和英国应用工程师学会 (IIE) 2006 年 3 月合并而成。英国电气工程师协会成立于 1871

年，是一家英国电子、电气、生产和信息技术专业人士尤其是电气工程师的专业组织。在与英国应用工程师学会合并成英国工程技术学会前，英国电气工程师协会是欧洲最大的专业工程师协会，在全世界有大约 120 000 个会员。

英国工程技术学会是世界上领先的专业工程和技术团体，在欧洲、北美洲以及亚太地区设有办公室，在全球 127 个国家拥有近 16 万名会员，是欧洲规模最大、全球第二的国际专业工程学会。

英国工程技术学会提供两种会员身份：个人会员身份和图书馆会员身份。其中，个人会员身份有学生或学徒会员、助理会员、普通会员、会士会员以及荣誉会士会员。

出版物

1) 期刊与杂志

❑ Engineering&Technology, monthly.

❑ E&T Education, published each semester (september, January, May).

❑ Wiring Matters.

❑ Flipside, published 8 times per year.

❑ Member News, three times per year.

❑ IET Biometrics.

❑ IET Circuits, Devices & Systems.

❑ IET Communications.

❑ IET Computers & Digital Techniques.

❑ IET Computer Vision.

❑ IET Control Theory & Applications.

❑ IET Electric Power Applications.

❑ IET Electrical Systems in Transportation.

❑ IET Generation, Transmission & Distribution.

❑ IET Image Processing.

❑ IET Information Security.

❑ IET Intelligent Transport Systems.

❑ IET Microwave Antennas & Propagation.

❑ IET Nanobiotechnology.

❑ IET Networks.

❑ IET Optoelectronics.

❑ IET Power Electronics.

❑ IET Radar, Sonar & Navigation.

❑ IET Renewable Power Generation.

❑ IET Science Measurement & Technology.

❑ IET Signal Processing.

❑ IET Software.

❑ IET Systems Biology.

❑ IET Wireless Sensor Systems.

❑ Electronics Letters, Semi – monthly.

❑ Micro & Nano Letters.

❑ The Journal of Engineering.

2）图书

❑ Buses, Bankers and the Beer of Revenge: an Eccentric Engineer collection; ISBN: 978 – 1 – 84919 – 581 – 2; 128pp.

❑ CMOS Digital Integrated Electronics: A First Course; ISBN: 978 – 1 – 61353 – 002 – 3; 417pp.

❑ Fundamentals of Electromagnetic Levitation: Engineering Sustainability through Efficiency; ISBN: 978 – 1 – 84919 – 663 – 5; 248pp.

❑ The Handbook of Electrical Resistivity – new materials and pressure effects; ISBN: 978 – 1 – 84919 – 149 – 4; 488pp.

❑ Introduction to Biomechatronics; ISBN: 978 – 1 – 89112 – 127 – 2; 600pp.

❑ An Introduction to Fractional Control; ISBN: 978 – 1 – 84919 – 545 – 4; 200pp.

❑ Control Theory: a guided tour, 3rd Edition; ISBN: 978 – 1 – 84919 – 227 – 9; 400pp.

❑ Developments in Control Theory towards Glocal Control; ISBN: 978 – 1 – 84919 – 533 – 1; 232 pp.

❑ Distributed Control and Filtering for Industrial Systems; ISBN: 978 – 1 – 84919 – 607 – 9; 450pp.

❑ Frequency – domain Control Design for High Performance Systems; ISBN: 978 – 1 – 84919 – 481 – 5; 456pp.

- Further Advances in Unmanned Marine Vehicles; ISBN: 978 – 1 – 84919 – 479 – 2; 400pp.
- Nonlinear and Adaptive Control Systems; ISBN: 978 – 1 – 84919 – 574 – 4; 350pp.
- Optimal Adaptive Control and Differential Games by Reinforcement Learning Principles; ISBN: 978 – 1 – 84919 – 489 – 1; 400pp.
- Designing Electronic Systems for EMC; ISBN: 978 – 1 – 89112 – 142 – 5; 304pp.
- Integral Equation Methods in Electromagnetics; ISBN: 978 – 1 – 89112 – 193 – 7; 550pp.
- MATLAB for Electrical and Computer Engineering Students and Professionals: With Simulink; ISBN: 978 – 1 – 61353 – 188 – 4; 450pp.
- Scattering of Waves by Wedges and Cones with Impedance Boundary Conditions; ISBN: 978 – 1 – 61353 – 003 – 0; 232pp.
- Lean Product Development: A manager's guide; ISBN: 978 – 1 – 84919 – 671 – 0; 248pp.
- Lightning Electromagnetics; ISBN: 978 – 1 – 84919 – 215 – 6; 976pp.
- High Voltage Engineering and Testing, 3rd Edition; ISBN: 978 – 1 – 84919 – 263 – 7; 750pp.
- Principles of Modern Radar: Advanced Techniques; ISBN: 978 – 1 – 89112 – 153 – 1; 600pp.
- Pulse Doppler Radar: principles, technology, applications; ISBN: 978 – 1 – 89112 – 198 – 2; 350pp.
- Tracking Filter Engineering – The Gauss – Newton and Polynomial Filters; ISBN: 978 – 1 – 84919 – 554 – 6; 320pp.
- Waveform Design and Diversity for Advanced Radar Systems; ISBN: 978 – 1 – 84919 – 265 – 1; 500pp.
- Sea Clutter: Scattering the K Distribution and Radar Performance, 2nd Edition; ISBN: 978 – 1 – 84919 – 589 – 8; 450pp.
- Modelling Distributed Energy Resources in Energy Service Networks; ISBN: 978 – 1 – 84919 – 559 – 1; 250pp.
- Offshore Wind Turbines: Reliability, availability & maintenance; ISBN: 978 – 1 – 84919 – 229 – 3; 296pp.
- Key Enablers for User – Centric Advertising across Next Generation Networks; ISBN: 978 – 1 – 84919 – 618 – 5; 288pp.
- Age Factors in Biometric Processing; ISBN: 978 – 1 – 84919 – 502 –

7；256pp.

3）标准

❏ Code of Practice for Electric Vehicle Charging Equipment Installation；IS-BN：978 - 1 - 84919 - 515 - 7.

❏ Code of Practice for Electric Vehicle Charging Equipment Installation；IS-BN：978 - 1 - 84919 - 514 - 0；92pp.

❏ Successfully Implementing a Plug - in Electric Vehicle Infrastructure；ISBN：978 - 1 - 84919 - 606 - 2.

❏ Successfully Implementing a Plug - in Electric Vehicle Infrastructure；ISBN：978 - 1 - 84919 - 605 - 5；112pp.

❏ Code of Practice for Electrical Safety Management；ISBN：978 - 1 - 84919 - 669 - 7；112pp.

4）会议录

❏ Radar International Conference on Radar Systems（CD）；ISBN：978 - 1 - 84919 - 676 - 5.

❏ 7th System Safety Conference Incorporating the Cyber Security Conference（CD）；ISBN：978 - 1 - 84919 - 680 - 2.

❏ Image Processing Conference —IPR（CD）；ISBN：978 - 1 - 84919 - 632 - 1.

❏ Road Transport Information and Control（RTIC）（CD）；ISBN：978 - 1 - 84919 - 674 - 1.

❏ The IAM and IET Asset Management Conference；ISBN：978 - 1 - 84919 - 693 - 2.

❏ The IET Professional Development Course on Electric Traction Systems；IS-BN：978 - 1 - 84919 - 683 - 3.

❏ CIRED Workshop - Integration of Renewables into the Distribution Grid；IS-BN：978 - 1 - 84919 - 628 - 4.

❏ The 6th IET International Conference on Power Electronics，Machines and Drives；ISBN：978 - 1 - 84919 - 616 - 1.

会议信息

❏ Robotics in Extreme Environments Seminar；2015. 10. 07；Birmingham，UK.

❏ Workshop on refrigeration and air conditioning；2015. 10. 07；Perak，Malaysia.

❏ Routes to Registration Workshop；2015. 10. 14；Coventry，UK.

❏ Renewable Power Generation RPG Conference；2015. 10. 17；Beijing，China.

❏ System Safety and Cyber Security Conference；2015. 10. 20；Bristol，UK.

- ❑ S&WW Network – Lifeskills event – Introduction to Management Workshop; 2015. 10. 20; Bridgwater, UK.
- ❑ Railway Electrification Seminar; 2015. 10. 22; London, UK.
- ❑ EVI – GTI Gas Turbine Instrumentation Seminar; 2015. 11. 03; London, UK.
- ❑ Annual Partnership Event 2015; 2015. 11. 04; London, UK.
- ❑ IET International Conference on Technologies for Active and Assisted Living (TechAAL) Conference; 2015. 11. 05; Surrey, UK.
- ❑ Elex Sandown Exhibition; 2015. 11. 05; Esher, UK.
- ❑ The 10th IET International Conference on Advances in Power system Control, Operation and Management; 2015. 11. 08; Tsim Sha Tsui, Hong Kong.
- ❑ Professional Registration Workshop; 2015. 11. 09; Southampton, UK.
- ❑ Joint PEI Churchill Medal Award; 2015. 11. 12; London, UK.
- ❑ Towards 5G Mobile Technology Vision to Reality Conference; 2015. 11. 19; London, UK.
- ❑ The Asset Management Conference; 2015. 11. 25; London, UK.
- ❑ Additive Manufacturing and 3D Printing Seminar; 2015. 12. 01; London, UK.
- ❑ Intelligent Signal Processing (ISP) Conference; 2015. 12. 01; London, UK.
- ❑ Passive Components for Power Electronics Seminar; 2015. 12. 01; Birmingham, UK.
- ❑ Aerospace Annual Symposium – All electric aircraft technology Conference; 2016. 01. 28; London, UK.
- ❑ Developments in Power System Protection – DPSP 2016 Conference; 2016. 03. 07; Edinburgh, UK.
- ❑ Power Electronics, Machines and Drives – PEMD 2016 Conference; 2016. 04. 19; Glasgow, UK.
- ❑ European High Power Electromagnetics EUROEM 2016 Conference; 2016. 07. 11; London, UK.

英国史密斯集团

英文名称：Smiths Group plc

网　　址：http：//smiths - group. com

机构简介

史密斯集团成立于 1851 年，总部设于英国伦敦，2014 年的收入约为 29.52 亿英镑，在全球 80 多个国家设有企业分支机构，在 50 多个国家拥有雇员 23 000 多名，设有 5 个业务部门。

（1）史密斯探测器（Smiths Detection）是全球最大的探测传感器制造商，这些探测传感器主要用于探测炸药、武器、化学剂、生物威胁、麻醉药、违禁品等。

（2）约翰克兰（John Crane）是世界上最大的密封及相关产品制造商。

（3）史密斯医疗（Smiths Medical）是全球专业的医疗器械和设备的提供商。

（4）史密斯英特康元器件（Smiths Interconnect）是重要的电子和射频部件制造商。

（5）Flex – Tek 公司为航空航天、医疗、工业、建筑和国内电器市场提供工程配件、加热和运动流体及燃气等。

出版物

报告

❑ Annual Report.

法　国

法国达索航空公司

英文名称：Dassault Aviation S. A.

网　　址：http：//www. dassault - aviation. com/

机构简介

法国达索航空公司由法国两家主要军用飞机制造商——马塞尔·达索飞机制造公司和布雷盖飞机制造公司于 1971 年合并而成，名为马塞尔·达索—布雷盖飞机制造公司（Aviation Marcel Dassault Breguet Aviation），1990 年改为现名。

法国达索航空公司隶属于法国达索集团，是全球航空业的领先者，主要从事军用飞机、民用飞机和航天产品的开发、生产和销售，也进行多种与航空航天相关的产品如电子产品的开发与生产。

达索航空公司旗下包括达索"隼"喷气公司（Dassault Falcon Jet）、达索"隼"服务公司（Dassault Falcon Service）、达索国际公司（Dassault International Inc.）等多个公司，还持有法国泰雷兹集团 26% 的股份。

达索航空公司现有 2 000 多架"猎鹰"喷气飞机和 1 000 多架作战飞机在役。

达索航空公司的总部设在巴黎，在圣克卢（Saint - Cloud）、比亚里茨（Biarritz）、梅里尼亚克（Merignac）、阿让特伊（Argenteuil）等十几个地方设有工厂或试验中心，2014 年的净收入达 3. 98 亿欧元，有 11 740 多名员工。

出版物

报告

❑ Annual Report.

法国科学技术信息研究所

英文名称：Institute for Scientific and Technical Information，INIST

网　　址／：http：//www. inist. fr/？ lang = en

机构简介

法国科学技术信息研究所成立于 1988
年，是法国主要的文献收藏中心，主要收藏
科学技术、医学、人文和社科等学科的文献，
可提供现代化的文献服务，如目录组织、翻
译、联机信息检索系统，文献对用户开放。

出版物

1）数据库

❑ Francis and Pascal.

❑ 期刊与杂志文章、会议录等出版物可以在 Refdoc 网站获取，网址：ht-
tp：//www. refdoc. fr/。

2）开放获取资源

❑ I－Revues，网址：http：//irevues. inist. fr/。

❑ Lara，网址：http：//lara. inist. fr/。

❑ OpenGrey，网址：http：//www. opengrey. eu/。

❑ Termsciences，网址：http：//www. termsciences. fr/。

空中客车集团防务与航天公司地理信息服务部门

英文名称：Airbus Defence and Space Geo – Information

网　　址：http：//www. geo – airbusds. com/

机构简介

空中客车集团防务与航天公司的地理信息服务部门的前身是欧洲宇航防务集团旗下的阿斯特里姆地理信息服务公司（Astrium Services），总部位于法国图卢兹，是世界地理信息市场公认的领先者，是 Pléiades 和 SPOT 卫星家族的运营商，拥有对高分辨率雷达卫星 TerraSAR – X 和 TanDEM – X 的独家商业开发权限。同时，依托全面的空间数据源和航空数据的获取能力，该部门还向用户提供无与伦比的对地观测影像和地理信息产品及服务组合。

空中客车集团防务与航天公司的地理信息服务部门的产品与业务服务于国防（如军事情报、军事测绘）、安全、国家空间数据基础设施、应急响应和危机管理、土地管理、测绘、环境、农业、石油和天然气开采等，该部门在全球有 20 个办事处，以及 100 多个经销商和合作伙伴，有 900 多名员工。

出版物

1) 简讯

❑ ImagineGEO.

2) 报告

❑ Geo Reports.

欧洲咨询公司

英文名称：Euroconsult

网　　址：http：//www. euroconsult – ec. com

机构简介

欧洲咨询公司成立于 1982 年，总部位于法国巴黎，是一家旨在为通信和太空领域提供评估和战略决策建议的知名国际咨询公司，在加拿大蒙特利尔、美国华盛顿、日本横滨等地均设有办公室。依靠其在太空市场的 30 多年的专业知识和经验，欧洲咨询公司服务来自全球约 50 个国家的约 600 家客户，其中不乏波音公司、美国航空航天局等著名机构。

欧洲咨询公司的研究主要聚焦于太空与卫星产业，包括结构、市场参与者、收入与动向等在内的评估；关注的市场领域包括广播与宽带、地球观测、政府空间事务、机上娱乐与通信、海上通信、卫星通信、卫星制造与发射等。

出版物

研究报告

❑ Earth Observation Requirements & Solutions in Latin America.

❑ Profiles of Government Space Programs.

❑ Mobile Satellite Communications Markets Survey：Prospects to 2024.

❑ Trends & Prospects for Emerging Space Programs.

❑ NASA Spending Outlook：Trends to 2016.

❑ Satellite Value Chain：The Snapshot.

❑ Satellite – Based Earth Observation：Market Prospects to 2023.

❑ Earth Observation：Data Distribution.

❑ Prospects for Satellite Communications and Broadcasting in Africa.

❑ Mobile Satellite Communications Markets Survey：Prospects to 2024.

❑ High Throughput Satellites：On Course for New Horizons.

会议信息

❑ World Satellite Business Week.

❑ Summit for Satellite Financing.

❑ Symposium on Satcom Market Forecasts.

❑ Summit on Earth Observation Business.

德　国

德国导航学会

德语名称: Deutsche Gesellschaft fuer Ortung und Navigation e. V, DGON

英文名称: German Institute of Navigation

网　　址: http://www.dgon.de/

机构简介

德国导航学会成立于 1951 年，是一个为公众服务的非营利性组织，设立的主要目的是协助与导航和定位相关的科学事业的开展、支持导航相关的研发活动、推动导航及定位领域的新应用，以促进陆地、海上、空中及内陆河道交通等的发展。

德国导航学会设有以下 7 个委员会。

（1）海上交通与导航委员会；

（2）空中交通与通用航空导航委员会；

（3）地面交通与陆地车辆导航委员会；

（4）雷达技术委员会；

（5）陀螺仪技术委员会；

（6）卫星导航委员会；

（7）交通远程信息技术委员会。

德国导航学会每年召开多场与导航技术相关的会议，并出版会议录等相应的出版物。

出版物

1）期刊与杂志

❏ European Journal of Navigation（EJN），ISBN：1571 – 473X.

2）会议录

❏ International Symposium Information on Ships.

❏ International Symposium on Certification of GNSS Systems & Services.

❏ Symposium Inertial Sensors and Systems.

❏ International Symposium on Precision Approach and Automatic Landing.

❏ Symposium ESAVS.

❏ International Radar Symposium.

会议信息

- ❏ 16th Marine Traffic Engineering Conference/International Symposium Information on Ships; 2015. 10. 14—16; Kolberg, Polen.

- ❏ Der Alpenraum und seine Herausforderungen an ORientierung, Navigation und Information saustausch（德语）; 2015. 11. 26—27; Wildhaus, CH.

- ❏ International Symposium on Enhanced Solutions for Aircraft and Vehicle Surveillance Applications; 2016. 04. 07—08; Berlin, Germany.

- ❏ Positionierung und Navigation für Intelligente Transportsysteme（德语）; 2016. 07. 05—06; Germany.

- ❏ International Symposium Information on Ships; 2016. 09. 01—02; Hamburg, Germany.

- ❏ DGON Inertial Sensors and Systems（ISS）Symposium Gyro Technology; 2016. 09; Karlsruhe, Germany.

- ❏ Der Alpenraum und seine Herausforderung an ORientierung, Navigation und Informationsaustausch（德语）; 2016. 11. 12; Germany.

德国工业设备有限公司

德语名称：Industrieanlagen – Betriebsgesellschaft mbH

英文名称：IABG

网　　址：http：//www. iabg. de/index_ en. php

机构简介

德国工业设备有限公司于 1961 年作为德国国防部和航空航天产业的中央分析与测试机构而成立，1993 年被私有化。

德国工业设备有限公司是欧洲领先的技术与科学服务提供商，提供涉及以下领域的分析、技术及操作解决方案，如自动化、信息通信、机动及能源环境、航空、空间、防务与安全等。公司在德国及欧盟拥有 1 000 多名员工。

出版物

小册子

- ❏ Automotive – Intelligent Automotive Services.
- ❏ Computer Aided Engineering – Simulation，Analysis，Optimisation.
- ❏ Durability – Stress and strain.
- ❏ Climate Simulation – All the year. Realistic. Reproducible.
- ❏ Material Characterisation – Material characterisation and damage analysis.
- ❏ Mechatronics – When testing meets intelligence.

会议信息

- ❏ The IT Security Expo and Congress；2015. 10. 06—08；Nürnberg，Germany.

意大利

莱昂纳多公司

英文名称：Leonardo Company

网　　址：http：//www. leonardocompany. com

机构简介

莱昂纳多公司的前身是意大利芬梅卡尼卡集团，由工业复兴集团公司（Istituto Per La Ricoctmzione Industriale，IRI）在 1948 年建立，2016 年 1 月改为现名。之后，芬梅卡尼卡集团先后建立了塞列尼亚（Selenia）、阿利塔利亚（Aeritalia）、阿莱尼亚（Alenia，由 Aeritalia 和 Selenia 合并成立）、安塞尔多能源公司（Ansaldo Energia）、阿古斯特维斯特兰公司（AgustaWestland）、安萨多布雷达公司（AnsaldoBreda）、塞莱克斯 ES 公司（SELEX ES）、安萨尔多公司（Ansaldo STS）等。

莱昂纳多公司是意大利主要的工业集团，也是高科技领域的领头羊，业务主要集中在直升机、防务电子与安全、航空、航天等领域，这部分的业务产生的收入占集团总收入的 86%，订单数量占集团订单总量的 80%，员工人数占集团员工总数的 81%。莱昂纳多公司主要在意大利、英国、美国和波兰等 4 个市场开展业务，2014 年公司收入达 146. 63 亿欧元，约有员工 54 380 人。

出版物

报告

❏ India 2030：security and defence challenges and policies of an emerging world power.

❏ The regularity of irregular war：Counterinsurgency and its implication.

❏ The restructuring of the aerospace and defence sector：trends and evolutionary dynamics.

❏ Italy in a changing world. Suggestions for Italy's foreign policy（Original Title：L'Italia in un mondo che cambia. Suggerimenti per la politica estera dell'Italia）.

❏ Annual Report.

❏ Occasional Paper.

荷 兰

爱思唯尔出版集团

英文名称：Elsevier B. V.

网　　址：http：//www. elsevier. com/

机构简介

爱思唯尔出版集团隶属于 RELX 集团（RELX Group plc），已经有 130 多年的历史。作为一家经营科学、技术和医学信息产品的世界一流出版集团，爱思唯尔出版集团长期致力于为用户提供优质灵活的信息解决方案，提高全球范围内研究人员的效率，从而推动科学、技术和医学的发展。

爱思唯尔出版集团的数字化平台包括 ScienceDirect、Scopus、Elsevier Research Intelligence 和 ClinicalKey，出版2 500多种期刊、33 000 多本图书。其出版物涉及多个学科领域，如：农业与生物科学，艺术与人文学科，天文学、天体物理与空间科学，建筑环境，商业、管理和会计，化学工程，化学，计算机科学，决策科学，牙科，药物发现，地球和行星科学，经济与财政，能源与动力，工程与技术，环境科学，辩论术，专业健康，免疫学，生命科学，材料科学，数学，医学，微生物与生态学，神经系统科学，看护，药物科学，药理学，物理，社会科学，毒物学，兽医科学和兽医药物等。

爱思唯尔出版集团总部位于荷兰的阿姆斯特丹，在全球多地设有办事机构，拥有 7 000 多名员工。

出版物

1）期刊与杂志

❏ Advanced Engineering Informatics.

❏ Applied Computing and Informatics.

❏ Astronomy and Computing.

❏ AEU – International Journal of Electronics and Communications.

❏ Electrochimica Acta.

❏ Solid State Communications.

❏ Microelectronics Reliability.

❏ Optics Communications.

❏ Communications in Nonlinear Science and Numerical Simulation.

- ❑ Catalysis Communications.
- ❑ Inorganic Chemistry Communications.
- ❑ Computer Physics Communications.
- ❑ Solid State Communications.
- ❑ Electrochemistry Communications.

2) 图书

- ❑ Acoustic Emission (AE) and Related Non – destructive Evaluation (NDE) Techniques in the Fracture Mechanics of Concrete.
- ❑ Adaptive Radar Resource Management.
- ❑ Additives for Polyolefins (Second Edition) .
- ❑ Adhesives Technology Handbook (Third Edition) .
- ❑ Advances in Composites Manufacturing and Process Design.
- ❑ Applications of Graphene and Graphene – Oxide based Nanomaterials.
- ❑ Advanced Theory of Constraint and Motion Analysis for Robot Mechanisms.
- ❑ Analog Circuit Design, Volume Three.

会议信息

- ❑ 10th Brain Research Conference; 2015. 10. 15; Chicago, USA.
- ❑ 16th Tetrahedron Symposium Asia Edition; 2015. 11. 10; Shanghai, China.
- ❑ 17th Tetrahedron Symposium; 2016. 06. 28; Sitges, Spain.
- ❑ Seventh International Conference on Engineering Failure Analysis; 2016. 07. 03; Leipzig, Germany.
- ❑ Biometrics 2015; 2015. 10. 13; Westminster, London.
- ❑ 4th Nano Today Conference; 2015. 12. 06; Dubai, UAE.

荷兰国际影像卫星公司

英文名称：ImageSat International N. V. , ImageSat

网　　址：http：//www. imagesatintl. com/

机构简介

荷兰国际影像卫星公司成立于 1997 年，是一家国际性的高分辨率卫星地球图像提供商，其数据由该公司的地球资源观测卫星（Earth Resource Observation Satellite，EROS）收集提供。2000 年 12 月，荷兰国际影像卫星公司发射了其第一颗卫星

EROS A,2006 年 4 月成功发射了其第二颗卫星 EROS B。在高清卫星图像领域，该公司的竞争力主要体现在：独家的服务包，对 EROS 卫星的独家运用，灵活的成像参数，国际化的操作，快速的图像获取和传送，有竞争力的价格，无风险的服务（先服务后付款）。

荷兰射电天文学研究所

英文名称：Netherlands Institute for Radio Astronomy，ASTRON

网　　址：http：//www. astron. nl/

机构简介

荷兰射电天文学研究所建立于1949 年，是一个非营利性组织，有员工约 160 人。

荷兰射电天文学研究所主要由荷兰科学研究组织（Netherlands Organisation for Scientific Research，NWO）资助，其他的资助机构包括欧盟委员会、荷兰政府等，还包括一些地区性的资助。荷兰射电天文学研究所设有 4 个重要的部门：天文小组，总务部门，射电天文台部门，研发部门。

荷兰射电天文学研究所从事天文与相关技术研发的基础研究、无线电望远镜等设备的制造、无线电望远镜的操作等，在国际射电天文学界有着重要作用。

会议信息

❑ CURSUS TOEGEPASTE RF TECHNIEK；2015. 11. 02—04；ASTRON.

挪　威

康斯伯格卫星服务公司

英文名称：Kongsberg Satellite Services AS，KSAT

网　　址：http：//www.ksat.no/

机构简介

康斯伯格卫星服务公司的历史可追溯至20世纪60年代，是总部位于挪威特罗姆瑟的一家商业卫星公司，约有135名员工。该公司由挪威康斯伯格集团和挪威航天有限公司（Space Norway AS）共同拥有，各持股50%。

康斯伯格卫星服务公司为80多颗卫星提供支持，包括高分辨率合成孔径雷达卫星和电光卫星等。特罗姆瑟网络操作中心（Tromsø Network Operations Centre）全天候运行，为卫星服务提供保障。

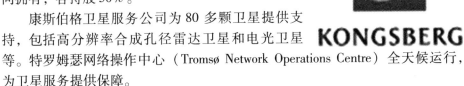

康斯伯格卫星服务公司主要提供海上态势感知和多任务快速反应服务，还通过位于斯瓦尔巴德的地面站——世界上唯一能够提供全轨道支持服务的地面站——为卫星拥有者提供以下服务，主要包括：

（1）遥测、追踪与指挥服务；

（2）发射与早期轨道阶段支持；

（3）数据获取、处理、传播及建档；

（4）客户供应设备的保护和操作。

出版物

小册子

❑ Company Profile.

❑ About KSAT.

❑ Welcome to Svalbard.

❑ Annual report 2012.

❑ Ground Station Network.

❑ Multi Mission Service.

西班牙

西班牙茵德拉系统公司

英文名称：Indra Sistemas，S. A.，Indra

网　　址：http：//www. indracompany. com/

企业概况

西班牙茵德拉系统公司的历史可追溯至1921 年。1992 年，西班牙将其在电子、IT、通信领域的重要公司合并，成立了一个新的全球性公司，并于 1993 年更名为茵德拉系统公司。

茵德拉系统公司的总部位于西班牙马德里，是领先的机载电子设备系统的供应商，又是欧洲重要的军用电子设备合同商。供应的产品包括用于欧洲歼击机和新型战斗机的电子设备，以及多用途显示器和火控装置等。该公司还是西班牙领先的咨询与技术公司，也是欧洲和拉丁美洲最突出的公司之一，主要提供商业解决方案、IT 服务、综合系统等，涉及的领域包括能源与工业、金融服务、电信与媒体、公共与医疗、运输与交通、安全与防务等。

茵德拉系统公司与全球 240 多家公司有正式的合作关系，如华为公司、IBM 公司、微软公司、日立数据系统公司（HITACHI Data Systems）、塞莱克斯通信公司（SELEX Communications）等。

茵德拉系统公司于 2000 年在北京设立了代表处，并于 2002 年创建了茵德拉信息技术系统有限公司，主要负责中国区域的空中交通管制、航空模拟、高速公路和隧道的交通控制系统、铁路访问控制系统和安全系统。

2014 年，茵德拉系统公司的营业额达到 30 亿欧元，在 149 个国家和地区拥有 39 000 多名员工，业务遍布全球 128 个国家和地区。

出版物

报告

❏ Annual Report.

第四部分

亚洲机构

日　本
印　度
土耳其
新加坡
以色列

日 本

电晕出版株式会社

日语名称: コロナ社

英文名称: Corona Publishing Co. , Ltd

网 址: http: //www. coronasha. co. jp

机构简介

电晕出版株式会社于 1927 年正式成立，主要出版有关电气工程学以及机械、金属、数学、原子能、化工等领域的专业性图书，涉及机械、核技术、电子电力学、情报科学、化学、生命科学、数学、医学、建筑、物理学、计量、环境等学科，每年大约出版新书 50~60 种。

出版物

1) 图书

❑ 生活支援工学概論。

❑ 石炭の科学と技術 – 未来につなぐエネルギー。

❑ ポイントマスター電子回路 トレーニングノート。

❑ 続 英語で学ぶ生物学 – 生物科学の新しい挑戦。

❑ 太陽エネルギー社会を築く材料テクノロジー（Ⅱ） – 材料プロセス編。

❑ 太陽エネルギー社会を築く材料テクノロジー（Ⅰ） – 材料・デバイス編。

❑ フィードバック制御理論 – 安定化と最適化。

❑ 例解 ディジタル信号処理入門。

❑ 磁気工学の基礎と応用。

❑ フィードバック制御の基礎と応用。

2) 词典

❑ 改訂コンピュータ用語辞典。

❑ 新版電気用語辞典。

❑ 新版音響用語辞典。

❑ 改訂電子情報通信用語辞典。

- ❏ 新版放射線医療用語辞典。
- ❏ 機械用語辞典。
- ❏ 原子力用語辞典。
- ❏ 土木用語辞典。
- ❏ 学術用語集・電気工学編（増訂 2 版）・計測工学編・原子力工学編。
- ❏ 新版精密工作便覧。
- ❏ 新安全工学便覧。
- ❏ 臨床 ME ハンドブック。
- ❏ 海洋工学ハンドブック。
- ❏ 新版ロボット工学ハンドブック。
- ❏ 塑性加工標準用語集。
- ❏ エネルギー便覧（資源編）。
- ❏ エネルギー便覧（プロセス編）。
- ❏ エネルギー・環境キーワード辞典。
- ❏ 生物工学ハンドブック。
- ❏ 光情報通信技術ハンドブック。
- ❏ 大電流工学ハンドブック。
- ❏ 光通信・光メモリ用語辞典。
- ❏ 新版画像電子ハンドブック。
- ❏ 映像情報メディア用語辞典。
- ❏ 改訂 ME 機器ハンドブック。
- ❏ 改訂医用超音波機器ハンドブック。
- ❏ ME 用語辞典。
- ❏ 生産システム便覧。
- ❏ モード解析ハンドブック。
- ❏ 塑性加工用語辞典。
- ❏ 混相流用語辞典。
- ❏ 原子炉水化学ハンドブック。
- ❏ 生物生産機械ハンドブック。
- ❏ 廃棄物小事典新訂版。
- ❏ 石炭利用技術用語辞。

3）講座

日本产业技术综合研究院

日语名称： 独立行政法人産業技術総合研究所

英文名称： National Institute of Advanced Industrial Science and Technology, AIST

网　　址： http：//www. aist. go. jp/

机构简介

日本产业技术综合研究院于 2001 年 4 月由原通产省工业技术院所属的 15 个国立研究所组建成立，是日本最大的公开研究机构之一，研究涉及能源与环境、生命科学与生物技术、信息技术与人因、材料与化学、电子与制造、日本地质勘查等。该研究院设有 9 个研究基地、5 个研究部门和 2 个研究中心，并设有日本国家计量研究院，致力于研究和开发计量标准和标准物质，特别是通过制定纳米长度标准和超高温温度标准，为工业和制造业技术的进步提供支持。

日本产业技术综合研究院还积极开展与国外机构的技术交流，积极开展国际标准比对，负责社会需要的测量技术人员的培训工作，有员工 2 900 多人。

出版物

1）期刊与杂志

❑ AIST TODAY（International Edition），季刊。

❑ Synthesiology – English edition，季刊。

2）报告

❑ AIST Report.

3）其他出版物

❑ AIST Brochure.

❑ AIST – Organization and Outline.

会议信息

❑ Japan Virtual Robotics Challenge（JVRC）；2015. 10. 07—10；Chiba, Japan.

日本船舶电装协会

英文名称： The Ship's Electric Installation Contractors' Association of Japan

网　　址： http：//www. ship – densou. or. jp/

机构简介

日本船舶电装协会成立于 1968 年，主要负责对会员企业/单位进行技术指导、培训，提供实施船舶电气装备技术的培训与实验，目的是推动日本船舶电气装备业务的进步和发展，促进船舶安全和性能的提高。

出版物

1）会议录（主要是讲座记录）

❑ 船舶電気装備技術講座［電気装備概論編］（初級）

❑ 船舶電気装備技術講座［電気艤装工事編］（初級）

❑ 船舶電気装備技術講座［電気機器編］（初級）

❑ 船舶電気装備技術講座［電気工学の基礎編］（初級）

❑ 船舶電気装備技術講座［電気艤装設計編］（中級）

❑ 船舶電気装備技術講座［試験・検査編］（中級）

❑ 船舶電気装備技術講座［電気装備技術基準編］（中級）

❑ 船舶電気装備技術講座［電気計算編］（中級）

❑ 船舶電気装備技術講座［高圧電気設備編］（上級）

2）报告

❑ 船舶電装工事（電路軽量化）の技術革新のための調査研究報告書

❑ 電線貫通部の工事方法に関する調査研究報告書

❑ 接着剤を用いた新しい電装工事方法に関する調査研究報告書

❑ 船舶電装工事の技術革新のための調査研究報告書

❑ 船舶電装工事の技術革新のための調査研究報告書

3）规则

❑ 船舶設備関係法令及び規則［資格更新研修用テキスト（強電用)］

❑ 船舶設備関係法令及び規則［資格更新研修用テキスト（弱電用)］
航海用レーダー

❑ 船舶設備関係法令及び規則［資格更新研修用テキスト（弱電用)］
GMDSS 設備・航海用具

❑ 船舶電気装備工事関係法令・規則集（CD 版）

日本电气计测器工业协会

日语名称：日本電気計測器工業会
英文名称：Japan Electric Measuring Instruments Manufacturers' Association，
JEMIMA
网　　址：http：//www. jemima. or. jp/english_ top. html

机构简介

日本电气计测器工业协会成立于
1948 年，1959 年设立了日本电气计测
器工业协会标准（JEMIMA standards，
JEMIS）。

日本电气计测器工业协会是其所处行业唯一一个日本协会，通过三大委员
会及下属委员会开展活动，如：进行日本国内外法规的调研，推动国际标准化
相关的活动，统计相关的活动，以及促进电气测量仪器电磁兼容、环境、安全
等相关技术发展的活动等。

日本电气计测器工业协会下设的委员会具体如下。

一、公共职能委员会

❑ 规划与推动委员会。

❑ 调研与统计委员会。

❑ 测量与控制东京展组委会。

❑ 测量与控制大阪展组委会。

❑ 公共关系委员会。

❑ 产品安全/电磁兼容委员会。

❑ 国际事务委员会。

❑ 董事会输出控制委员会。

❑ 知识产权委员会。

❑ 零部件与材料采购委员会。

❑ 绿色产品委员会。

❑ 校准服务委员会。

❑ 能源/低碳委员会。

❑ 先进技术战略研究委员会。

二、产品委员会

❑ 指示仪器委员会。

❑ 电计量委员会。

❑ 电子测量仪器与系统委员会。

❑ 温度测量委员会。

❑ 爆炸保护委员会。

❑ 环境测量委员会。

❑ 辐射测量委员会。

三、ISO, IEC 国家委员会

❑ ISO/TC30 日本国家委员会。

❑ IEC/TC45 日本国家委员会。

❑ IEC/TC65 日本国家委员会。

日本电气计测器工业协会总部位于东京，在大阪设有办事机构，拥有约86 家常规会员和约 36 家支持会员，每年组织测量与控制展览，还组织相关的研讨会，以促进相关技术及信息的交流。

出版物

1）标准

❑ Long – term Stability of a Magnetic Flow Meter.

❑ Face – to – Face Dimensions of a Magnetic Waterworks Meter.

❑ Voltage Variation and Flicker Tolerable Value of Low – voltage Power Supply Systems Used Industrial Process Measurement and Control Equipment Less Than 16 A in Rated Current.

❑ Tolerable Values of Electromagnetic Wave Interference Characteristics of Industrial Process Measurement and Control Equipment and Measurement of Them.

2）调查报告

❑ Security Export Control Textbook for Clear Understanding – From ABC to Practical Operation, 2 Edition.

❑ Mid – term Forecast of Electric Measuring Instruments 2013—2017.

会议信息

❑ Measurement and Control Show, October every year.

❑ Measurement and Control Show 2015 TOKYO；2015. 12. 02—04；Tokyo, Japan.

日本电子情报通信学会

日语名称：电子情报通信学会

英文名称：Institute of Electronics, Information and Communication Engineers, IEICE

网　　址：http：//www. ieice. org/

机构简介

日本电子情报通信学会的历史可追溯至 1911 年成立的第二研究小组（Second Study Group），1914 年该小组更名为电报电话研究会（Study Group on Telegraph and Telephone）。1917 年 5 月，日本电报电话工程师学会成立，1937 年更名为日本电气通信工程师学会（Institute of Electrical Communication Engineers of Japan），1967 年更名为日本电子与通信工程师学会（Institute of Electronics and Communication Engineers of Japan），1987 年改为现名，以表明其关注领域延伸到信息技术领域。

日本电子情报通信学会是日本重要的学术团体，下设 4 个委员会：工程学委员会、通信委员会、电子委员会、情报与系统委员会，还设有一个人类通信小组。日本电子情报通信学会拥有各种会员 31 000 多人，在日本有 20 多个分部。

出版物

1）期刊与杂志

❑ Journal of IEICE, monthly.

2）学报

❑ IEICE Transactions on Communications.

❑ IEICE Transactions on Electronics.

❑ IEICE Transactions on Information and System.

❑ IEICE Transactions on Fundamentals of Electronics, Communications and Computer Sciences.

3）技术报告

❑ The Technical Report of The Proceeding of The Institute of Electronics; Information and communication Engineers.

4）其他出版物

❑ ESS – ENCE，英语，每月以邮件形式发送给会员。

会议信息

❑ Radio Communication Systems（RCS）——Topics：Wireless Communica-

tion Schemes, Wireless Communication Systems, Wireless Standards, etc;
2015. 10. 01—02; Yokosuka.

❑ Fuji Electric FA Components & System Co. , Ltd. Electromechanical Devices (EMD); 2015. 10. 02.

❑ Theoretical Foundations of Computing (COMP); 2015. 10. 02.

❑ Thought and Language (TL) ——Topics: resource, language and learning, co – creation in a place, thought and language, etc. ; 2015. 10. 04; WASEDA University.

❑ Nonlinear Problems (NLP), Circuits and Systems (CAS); 2015. 10. 05—06.

❑ Satellite Telecommunication (SAT) ——Topics: Satellite Communications, etc. ; 2015. 10. 07—08; Osaka University.

❑ International Convention Complex Computer System (CPSY), System Architecture (IPSJ – ARC) ——Topics: Emerging Computer Systems Exhibition; 2015. 10. 08.

❑ Pattern Recognition and Media Understanding (PRMU); 2015. 10. 08—09.

❑ Multimedia and Virtual Environment (MVE), Virtual Reality (HI – SIG – VR); 2015. 10. 08—09.

❑ Wideband System (WBS) ——Topics: Green Wireless System, Poster Session, etc. ; 2015. 10. 08—09; WASEDA University.

❑ Component Parts and Materials; 2015. 10. 14; Kikai – Shinko – Kaikan Bldg.

❑ Network Systems (NS); 2015. 10. 15—16; Akita University.

❑ Information Networks (IN) ——Topics: Contingency Plan/BCP, Robustness, Security and Privacy, Authentication/ID management, Web Service/SOA/ROA Platform, Social Networking Service (SNS), etc. ; 2015. 10. 15—16; Osaka University.

❑ Organic Molecular Electronics (OME) ——Topics: Organic Thin Film, Organic Device, etc. ; 2015. 10. 16; Kikai – Shinko – Kaikan Bldg.

❑ Reliability (R); 2015. 10. 16.

❑ Internet Architecture (IA) ——Topics: Network R&D Testbed Operation and Utilization, etc. (cosponsored by ADVNET); 2015. 10. 19; University of Tokyo.

❑ Safety (SSS); 2015. 10. 20.

❑ Electron Device (ED); 2015. 10. 22—23.

❑ Optical Fiber Technology (OFT); 2015. 10. 22—23.

❑ Antennas and Propagation (AP) ——Topics: Antenna and Propagation;

2015. 10. 22—23；Yamaguchi, JAPAN.

❑ Electromagnetic Compatibility (EMCJ), Electromagnetic Compatibility (IEE – EMC), Microwave Engineering (MW), Electronics Simulation Technology (EST) ——Topics：Microwave, Electromagnetic Analysis, EMC, etc.；2015. 10. 22—23；Tohoku University.

❑ Magnetic Recording (MR), Multi – media Storage (ITE – MMS) ——Topics：Recording Head, Spintronics, etc；2015. 10. 22—23；Osaka University.

❑ Organic Molecular Electronics (OME) ——Topics：Organic devices and sensors, etc.；2015. 10. 23；Osaka University.

❑ Well – being Information Technology (WIT) ——Topics：Ergonomics and Well – being Information Technology, etc.；2015. 10. 25—26；Kawatana, JAPAN.

❑ Integrated Circuits and Devices (ICD), Image Engineering (IE), VLSI Design Technologies (VLD), System and LSI Design Methodology (IPSJ – SLDM)；2015. 10. 26—27.

❑ Short Range Wireless Communications (SRW) ——Topics：Network · MAC, sensor, etc.；2015. 10. 26；Tokyo, JAPAN.

❑ Silicon Device and Materials (SDM) ——Topics：Process Science and New Process Technology；2015. 10. 29—30；Tohoku University.

❑ Opto – Electronics (OPE), Lasers and Quantum Electronics (LQE), Optical Communication Systems (OCS)；2015. 10. 29—30；Beppu, JAPAN.

❑ Electromagnetic Theory (EMT), Electromagnetic Theory (IEE – EMT) ——Topics：Electromagnetic Theory, etc.；2015. 10. 29—31；Miyazaki, JAPAN.

❑ Space, Aeronautical and Navigational Electronics (SANE) ——Topics：Radar signal processing and general issues；2015. 10. 30.

❑ Nonlinear Problems (NLP) ——Topics：Nonlinear Problems, etc.；2015. 10. 31—11. 01.

❑ Educational Technology (ET) ——Topics：Advanced Education/Learning Support, etc.；2015. 10. 31；Yufuin, JAPAN.

❑ Antennas and Propagation (AP), Radio Communication Systems (RCS), Wireless Power Transfer (WPT), Satellite；2015. 11. 04—06；Okinawa, JAPAN.

❑ Silicon Device and Materials (SDM) ——Topics：Process, Device, and Circuit Simulation, etc.；2015. 11. 05—06；Kikai – Shinko – Kaikan Bldg.

❑ Ambient intelligence and Sensor Networks (ASN) ——Topics：Agriculture

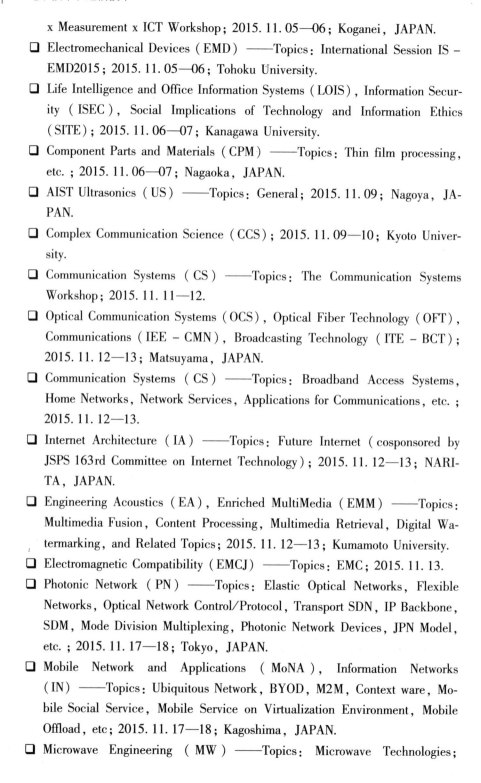

x Measurement x ICT Workshop; 2015. 11. 05—06; Koganei, JAPAN.

❑ Electromechanical Devices (EMD) ——Topics: International Session IS – EMD2015; 2015. 11. 05—06; Tohoku University.

❑ Life Intelligence and Office Information Systems (LOIS), Information Security (ISEC), Social Implications of Technology and Information Ethics (SITE); 2015. 11. 06—07; Kanagawa University.

❑ Component Parts and Materials (CPM) ——Topics: Thin film processing, etc. ; 2015. 11. 06—07; Nagaoka, JAPAN.

❑ AIST Ultrasonics (US) ——Topics: General; 2015. 11. 09; Nagoya, JAPAN.

❑ Complex Communication Science (CCS); 2015. 11. 09—10; Kyoto University.

❑ Communication Systems (CS) ——Topics: The Communication Systems Workshop; 2015. 11. 11—12.

❑ Optical Communication Systems (OCS), Optical Fiber Technology (OFT), Communications (IEE – CMN), Broadcasting Technology (ITE – BCT); 2015. 11. 12—13; Matsuyama, JAPAN.

❑ Communication Systems (CS) ——Topics: Broadband Access Systems, Home Networks, Network Services, Applications for Communications, etc. ; 2015. 11. 12—13.

❑ Internet Architecture (IA) ——Topics: Future Internet (cosponsored by JSPS 163rd Committee on Internet Technology); 2015. 11. 12—13; NARITA, JAPAN.

❑ Engineering Acoustics (EA), Enriched MultiMedia (EMM) ——Topics: Multimedia Fusion, Content Processing, Multimedia Retrieval, Digital Watermarking, and Related Topics; 2015. 11. 12—13; Kumamoto University.

❑ Electromagnetic Compatibility (EMCJ) ——Topics: EMC; 2015. 11. 13.

❑ Photonic Network (PN) ——Topics: Elastic Optical Networks, Flexible Networks, Optical Network Control/Protocol, Transport SDN, IP Backbone, SDM, Mode Division Multiplexing, Photonic Network Devices, JPN Model, etc. ; 2015. 11. 17—18; Tokyo, JAPAN.

❑ Mobile Network and Applications (MoNA), Information Networks (IN) ——Topics: Ubiquitous Network, BYOD, M2M, Context ware, Mobile Social Service, Mobile Service on Virtualization Environment, Mobile Offload, etc; 2015. 11. 17—18; Kagoshima, JAPAN.

❑ Microwave Engineering (MW) ——Topics: Microwave Technologies;

2015. 11. 19—20；University of the Ryukyus.

❑ Reliability（R）；2015. 11. 19.

❑ Mathematical Systems Science and its applications（MSS），Circuits and Systems（CAS），Algorithms（IPSJ – AL）；2015. 11. 12—21；Ibusuki，JAPAN.

❑ Space，Aeronautical and Navigational Electronics（SANE）——Topics：IC-SANE 2015；2015. 11. 23—24；Bangkok，Thailand.

❑ Information Theory（IT）——Topics：Lectures for Young Researchers（Invited talks only）；2015. 11. 24.

❑ Space，Aeronautical and Navigational Electronics（SANE）——Topics：The 13th workshop on subsurface electromagnetic measurement；2015. 11. 26—27；Tohoku University.

❑ Safety（SSS）；2015. 11. 26.

❑ Communication Quality（CQ），Information and Communication Management（ICM），Network Systems（NS）——Topics：Network Quality，Network Measurement and Management，Network Virtualization，Network Service，General；2015. 11. 26—27；Niigata University.

❑ Image Media Quality（IMQ）；2015. 11. 27.

❑ Microwave and Millimeter – wave Photonics（MWP）——Topics：Transportation Systems，etc. ；2015. 11. 27；Kikai – Shinko – Kaikan Bldg.

❑ Opto – Electronics（OPE），Organic Molecular Electronics（OME）；2015. 11. 27；Kikai – Shinko – Kaikan Bldg.

❑ Theoretical Foundations of Computing（COMP）；2015. 12. 01.

❑ Human Information Processing（HIP），Human Information（ITE – HI），Consumer Electronics（ITE – CE）；2015. 12. 01—02；Tohoku University.

❑ Audio Visual and Multimedia Information Processing（IPSJ – AVM），Communication Systems（CS），Image Engineering（IE），Broadcasting Technology（ITE – BCT）——Topics：Image Coding，Streaming，etc. ；2015. 12. 03—04.

❑ Educational Technology（ET），Social Implications of Technology and Information Ethics（SITE），Computers in Education（IPSJ – CE），Collaboration and Learning Environment（IPSJ – CLE）——Topics：Use of Learning Data，etc. ；2015. 12. 04—05；Community Fukui，JAPAN.

❑ Software Enterprise Modeling（SWIM）——Topics：Model implementation，etc. （Work Shop）；2015. 12. 05；Tokyo polytechnic University.

❑ Well being Information Technology（WIT）——Topics：Well – being Information Technology, etc. ; 2015. 12. 09; Tokyo, JAPAN.

❑ Wireless Power Transfer (WPT) ——Topics: 2015 Asian Wireless Power Transfer Workshop (AWPT2015) ; 2015. 12. 10—11.

❑ Opto – Electronics (OPE) ; 2015. 12. 10—11.

❑ Antennas and Propagation (AP) ——Topics: Antenna and Propagation, 50th anniversary; 2015. 1210—11; Kikai – Shinko – Kaikan Bldg.

❑ Engineering Acoustics (EA) ——Topics: General topics; 2015. 12. 11—12; Kanazawa University.

❑ Microwave Engineering (MW) ——Topics: Students Session/Microwave Technologies; 2015. 12. 17—18; Tokyo University of Science.

❑ Network Systems (NS), Radio Communication Systems (RCS) .

❑ Information Networks (IN), Internet Architecture (IA) ——Topics: Performance Analysis and Simulation, Robustness, Traffic and Throughput Measurement, Quality of Service (QoS) Control, Congestion Control, Overlay Network/P2P, IPv6, Multicast, Routing, DDoS, etc. ; 2015. 12. 17—18; Hiroshima City University.

❑ Safety (SSS) ; 2015. 12. 17.

❑ Antennas and Propagation (AP) ——Topics: Measurement Technique of Radio Equipment and Antenna Systems; 2015. 12. 18; Miyako, JAPAN.

❑ Electromagnetic Compatibility (EMCJ), * (IEE – EMC) ——Topics: Power electronics, EMC; 2015. 12. 18; Aichi – ken, JAPAN.

❑ Lasers and Quantum Electronics (LQE) ; 2015. 12. 18.

❑ Information Security (ISEC) ; 2015. 12. 18; Kikai – Shinko – Kaikan Bldg.

❑ Reliability (R) ; 2015. 12. 18.

❑ Ultrasonics (US) ——Topics: High Power Ultrasound, General; 2015. 12. 21; Tokyo, JAPAN.

❑ Pattern Recognition and Media Understanding (PRMU) ; 2015. 21. 21—22.

❑ Short Range Wireless Communications (SRW) ——Topics: WLAN · WPAN · Sensor networks etc. ; 2015. 12. 21.

❑ Microwave Engineering (MW) ——Topics: Microwave Technologies/50th Anniversary Special Talks; 2016. 01. 14—15; Kikai – Shinko – Kaikan Bldg.

❑ Antennas and Propagation (AP) ——Topics: Antenna and Propagation; 2016. 01. 14—15; Takushoku University.

❑ Radio Communication Systems (RCS), Information Theory (IT), Signal Processing (SIP) ——Topics: Signal Processing for Wireless Communications, Learning, Mathematical Science, Communication Theory, etc. ; 2016. 01. 18—19; Osaka, JAPAN.

- [ ] Communication Quality (CQ); 2016. 01. 21—22; University of Tsukuba.
- [ ] Space, Aeronautical and Navigational Electronics (SANE) ——Topics: Positioning, navigation, radar and general; 2016. 01. 21—22; Nagasaki, JAPAN.
- [ ] Network Systems (NS); 2016. 01. 21—22.
- [ ] Information Networks (IN) ——Topics: Contents Delivery/Contents Exchange, Social Networking Service (SNS), Data Analysis/Processing Platform, Big Data, etc. ; 2016. 01. 21—22; Nagoya, JAPAN.
- [ ] Pattern Recognition and Media Understanding (PRMU), * (IPSJ – CVIM), Multimedia and Virtual Environment (MVE); 2016. 01. 21—22.
- [ ] Communication Systems (CS), Optical Communication Systems (OCS) —— Topics: Network Core/Metro Systems, Submarine Transmission Systems, Optical Access Systems/Next Generation PON, Ethernet, Optical Transport Network (OTN), Transmission Monitoring and Supervisory Control, Optical Transmission System Design/Tools, Mobile Optical Network; 2016. 01. 21—22; Kagoshima University.
- [ ] Information and Communication Management (ICM), Life Intelligence and Office Information Systems (LOIS) ——Topics: Practical Use of Lifelog, Office Information System, Business Management, etc. ; 2016. 01. 21—22; Fukuoka Institute of Technology.
- [ ] Mathematical Systems Science and its applications (MSS), Software Science (SS); 2016. 01. 25—26; Shiinoki – Geihin – Kan.
- [ ] Knowledge – based Software Engineering (KBSE); 2016. 01. 25—26.
- [ ] Technology Electromagnetic Compatibility (EMCJ), Wireless Power Transfer (WPT) ——Topics: Communication, Wireless Power Transmission, EMC; 2016. 01. 28—29; Kumamoto National College.
- [ ] Lasers and Quantum Electronics (LQE), Electronics Simulation Technology (EST), Opto – Electronics (OPE), Electromagnetic Theory (EMT), Photonic Network (PN), Microwave and Millimeter – wave Photonics (MWP), Electromagnetic Theory (IEE – EMT); 2016. 01. 28—29.
- [ ] Neurocomputing (NC), Nonlinear Problems (NLP) ——Topics: Implementation of Neuro Computing, Analysis and Modeling of Human Science, etc. ; 2016. 01. 28—29.
- [ ] Ultrasonics (US), Engineering Acoustics (EA) ——Topics: [Joint Meet-

ing on Acoustics and Ultrasonics Subsociety〕Engineering/Electro Acoustics, Ultrasonic and Underwater Acoustics, and Related Topics; 2016. 01. 28—29; Kansai University.

❏ Internet Architecture (IA) ——Topics: Sensor Network, etc. ; 2016. 01. 29; Kikai – Shinko – Kaikan Bldg.

❏ Educational Technology (ET) ——Topics: Embodied Knowledge, Skill Support, etc. ; 2016. 01. 30; Kansai University.

❏ Satellite Telecommunication (SAT), Space, Aeronautical and Navigational Electronics (SANE) ——Topics: Satellite Application and General; 2016. 02. 16—17; Hiroshima Institute of Technology.

❏ Pattern Recognition and Media Understanding (PRMU), Cloud Network Robotics (CNR); 2016. 02. 18—19.

❏ Antennas and Propagation (AP) ——Topics: Antenna and Propagation, Company special edition; 2016. 02. 18—19; Iwaki, JAPAN.

❏ Software Enterprise Modeling (SWIM) ——Topics: Evaluation of business model and reliability, Student session, etc. ; 2016. 02. 26; Kikai – Shinko – Kaikan Bldg.

❏ Radio Communication Systems (RCS), Complex Communication Sciences (CCS), Smart Radio (SR), Short Range Wireless Communications (SRW) ——Topics: Mobile Communication Workshop; 2016. 03. 02—04; Tokyo Institute of Technology.

❏ Microwave Engineering (MW), Integrated Circuits and Devices (ICD) ——Topics: Microwave Integrated Circuit/Microwave Technologies; 2016. 03. 02—04; Hiroshima University.

❏ Network Systems (NS), Information Networks (IN) ——Topics: General; 2016. 03. 03—04; Seagaia, JAPAN.

❏ Communication Systems (CS), Circuits and Systems (CAS) ——Topics: Network Processor, Signal Processing Circuits for Communication, Wireless LAN/PAN, etc. ; 2016. 03. 03—04.

❏ Mathematical Systems Science and its applications (MSS); 2016. 03. 03—04.

❏ Knowledge – based Software Engineering (KBSE); 2016. 03. 03—04.

❏ Educational Technology (ET) ——Topics: E – Learning and ICT Cooperative Use by University etc. ; 2016. 03. 05; Kagawa University.

❏ Photonic Network (PN) ——Topics: Photonic network technologies, etc. ; 2016. 03. 07—08; Okinawa, JAPAN.

❏ Information Theory (IT), Information Security (ISEC), Wideband System

（WBS）——Topics：joint meeting of IT, ISEC, and WBS；2016. 03. 10—11；Tokyo, JAPAN.

❑ Safety（SSS）；2016. 03. 10.

❑ Information and Communication Management（ICM）——Topics：Element Management, Management Functionalities, Operations and Management Technologies；2016. 03. 10—11.

❑ Antennas and Propagation（AP）——Topics：Antenna and Propagation；2016. 03. 10—11.

❑ Electromagnetic Compatibility（EMCJ）——Topics：EMC；2016. 03. 11；Kikai – Shinko – Kaikan Bldg.

❑ Pattern Recognition and Media Understanding（PRMU）, Biometrics（BioX）；2016. 03. 24—25.

❑ Engineering Acoustics（EA）, Signal Processing（SIP）, Speech（SP）——Topics：Engineering/Electro Acoustics, Speech, Signal Processing, and Related Topics；2016. 03. 28—29.

❑ 2015 International Symposium on Communications and Information Technologies（ISCIT 2015）；2015. 10. 07—09；Nara, Japan.

❑ The 2015 International Symposium on Intelligent Signal Processing and Communication Systems（ISPACS 2015）；2015. 11. 09—12；Nusa Dua, Indonesia.

❑ 2015 International Symposium on Nonlinear Theory and its Applications（NOLTA 2015）；2015. 12. 01—04；Hong Kong, China.

❑ 21st Asia and South Pacific Design Automation Conference（ASP – DAC 2016）；2016. 01. 25—28；Macao, China.

❑ The 8th International Workshop on Image Media Quality and its Applications（IMQA 2016）；2016. 03. 10—11；Nagoya, Japan.

❑ The 21th Asia – Pacific Conference on Communications（APCC2015）；2016. 10. 14—16；Kyoto, Japan.

❑ 37th IEEE International Telecommunication Energy Conference（INTELEC 2015）；2016. 10. 18—22；Osaka, Japan.

❑ IEEE Conference on Standards for Communications & Networking（IEEE CSCN）；2016. 10. 28—30；Tokyo, Japan.

❑ International Conference on Information and Communication Technology Convergence 2015（ICTC 2015）；2016. 10. 28—30；Jeju Island, Korea.

❑ 2015 International Symposium on Antennas and Propagation（ISAP2015）；2015. 11. 09—12；Tasmania, Australia.

- ❑ 2016 International Symposium on Antennas and Propagation（ISAP2016）；
  2016. 10. 24—28；Okinawa，Japan.
- ❑ The 4th ENRI International Workshop on ATM/CNS（EIWAC2015）；
  2016. 11. 17—19；Tokyo，Japan.
- ❑ 4th International Conference on Renewable Energy Research and Applications（ICRERA2015）；2016. 11. 22—25；Palermo，Italy.

日本电子信息技术产业协会

日语名称：電子情報技術産業協会

英文名称：Japan Electronics and Information Technology Industries Association, JEITA

网　　址：http：//www.jeita.or.jp/english/

机构简介

日本电子信息技术产业协会于 2000 年由日本 **JEITA**
电子产业协会（Electronic Industries Association of
Japan）和日本电子产业发展协会（Japan Electronic Industries Development Association）合并成立。

日本电子信息技术产业协会是一家行业团体，旨在促进电子设备、电子元件的正常生产、贸易和消费，推动电子信息技术产业的综合发展，为日本的经济发展和文化繁荣作出贡献，目前正积极致力于解决电子材料、电子元器件、最终产品等众多领域的各种课题。

日本电子信息技术产业协会的附属协会、团体有：

（1）日本电气制造商协会（The Japan Electrical Manufacturers' Association, JEMA）；

（2）通信与信息网络协会（Communications and Information network Association of Japan, CIAJ）；

（3）日本数字内容协会（Digital Content Association of Japan, DCAJ）；

（4）家电产品协会（Association for Electric Home Appliances, AEHA）；

（5）家电产品 PL 中心（Electric Home Appliances PL Center）；

（6）日本电子封装与电路工业会（Japan Electronics Packaging and Circuits Association, JPCA）；

（7）日本电子元件性能中心（Reliability Center for Electronic Components of Japan, RCJ）；

（8）日本半导体设备协会（Semiconductor Equipment Association of Japan, SEAJ）；

（9）日本电气测量仪器制造商协会（Japan Electric Measuring Instruments Manufacturers' Association, JEMIMA）；

（10）商用机器信息系统产业协会（Japan Business Machine and Information System Industries Association, JBMIA）；

（11）超级先进电子技术协会（Association of Super – Advanced Electronics Technology, ASET）；

（12）关西电子工业振兴中心（Kansai Electronic Industry Development Center, KEC）；

（13）国际计算机化合作中心（Center of the International Cooperation for Computerization, CICC）；

（14）光电产业与技术发展协会（Optoelectronic Industry and Technology Development Association, OITDA）；

（15）TRON 协会（TRON Association）；

（16）国际超导技术研究中心（International Superconductivity Technology Center, ISTEC）；

（17）日本环境认证机构（Japan Audit and Certification Organization for Environment, JACO）；

（18）日本半导体尖端技术公司（Semiconductor Leading Edge Technologies, Inc. , Selete）；

（19）半导体技术学术研究中心（Semiconductor Technology Academic Research Center, STARC）；

（20）电磁环境实验所认定中心（Voluntary EMC Laboratory Accreditation Center Inc. , VLAC）。

出版物

1）标准

❑ AV&IT Technology Standardization.

❑ Information & Communications Standardization.

❑ Industrial Electronics Equipment Standardization.

❑ Electronic Components Standardization.

❑ Electronic Devices Standardization.

❑ Electronics Assembly System Standardization.

❑ Electronic Materials Standardization.

❑ Infomation Technology Standardization.

❑ Three – dimensional CAD Information.

❑ Printed Electronics Standardization.

2）其他出版物

❑ Industry Review: Electronics and Information Technology Industries in Japan.

❑ RENKEI Control Guidebook: Energy use optimisation technology by Green IT – From Introduction through Saving Verification.

❑ AV&IT 機器世界需要動向 ～2019 年までの展望～。

❑ AV&IT 機器世界需要動向 ～2018 年までの展望～。

- 2015 民生用電子機器国内出荷データ集。
- 移動電話に関する市場調査報告書。
- 主要電子機器の世界生産状況 2013 年~2015 年。
- 2024 年までの電子部品技術ロードマップ - ~変化する将来の生活環境と世界をリードする電子部品の動向~。
- フラットパネルディスプレイ（FPD）の人間工学シンポジウム2014 講演資料。
- 平成 26 年度 ソフトウェアに関する調査報告書 I、II、III（IS – 15 – 情シ – 1、2、3）。
- 平成 26 年度 クラウド利用におけるサービス品質の可視化（IS – 15 – 情シ – 6）。
- 端末装置に関する調査報告書（IS – 15 – 情端 – 5）。
- 磁気記憶装置に関する調査報告書（IS – 15 – 情端 – 4）。

日本光电产业与技术发展协会

英文名称：Optoelectronics Industry and Technology Development Association，OITDA

网　　址：http：//www. oitda. or. jp/

机构简介

日本光电产业与技术发展协会成立于1980 年，目的是推动光电产业和光电技术的发展进步，其研究涉及以下内容。

（1）光电技术路线图：提出光电技术在信息处理、通信、输入/输出等领域的具体需求。

（2）光电技术趋势：由光电技术趋势研究委员会对国内外当前状态及未来观点发展趋势，从多个角度进行连续跟踪和研究。

（3）光电产业趋势：每年进行调查并分析当前国内光电产业的规模并预测未来的趋势。

（4）产业—学术—政府合作：加强产业、学术与政府在光电领域的多角度合作，并促进最新的光电技术信息的交流。

除此之外，协会还支持新技术的开发，通过项目研发使自己始终走在技术发展前列，支持风险企业通过光电应用开发新设备和新系统。

日本光电产业与技术发展协会设有光电产业与技术标准化总委员会，建立光电产业的国内标准和国际标准，如通过创建 OITDA Standards 来推动国际标准化。协会还与国际光电协会（International Optoelectronics Associations，IOA，非正式组织）的会员展开广泛的合作与交流。

出版物

1）报告

❏ Annual Report.

2）标准

❏ File allocation system with minimized reallocation.

❏ Evaluation method of performance for dye – sensitized solar devices.

3）技术论文

❏ Discussion process of the standardization of wavelength selective switch interface specification.

❏ Fiber optic active components and devices – Test and measurement procedures – GPON transceivers.

❏ Investigation of examinations and measurements – Light – blocking performance of optical adaptor with shutter.

❑ Fiber optic active components and devices – Performance standard template – Wavelength tunable laser diode module for Dense WDM transmission.

❑ Dynamic Crosstalk Measurement for Wavelength Selective Switch.

会议信息

❑ International Optoelectronics Exhibition 2015（InterOpto 2015）；2015. 10. 14—16；Yokohama，Japan.

日本应用电磁学和力学学会

英文名称：Japan Society of Applied Electromagnetic and Mechanics，JSAEM

网　　址：http：//www. jsaem. gr. jp/index－e. html

机构简介

日本应用电磁学和力学学会成立于 1991 年，是世界上第一个促进应用电磁学的学会，主要目标是促进日本与国际间关于电磁力和从量子级现象到系统级现象的合作研究，主要研究方向是电磁、力学和材料科学。

日本应用电磁学和力学学会通过组织或赞助学术会议来促进联合研究和信息交流，最终促进新的研究领域和新技术的开发。该学会关注的领域包括：

（1）智能高密度电磁的应用；

（2）DDS 与电磁能的融合技术；

（3）智能电磁材料与结构的适应设计；

（4）无铅压电陶瓷。

出版物

1）期刊与杂志

❑ 日本 AEM 学会誌——Journal of the Japan Society of Applied Electromagnetics and Mechanics.

❑ International Journal of Applied Electromagnetics and Mechanics，季刊。

2）其他出版物

❑ Studies in Applied Electromagnetics and Mechanics.

❑ JSAEM Studies in Applied Electromagnetics and Mechanics.

❑ "Application of ElectroMagnetic Forces" series.

❑ 数値電磁界解析法の基礎、坪井始、内藤督 編著。

❑ 実践数値電磁界解析法、坪井始、内藤督 編著。

❑ 解析電磁気学と電磁構造、宮健三 著。

❑ メカトロニクスと運動制御入門、長屋幸助、長南征二、高木敏行、江鐘偉 著。

❑ 超電導の数理と応用、宮健三、吉田義勝 編著。

❑ 電磁現象と逆問題、小島史男、上坂充 編著。

会议信息

❑ 第 24 回 MAGDA コンファレンス，電磁現象及び電磁力に関するコンフアレンス；2015. 11. 12—14；东北大学，仙台，日本。

❑ 10th International Symposium on Advanced Science and Technology in Experimental Mechanics（10th ISEM '15 – Matsue）；2015. 11. 01—04；Matsue City，Japan.

日刊海事通信社

日语名称: 日刊海事通信社

网　　址: http: //www. kaijitsushin. jp/

机构简介

日刊海事通信社成立于 1949 年，同年报纸《日刊海事通信》开始发行。该通信社主要通过出版的刊物及其他出版物，向海运协会、造船及船舶工业协会等用户提供海运通信领域的信息。

出版物

1) 报纸

❏ 「日刊海事通信」每周 4 期。

2) 期刊与杂志

❏ 「フェリー·旅客船ガイド」，每年 2 期，4 月、10 月出版。

❏ 「海の情報誌 Marine」，每年 2 期，1 月、7 月出版。

❏ 「新造船工事予定表」，每年 4 其，1 月、4 月、7 月、10 月出版。

3) 年鉴

❏ 「海運·造船会社要覧」。

印　度

印度巴拉特电子有限公司

英文名称：Bharat Electronics Limited，BEL

网　　址：http：//www. bel - india. com

机构简介

印度巴拉特电子有限公司由印度国防部于 1954 年创立，位于班加罗尔，2014 至 2015 财年公司收入约达 66. 95 亿卢比（约 1. 02 亿美元），有员工 9 700 多人。

印度巴拉特电子有限公司主要是为了满足印度国防领域对电子产品的需求，其产品和服务涉及火控系统、雷达、军事通信、海军系统、电子战系统、C^4I 系统、电信、音视频广播、光电设备、坦克电子设备、太阳能光伏系统、嵌入式软件与电子元件等。此外，公司还提供整套系统解决方案，为满足印度和海外市场多个领域的客户需求服务。

印度巴拉特电子有限公司有 1 个子公司和 2 个合资公司。

（1）BEL Optronic Devices Limited（简称 BELOP）是印度巴拉特电子有限公司的子公司，位于浦那（Pune）的工业区，其成立是为了进行研发和制造供军方和安全领域及商业领域使用的图像增强管（Image Intersifier Tubes）以及高压电电源供应器。

（2）BEL - Thales Systems Limited 是巴拉特电子有限公司与泰雷兹集团在印度国防部批准于 2013 年批准、2014 年成立的公司，双方分别持股 74% 和 26%，负责民用及防务用雷达的设计、开发与供应，产品销往印度和全球市场。

（3）GE BE Pvt Limited（GEBEL）是印度巴拉特电子有限公司与通用电气医疗器械集团于 1997 年合资成立的公司，主要生产 CT Max 和先进的 X 射线管。

出版物

报告

❑ Annual Report.

土耳其

土耳其军用电子工业公司

英文名称：Aselsan A. S.

网　　址：http://www. aselsan. com. tr

机构简介

土耳其军用电子工业公司于 1975 年由土耳其军事基金会（Turkish Army Foundation）及两家私营企业合资组建，目的是为土耳其三军提供现代化的电子设备。目前，土耳其

武装部队基金会（Turkish Armed Forces Foundation）持有该公司 84.58% 的股份。

土耳其军用电子工业公司是土耳其一家主要的军用航空电子公司，是被列入防务新闻杂志的"世界百强军工企业"名单的第一个也是唯一一个土耳其国防工业公司。

2014 年，公司收入达 11.41 亿美元，有员工 4 200 多人，设有 5 个业务部门，分别是：

（1）通信与信息技术业务部门；

（2）微电子、指导与电光业务部门；

（3）雷达与电子战系统业务部门；

（4）防务系统技术业务部门；

（5）运输、安全、能源与自动化系统业务部门。

出版物

报告

❑ Annual Report.

新加坡

世界科技出版公司

英文名称：World Scientific Publishing Company，WSPC

网　　址：http://www.worldscientific.com/

机构简介

世界科技出版公司成立于1981 年，在 20 多年的时间里员工人数从 5 名发展到 600 多名。公司总部设在新加坡，在中国北

京、中国香港、中国台北、美国新泽西、英国伦敦、印度金奈等地拥有子公司或办事机构，现已经成为亚太地区最大的国际性科学出版商。

世界科技出版公司每年出版约 600 多种图书、130 多种各个领域的期刊，许多出版物受到哈佛大学、加州理工大学、斯坦福大学、普林斯顿大学等名校的推崇。其出版物涉及的学科包括亚洲研究、计算机科学、工程与声学、材料科学、纳米技术与纳米科学、非线性科学、混沌与动态系统、物理学、社会科学、生命科学/生物学、数学、医学、环境科学、经济与金融、商务管理、化学、建筑及建造管理等。

出版物

1）期刊与杂志

❏ International Journal of Structural Stability and Dynamics.

❏ International Journal of Reliability, Quality and Safety Engineering.

❏ Coastal Engineering Journal (CEJ).

❏ Journal of Earthquake and Tsunami (JET).

❏ China Quarterly of International Strategic Studies.

❏ TECHNOLOGY.

❏ Taiwan Veterinary Journal.

❏ Journal of Interconnection Networks.

❏ Functional Materials Letters (FML).

❏ NANO.

❏ International Journal of Nanoscience.

2）图书

- ❏ The Handbook on Reasoning – Based Intelligent Systems.
- ❏ Emergent Information: A Unified Theory of Information.
- ❏ Consciousness and Robot Sentience.
- ❏ Handbook of Carbon Nano Materials (In 2 Volumes).
- ❏ Innovative Thermoelectric Materials: Polymer, Nanostructure and Composite Thermoelectrics.
- ❏ X – Ray Scattering from Semiconductors and Other Materials.
- ❏ Scanning Transmission Electron Microscopy of Nanomaterials: Basics of Imaging and Analysis.
- ❏ Materials Thermodynamics: With Emphasis on Chemical Approach.
- ❏ Fundamentals of Atomic Force Microscopy: Part I: Foundations.
- ❏ Bio – Inspired Nanomaterials and Applications: Nano Detection, Drug/Gene Delivery, Medical Diagnosis and Therapy.
- ❏ Physical Properties of Carbon Nanotubes.
- ❏ Molecular Electronics: An Introduction to Theory and Experiment.
- ❏ Nanostructured Superconductors.
- ❏ Nanotechnology Challenges: Implications for Philosophy, Ethics and Society.
- ❏ Molecular Electronics: Commercial Insights, Chemistry, Devices, Architecture and Programming.
- ❏ Principles of Nanotechnology: Molecular – Based Study of Condensed Matter in Small Systems.
- ❏ Introduction to Nanoscience and Nanomaterials.

以色列

以色列埃尔比特系统公司

英文名称：Elbit Systems Ltd，ESLT

网　　址：http：//www.elbitsystems.com/elbitmain/

机构简介

埃尔比特系统公司由以色列埃尔隆电子实业公司于 1966 年组建成立，融合了以色列国防部研究所在特殊计算机设计和埃尔隆在电子

产品研制方面的专业实力。公司成立后迅速发展壮大，业务扩展到以色列飞机使用的导航系统、后勤支持的武器交付、梅卡瓦坦克使用的火控系统、以色列航空工业公司"狮"战斗机使用的作战航空电子包等，业务涉及军用飞机和直升机系统、头盔系统、商用飞行系统及航空结构、无人机和无人水面舰艇、陆地车辆系统、C⁴I 系统、情报与网络系统、光电与对抗系统、国土安全系统、电子战与信号情报系统等。

埃尔比特系统公司的总部位于以色列海法，2014 年的收入达 29.58 亿美元，约有 11 850 名员工，主要有以下子公司。

（1）埃尔比特系统埃洛普光电公司（Elbit Systems Electro – Optics – Elop Ltd.，Elop）有 70 多年的历史，位于雷霍沃特，主要负责用于国防、太空和国土安全领域的电光系统的设计制造。

（2）埃尔比特系统陆地与 C⁴I 公司（Elbit Systems Land and C⁴I Ltd.，ESLC）位于内坦亚，主要业务涉及路基系统、军用车辆产品、C⁴I 系统、通信系统与装备等。

（3）埃尔比特系统埃利斯拉电子战与信号情报公司（Elbit Systems EW and SIGINT – Elisra ltd.，Elisra）位于以色列伯尼布莱克，提供电子战、信号情报、红外无源预警系统和 C⁴ISR 技术解决方案。

（4）埃尔比特系统美国公司（Elbit Systems of America）主要在美国的阿拉巴马州和德克萨斯州开展业务，为美国军队、国土安全和医疗设备领域的客户提供产品与系统解决方案，是美国对外军售和对外军事资助（Foreign Military Financing，FMF）项目的承包商之一。

出版物

1) 报告

❑ Annual Report.

2) 手册

❑ Company Brochures.

第五部分

大洋洲机构

澳大利亚

澳大利亚

澳大利亚联邦科学与工业研究组织

英文名称：Commonwealth Scientific and Industrial Research Organisation，CSIRO

网　　址：http：//www. csiro. au/

机构简介

澳大利亚联邦科学与工业研究组织是澳大利亚最大的国家级科研机构，前身是于 1926 年成立的澳大利亚科学与工业顾问委员会（Advisory Council of Science and Industry）。

澳大利亚联邦科学与工业研究组织的总部位于堪培拉，在澳洲国立大学设有分部。在近一个世纪的发展中，该组织取得了多项重要的研究成果，如：发明了原子吸收光谱法，开发了世界上第一种塑料钞票，发明了航空驱虫剂和基因粘贴技术。该组织在信息通信技术方面的研究也取得了一系列成果，例如 Panoptic 搜索引擎（现改称 Funnelback）、votApedia 电话问卷系统和 Annodex 视频内容标注系统。该组织在太空领域与 NASA 和欧洲航空航天局都有合作。

出版物

1）期刊与杂志

❏ Double Helix.

❏ Animal Production Science.

❏ Australian Health Review.

❏ Australian Journal of Botany.

❏ Australian Journal of Chemistry.

❏ Australian Journal of Primary Health.

❏ Australian Journal of Zoology.

❏ Australian Mammalogy.

❏ Australian Systematic Botany.

❏ Crop & Pasture Science.

❏ Emu.

❏ Environmental Chemistry.

❏ Exploration Geophysics.

- ❑ Functional Plant Biology.
- ❑ Health Promotion Journal of Australia.
- ❑ Healthcare Infection.
- ❑ Historical Records of Australian Science.
- ❑ International Journal of Wildland Fire.
- ❑ Invertebrate Systematics.
- ❑ Marine & Freshwater Research.
- ❑ Microbiology Australia.
- ❑ Pacific Conservation Biology.
- ❑ Preview.
- ❑ Proceedings of the Royal Society of Victoria.
- ❑ Reproduction, Fertility and Development.
- ❑ Sexual Health.
- ❑ Soil Research.
- ❑ The Rangeland Journal.
- ❑ The South Pacific Journal of Natural and Applied Sciences.
- ❑ Wildlife Research.

2) 图书

- ❑ Mt Stromlo Observatory.
- ❑ Probing the New Solar System.
- ❑ Airborne Surveys and Monitoring of the Earth – Application to the Mitigation of Natural and Anthropogenic Hazards.
- ❑ Australia 2050: Structuring conversations about our future.

3) 数据库

- ❑ Research Publications Repository.
- ❑ Data Access Portal.

会议信息

- ❑ One Health and EcoHealth; 2016. 12. 04—07; Melbourne, Australia.
- ❑ Approved Persons Course for thermal processing of low – acid foods; 2015. 11. 09—13; Werribee Vic Australia.

附 录：机构中英文名称对照表

序号	机构英文名及简称	机构中文名
1	Aerospace & Electronics Systems Society（AESS）	IEEE 航天与电子系统协会
2	Aerospace Corporation（Aerospace）	航空航天公司
3	Airbus Defence and Space Geo – Information	空中客车集团防务与航天公司地理信息服务部门
4	Aircraft Electronics Association（AEA）	航空电子协会
5	American Institute of Aeronautics & Astronautics（AIAA）	美国航空航天学会
6	Analysis Tech Inc.（Analysis Tech）	美国分析技术公司
7	Applied Computational Electromagnetics Society（ACES）	美国应用计算电磁学学会
8	Applied Hydro – Acoustics Research, Inc.（AHA）	应用水动力声学研究公司
9	Applied Research Associates, Inc.（ARA）	应用研究联合公司
10	Applied Technology Associates（ATA）	应用技术联合公司
11	Armed Forces Communication and Electronic Association（AF-CEA）	美国武装部队通信与电子协会
12	Aselsan A. S.	土耳其军用电子工业公司
13	ASM Electronic Device Failure Analysis Society（EDFAS）	ASM 电子设备故障分析学会
14	Association Connecting Electronics Industries（ACEI）	IPC 国际电子工业联接协会
15	Association for Educational Communications and Technology（AECT）	教育通信与技术协会
16	Association for Information Science and Technology（ASIS&T）	情报科学与技术学会
17	Association of Public Safety Communications Officials International（APCO）	国际公共安全通信官协会
18	Ball Aerospace & Technologies Corporation（BATC）	鲍尔航空航天技术公司
19	Bharat Electronics Limited（BEL）	印度巴拉特电子有限公司
20	British Marine Electrical and Electronics Association（BMEEA）	英国船舶电子电气协会
21	CAE Inc.（CAE）	加拿大航空电子工业有限公司
22	Committee on Earth Observation Satellites（CEOS）	国际对地观测卫星委员会
23	Commonwealth Scientific and Industrial Research Organisation（CSIRO）	澳大利亚联邦科学与工业研究组织
24	Communications and Security Establishment Canada（CSEC）	加拿大通信安全学会

（续）

序号	机构英文名及简称	机构中文名
25	Communications – Electronics Command（CECOM）	美国陆军通信电子司令部
26	Corona Publishing Co.，Ltd	电晕出版株式会社
27	Dassault Aviation S. A.（DASSAULT AVIATION）	法国达索航空公司
28	Defense Systems Information Analysis Center（DSIAC）	国防系统信息分析中心
29	DigitalGlobe，DG（DigitalGlobe）	美国数字地球公司
30	Dish Network Corporation（DISH）	碟形网络公司
31	Elbit Systems Ltd（ESLT）	以色列埃尔比特系统公司
32	Electrical Manufacturing & Coil Winding Association（EMC-WA）	机电制造与绕线协会
33	Electron Microscopy and Analysis Group（EMAG）	电子显微镜与分析小组
34	Electronics Technicians Association，International（ETA）	国际电子技师协会
35	Electrostatic Discharge Association（EDA）	国际静电放电协会
36	Elsevier B. V.	爱思唯尔出版集团
37	Euroconsult	欧洲咨询公司
38	European Committee for Electrotechnical Standardization（CENELEC）	欧洲电气标准化委员会
39	European Organisation for the Exploitation of Meteorological Satellites（EUMETSAT）	欧洲气象卫星开发组织
40	European Satellite Operator's Association（ESOA）	欧洲卫星运营商协会
41	Frost & Sullivan	弗若斯特沙利文公司
42	German Institute of Navigation（DGON）	德国导航学会
43	Glenn Research Center（GRC）	戈兰研究中心
44	IABG	德国工业设备有限公司
45	IHS Jane's Information Group（Jane's）	简氏信息出版集团
46	ImageSat International N. V.（ImageSat）	荷兰国际影像卫星公司
47	Indra Sistemas, S. A.（Indra）	西班牙茵德拉系统公司
48	Institute for scientific and technical information（INIST）	法国科学技术信息研究所
49	Institute of Automation and Electrometry, Siberian Branch of the Russian Academy of Sciences（IA&E, SB RAS）	俄罗斯自动化和电测法研究所
50	Institute of Electrical and Electronics Engineers, Inc.（IEEE）	美国电子电气工程师协会
51	Institute of Electronics, Information and Communication Engineers（IEICE）	日本电子情报通信学会
52	Integrated System Consultants, Inc.（ICI）	综合系统咨询公司

（续）

序号	机构英文名及简称	机构中文名
53	International Association for Marine Electronics Companies (CIRM)	国际船舶电子公司协会
54	International Association for Radio, Telecommunications and Electromagnetics (iNARTE)	国际无线电与电信工程师协会
55	International Committee on Global Navigation Satellite Systems (GNSS) (ICG)	全球导航卫星系统国际委员会
56	International Federation for Information Processing (IFIP)	国际信息处理联合会
57	International Global Navigation Satellite Systems Society Inc. (IGNSS)	国际全球导航卫星系统协会
58	International Maritime Satellite Organization (INMARSAT)	国际海事卫星组织
59	International Microelectronics Assembly and Packaging Society (IMAPS)	国际微电子组装与封装协会
60	International Telecommunication Union (ITU)	国际电信联盟
61	International Telecommunications Satellite Organization (INTELSAT)	国际通信卫星组织
62	International Union of Radio Science (URSI)	国际无线电科学联盟
63	Japan Electric Measuring Instruments Manufacturers' Association (JEMIMA)	日本电气计测器工业协会
64	Japan Electronics and Information Technology Industries Association (JEITA)	日本电子信息技术产业协会
65	Japan Society of Applied Electromagnetic and Mechanics (JSAEM)	日本应用电磁学和力学学会
66	John Wiley & Sons, Inc.	约翰威立国际出版公司
67	JSC Navigation Information Systems (JSCNIS)	俄罗斯导航信息系统公司
68	JSC Institute of Aircraft Equipment (NIIAO)	航空设备科学研究院
69	Kongsberg Satellite Services AS (KSAT)	康斯伯格卫星服务公司
70	Kotel'nikov Institute of Radio – engineering and Electronics of RAS (IRE)	俄罗斯科学院无线电工程和电子学研究所
71	L – 3 Communications Inc. (L – 3)	L – 3 通信公司
72	Leonardo Company	莱昂纳多公司
73	Lockheed Martin Corporation (LMT)	洛克希德·马丁公司
74	National Geospatial – Intelligence Agency (NGA)	美国国家地理空间情报局
75	National Institute of Advanced Industrial Science and Technology (AIST)	日本产业技术综合研究院
76	National Marine Electronics Association (NMEA)	国家船舶电子协会

（续）

序号	机构英文名及简称	机构中文名
77	NATO Science and Technology Organization Collaboration Support Office（STO – CSO）	NATO 军事科学与技术组织
78	Netherlands Institute for Radio Astronomy（ASTRON）	荷兰射电天文学研究所
79	Office of Naval Research（ONR）	美国海军研究局
80	Omsk Research Institute of Communications and Electronics（ONIIP）	鄂木斯克仪器制造研究院
81	Optoelectronics Industry and Technology Development Association（OITDA）	日本光电产业与技术发展协会
82	Optoelectronics Industry Development Association – North America（OIDA）	美国光电产业发展协会
83	Orbital ATK Inc	轨道阿连特公司
84	Physical Acoustics Companies（PAC）	美国物理声学公司
85	Radio Technical Commission for Aeronautics（RTCA）	美国航空无线电委员会
86	Russia Mars Konzern	俄罗斯"火星"康采恩
87	SciTech Publishing, Inc.	科技出版社
88	Scottish Optoelectronics Association（SOA）	苏格兰光电协会
89	Skybox Imaging, Inc.	Skybox Imaging 公司
90	Smiths Group plc	英国史密斯集团
91	Society for Information Display（SID）	信息显示协会
92	Society of Cable Telecommunications Engineers（SCTE）	美国电缆电信工程师协会
93	St. Petersburg Radio Technology Equipment Plant	圣彼得堡无线电技术设备厂
94	State Corporation for Assistance to Development, Production and Export of Advanced Technology Industrial Product «Russian Technologies»（State Corporation Rostec）	俄罗斯工业与科技集团
95	Surrey Satellite Technology Ltd.（SSTL）	萨里卫星技术有限公司
96	Teal Group Corp	蒂尔集团咨询公司
97	Technica Corporation（Technica）	Technica 公司
98	Telecommunications Industry Association（TIA）	美国电信行业协会
99	Texas Instruments Inc.（TI）	德克萨斯仪器公司
100	The Institution of Engineering and Technology（IET）	英国工程技术学会
101	The Intersputnik International Organization of Space Communications（Intersputnik）	俄罗斯国际卫星组织
102	The Ship's Electric Installation Contractors' Association of Japan	日本船舶电装协会
103	TriQuint Semiconductor Inc	美国 TriQuint 半导体公司

（续）

序号	机构英文名及简称	机构中文名
104	U. S. Army Research, Development and Engineering Command（RDECOM）	美国陆军研发与工程司令部
105	Ultra Electronics Holdings Plc（ULE）	英国超级电子公司
106	Ultrasonics, Ferroelectrics, and Frequency Control Society, IEEE UFFC	IEEE 超声学、铁电体与频率控制协会
107	US Army's Communications – Electronics Command – Night Vision and Electronic Sensors Directorate,（NVESD）	美国陆军夜视与电子传感器委员会
108	World Scientific Publishing Company（WSPC）	世界科技出版公司
109	Xplor International, The Electronic Document Systems Association（Xplor International）	电子文档系统协会